Revelation Revealed

Of Jesus Christ and Things Soon to Come

First Edition

Dr. J. Ronald Nyberg, Jr.
(A.A., A.S., B.S., M.A., Ph.D.)

Author of Top 10 Bible Doctrines and other materials,
see **https://RonNyberg.org**.

ISBN-13: 978-1-940356-01-3

i. Preface

Revelation Revealed attempts to literally reveal and explain the meaning of the Book of Revelation. The Bible is the only 100% accurate detailed prophetic book of any in the world, and has been since the Old Testament was completed, and then the New Testament in the 1st century. Yes, there are other books that claim to be prophetic, but none exist except those so vague or wrong in their predictions. The Bible is approximately 20% prophecy, and 100% true. The final Book in the Bible (the Book of Revelation), provides the most detailed description of all Books in the world (including the Bible), of the final events for all human history.

There are many books written about Revelation. Most merely provide or pick out a few of the most interesting or apocalyptic events described therein to elaborate or pontificate. Most also spend their time quoting other authors and not the Bible. Almost none address all the specific and most difficult statements to interpret or understand. Even fewer address the entire Book to understand it by means of a literal exegetical exposition.

Biblical Inspiration note: The correct Biblical Inspiration view is the Verbal Plenary view, where verbal means *"in the form of words"* and plenary means *"full or complete."* This means each and every (all) the words themselves were supernaturally inspired through many prophets and apostle's unique personalities in order to provide man with a multifaceted perspective of divine communication shaped in human molds and to ensure every word from God was written with God's exact meaning and intent, so that *"all Scripture is given by inspiration of God, and is profitable"* (**2Ti. 3:16**). God's true Word did not come *"by the will of man"* so we have *"a more sure word of prophecy,"* so that *"no prophecy of the Scripture is of any private interpretation"* (**2Pe. 1:19-21**). This means every word is inspired and important, God wants us to understand His Word, and God's Word can be interpreted correctly, there is a correct interpretation that is not private, especially when read and led by God's Holy Spirit, Who *"will guide you into all truth"* (**John 16:13**). Thus, God's Word is without error and authoritative above all other writings.

Biblical Interpretation note: In order for us to best understand God's Word, we need to have believed God's Word by trusting God, so we are indwelt and filled by God's Spirit, and confessed of all known sin. I believe that Jesus Christ died, was buried, and rose again from the dead to save me from my sin, and by this grace, through faith (**_Eph. 2:8-9_**), God has given me eternal life (**_John 3:16_**) and His Spirit is guiding me into all truth (**_John 16:13_**). I believe the literal, historical-grammatical methodology is the most accurate way to interpret any literature, especially the Scripture, since every word is inspired and key to understanding God's full counsel. Understanding and interpreting the words within their grammatical constructs and historical context, is the best way to most accurately "_study_" and understand the meaning of "_the Word of truth_" (**_2Ti. 2:15_**). Rightly interpreting God's Word and hiding it in your heart enables one to "_cleanse his way_," "_take heed_," and thus "_not sin_" against God, and allow His Word to be "_a lamp unto my feet and a light unto my path_" (**_Psa. 119:9-10, 105_**).

Therefore, my intent for _Revelation Revealed_ is to provide an understandable word-for-word or verse-by-verse commentary with a literal interpretation or exposition that provides main views on the most difficult, less explained prophecies. This does not contain wild conjectures like many symbolic, spiritual, or non-literal books about Revelation, but does contain some of the most amazing prophecies.

Revelation Revealed provides summary timelines, definitions, and the purpose and promise of prophecy in this one-of-a-kind Book of Revelation. I guarantee all readers will learn and be amazed (as I was and am) of the specific details and time frames of many incredibly amazing events, people, places, and creatures that are promised and predicted to come to earth and to heaven very quickly.

Process note: I must confess my process was to read and keep rereading Revelation over and over again from the KJV to begin observation. I then read many top different translations (NKJV, NASB, NIV...). Then, I personally translated the entire Book of Revelation, focusing on numerous word studies, especially where many translations differed. During this process, I came up with numerous questions. As I reread with these questions in mind, I found that Revelation itself revealed most of the answers (even citing directly and literally the meaning of various metaphors), and then leveraged numerous cross references from the rest of the Bible, which provided me the best authoritative framework to refine interpretation. This reduced my questions considerably. I then continued to pray and ask God to reveal specific tougher passages and amazingly felt His Spirit leading me to what seemed to be clear common-sense answers. Some took more prayer than others. After taking a position and being open minded where Revelation seemed to be intentionally less concrete, I consulted many commentaries, books, and reference notes by other Christians to learn other views. This was both educational, expanding of my vantage point, and very disappointing. Most of the toughest passages were not addressed or summarily dismissed with broad brush strokes or wild speculations. I have to admit, that I even looked at several false religions and cultist perspectives that got even wilder or historically revising events that they wanted *"things which must shortly come to pass"* to fit into. I then put together lessons to teach. Then, prayerfully taught three dozen church members, which provided even more questions and answers from the Spirit refining again. Though I plan to study, revise, and teach this many more times, I felt it best to compile into this book so many others could leverage in their ongoing study.

Although more difficult to read, I intentionally list the Scripture references in the text (not as footnotes or end notes), since there are so many, they are most important, and it would be too cumbersome to turn back and forth. This is a reference book and Scripture is the primary authority of each point, far above what this author or any other may state **Revelation Bible quotes are italicized and in bold** with the **Biblical references also underlined** for emphasis and not to miss the clear authority and for easy lookup. Numerous Greek words (>330) are included in italics in this format (*Gr:Transliterated Word-Definition; possible additional note or clarification*) *to provide a* better understanding of the meaning of key words and to provide their English transliteration for easier reading and pronunciation. I intentionally chose not to cite many other authors, but significantly quoted or cited Scripture (which ironically few books do on Revelation), but this approach always provides the only guaranteed key to understanding difficult prophetic pictures or passages.

Brief Book Description: *Revelation Revealed* unveils a rare, literally interpreted book that is clear, concise, yet comprehensive on the Book of Revelation. It is a Scriptural study, teaching materials, and reference book of the Book of Revelation, which is *"the revelation of Jesus Christ"* and *"things which must shortly come to pass"* (**Rev. 1:1**). Since *"no prophecy of the Scripture is of any private interpretation,"* this book let's God's Revelation (Scripture), not man's opinion (quoting other books), provide a public nonfictional understanding of what God says was, is, and is soon to come. *Revelation Revealed* details promises, plans, and direct words of the most important Person, Jesus Christ. It leaps past His 1st Coming in guised glory, humbled, crucified, buried, resurrected, ascended, followed, and rejected by Israel. It springs to the spectacular God-man, in all His current and coming glory, and soon coming future of all, humbled in reverence, on bent knees, then raised to our eternal destiny.

Why Published: This is an indispensable must have reference book, organized by Revelation chapter, topic, paragraph, and verse for ease and fast future finding. It provides clarity on the most important life-changing apocalyptic literature ever written. It includes exciting revelation of the most influential persons in human history, our current place in God's timeline, is from the greatest and only 100% true end times prophecy, and promises blessing from God Himself, to all who read, heed, and keep these prophecies.

A plethora of books exist for parts of Revelation, although few cover the entire book. Some summarize or interpret the Book symbolically with little detail or Scriptural cross referencing. Many push personal opinion or quote opinions of men leveraging little Biblical authority. Almost none address every specific and most difficult predictions to interpret or understand. Even fewer address the entire Book to understand it by means of a literal exposition. Many depend on past popularity, which often has fallen from favor. Seminaries and others publish commentaries where Revelation's 22 chapters are explained in fewer pages than the actual Biblical text. Most are 1/27th of a NT commentary or 1/66th of the entire Bible. Other authors sensationalize sections of Revelation. Many great books and authors render an entire book based on a few verses or chapter(s), (e.g., the 4 Riders of the Apocalypse, Heaven, 7 Churches, the Kingdom or Millennium, Mark of the Beast or the infamous "666," Babylon, Judgment Day, Hell, Rapture, the Tribulation, 2nd Coming), or publish illustrations, main views, insights, applications, or lessons. Teaching books may be found engaging sound pedagogy but lacking Biblical expertise and theological accuracy. Almost none are comprehensive, and many display denominational bias. Others are published past pulpit messages. Many have strong value, for their intended, limited purpose. Revelation Revealed is for those who don't want to read 10 books but would rather have 1 definitive book that has it all.

Why Unique:

- *Revelation Revealed* uses a literal hermeneutic or interpretation
- Includes every word of the Book of Revelation
- Concise and precise, yet comprehensive coverage of all verses (doesn't cherry pick or skip due to difficulty)
- Numerous Scripture cross references (>2,000) and Scripture quotes (>500) without lots of fluff or undefined scholarly words
- Answers the top 10 prophetic questions (>400 total)
- Numerous word studies and Greek definitions (>330)
- >80 engaging introductory lesson hooks or context setting
- >45 main views, rationale, and rebuttal
- >190 personal applications end times predictions
- Great reference book to use again and again
- Outlines Revelation and titles all chapters and paragraphs
- Timelines of the final events of history (>40 events)
- Several 1-page detailed summary charts
- Ideal for exegetical, expository, or verse-by-verse preaching or teaching
- Adaptable curriculum for 30-52 lessons (depending on discussion; all info in "{}" is for teacher; handouts for class includes everything else; each chapter/lesson includes an Introduction/Hook, Scriptural Observation/Interpretation/ Commentary, and practical Application questions and answers)
- Protects from proselytizing by cults and political correctness

Exhaustive commentaries of 1,000+ pages are tough to finish without getting disconnected from Revelation. Summary commentaries may be brief, but not comprehensive, and skip difficult prophecies. Most commentaries mainly quote authors from their denominational viewpoint. Very few approach Revelation from a literal hermeneutic or interpretation. There are a few good literal commentaries, and most are 500+ pages. Even fewer: provide applications, are designed as a reference book, have summarizing charts, include every word of Revelation, have word studies, articulate main views, provide a preaching/teaching format, include timelines, and are as short and comprehensive as Revelation Revealed. You get this complete, unique work, with about 40 pages of outlines, images, charts, and references (visual summaries, timelines, and reference hooks), about 45 pages of engagement hooks and applications (great preaching and teaching format), about 150 pages of complete Revelation text with concise and comprehensive commentary (many others are either under 50-page summaries or over 500 page exhaustive commentaries). May God fulfill His promised blessing to you as you read, heed, and keep the words of Revelation.

The Great Challenge: My great challenge was a double-edged sword, where the greatest strength is also the greatest weakness. The reason why other Revelation books don't attempt a single book that is comprehensive, yet concise, is because they only understand part of it, so that's what they write about. The second big reason is it is almost overwhelming to read a book with all the different epic topics, judgments, people, creatures, scenes, and soon and eternal predictions. In fact, those two reasons are why most don't read the actual Book of Revelation. Then organizing a single book with detailed outlines, lessons, definitions, views, chapters, paragraphs, verses, and title reference hooks is more difficult to read as it includes numbers and letters, questions and answers, interpretations and applications, summary overviews, yet detailed word analyses, top views, while staying within the context and flow of paragraphs, keeping every word of Revelation included without making it easier to read with tangential stories that would have made a 200 page book 500 pages. **So, my challenge was to write it, yours is to read it and to use it.** If you only use it as a reference in time of need, it will be worth its weight. If you use it like a commentary or dictionary to teach others, you will love it. If you use it to worship God and His Son Jesus Christ, you'll find it life changing. If you use it only to look at the 1-page summaries to pull the entire book and details into a manageable picture, fantastic. If you read only the different views to understand how different denominations and religions view the greatest prophecy ever written, you will be the wiser. If you read it only to see how end times prophetic events and people fit on timeline charts, it will help you visually know where you are, will be in the near future, and how these events sequentially fit together. If you are brave enough to steadily read its entirety, I guarantee you will be overwhelmed in heart, mind, and soul, but blessed immensely. In fact, if you read, heed, and keep these prophecies, God promises you a blessing. If you don't know God, this book can lead you to be eternally saved (by faith in Jesus Christ alone). All readers will know what is coming, gain a peace that passes all understanding, and a burden to make a difference while there is still time.

Purpose: The intent of this book is first to glorify God and readily provide this resource at minimal cost to as many as possible. Sub-goals: 1) Educate and lead the unsaved to the truth. 2) Equip, mature, and protect the saved. 3) Stimulate deep thought and love for the depth and riches of God and His Word. 4) Provide a basic tailorable curriculum for all those who preach or teach in Bible studies, churches, Christian schools, colleges, universities, and seminaries. Minimally, learners should be able to provide the outline of Revelation, its purpose, promise, key events, major timeline, and point to major Scripture references from memory. More advanced outcomes include the ability to understand and discuss the concluding events of the Church Age, the final 7 years of Israel's history, the importance of the top 3 Millennial views, and defend their faith. All should have this as a concise reference with Scripture for further study.

Intended Reader: Target readers are conservative Christians who interpret Scripture literally and desire to understand one of the most difficult prophetic Books in the Bible, such as: professors at seminaries, universities, or colleges, especially Bible Colleges, pastors, Christian high school or middle school teachers, Sunday school, Bible study, or small group teachers or leaders, lay-people, both saved or unsaved, that are seeking to understand what God's Word in Revelation literally says, means, and how to actually apply it in their lives. It is not ideal for readers who want an easy light read, unless seeking a strong reference book or needing answers to a specific passage, timeline, or topic.

See https://RonNyberg.org for other free materials.

May God bless you greatly as He reveals more each time you look at His Word on this life changing Book, and the Revelation of Himself and of the final events of all human history!

ii. Table of Contents

i. Preface.. i

ii. Table of Contents viii

iii. List of Figures.. ix

iv. Abbreviations x

1 – *Revelation 1:1-8* (Introduction-Revelation of Jesus and Future)........ 1

2 – *Revelation 1:9-20* (Vision, Words, and Book Outline from Jesus) 8

3 – *Revelation 2:1-7* (To Churches—1: Ephesus) 14

4 – *Revelation 2:8-11* (To Churches—2: Smyrna) 18

5 – *Revelation 2:12-17* (To Churches—3: Pergamos) 22

6 – *Revelation 2:18-29* (To Churches—4: Thyatira) 26

7 – *Revelation 3:1-6* (To Churches—5: Sardis)................................... 31

8 – *Revelation 3:7-13* (To Churches—6: Philadelphia) 36

9 – *Revelation 3:14-22* (To Churches—7: Laodicea) 42

10 – *Revelation 4:1-11* (God Worshiped on His Heavenly Throne) 48

11 – *Revelation 5:1-14* (Jesus Worshiped and Worthy to Judge) 56

12 – *Revelation 6:1-17* (*6/7 Seal Judgments of the Tribulation*) 65

13 – *Revelation 7:1-17* (144,000 Jewish Witnesses and Trib Saints)...... 74

14 – *Revelation 8:1-13* (7th Seal and 1st 4 Trumpet Judgments)............ 82

15 – *Revelation 9:1-12* (5th Trumpet and 1st Woe Judgment) 88

16 – *Revelation 9:13-21* (6th Trumpet and 2nd Woe Judgment) 93

17 – *Revelation 10:1-11* (A Book Not to Write, But Eat)....................... 97

18 – *Revelation 11:1-14* (The 2 Witnesses)..................................... 102

19 – *Revelation 11:15-19* (The 7th Trumpet Sounds) 108

20 – *Revelation 12:1-17* (The Woman, Son, Michael, and Dragon)..... 111

21 – *Revelation 13:1-18* (The Antichrist, 666, and False Prophet) 123

22 – *Revelation 14:1-20* (Heavenly Singing and Coming Judgment) 132

23 – *Revelation 15:1-8* (God's Glory Praised Before 7 Last Plagues).... 137

24 – *Revelation 16:1-21* (7 Vial Judgments Including Armageddon).... 141

25 – *Revelation 17:1-18* (The Great Harlot and Babylonian Beast)...... 149

26 – *Revelation 18:1-24* ("Babylon the Great is Fallen") 160

27 – *Revelation 19:1-21* (The Wedding, 2nd Coming, and Judgment)... 167

28 – *Revelation 20:1-15* (Millennial Rule and Great White Throne) 176

29 – *Revelation 21:1-27* (A New Heaven, Earth, and Jerusalem) 186

30 – *Revelation 22:1-21* (Obey Completed Word, Jesus Comes Soon) 196

v. End Notes 207

vi. Bibliography (with notes) 210

iii. List of Figures

(Format: Figure # – Chapter #.Figure # in Chapter)

Figure 1 – 1.1 **Revelation Overview**...7

Figure 2 – 1.2 **St. John's Vision of the Seven Candlesticks[1]**.................13

Figure 3 – 8.1 **Main Rapture Views**..36

Figure 4 – 10.1 **St. John Kneeling Before Christ & the 24 Elders[3]**.........53

Figure 5 – 10.2 **Revelation Timeline of 7 Key Events Defined**..............55

Figure 6 – 11.1 **The Hymn in Adoration of the Lamb[7]**.....................62

Figure 7 – 11.2 **Revelation Timeline Overview**..............................64

Figure 8 – 12.1 **The Four Horsemen of the Apocalypse[8]**.....................67

Figure 9 – 12.2 **The Opening of the Fifth and Sixth Seals[9]**.................72

Figure 10 – 13.1 **Four Angels Holding Back the Winds, and the Marking of the Elect[10]**...81

Figure 11 – 14.1 **The Four Angels of Death[12]**................................87

Figure 12 – 15.1 **The Opening of the Seventh Seal and the Eagle Crying 'Woe'[14]**...91

Figure 13 – 17.1 **St. John Eating the Book[19]**.................................101

Figure 14 – 19.1 **Seals, Trumpets, and Vials Overview**......................108

Figure 15 – 20.1 **The Woman of the Apocalypse and the Seven-Headed Dragon[20]**...113

Figure 16 – 20.2 **Saint Michael Fighting the Dragon[22]**......................122

Figure 17 – 21.1 **The Beast with the Lamb's Horns and the Beast with Seven Heads[25]**...130

Figure 18 – 24.1 **Revelation Timeline Overview of 40+ Events**..........148

Figure 19 – 25.1 **The Whore of Babylon[33]**.................................159

Figure 20 – 28.1 **Main Millennial Views**.....................................178

Figure 21 – 28.2 **The Angel with the Key of the Bottomless Pit[34]**.......184

*In addition, there are 4 tables (not listed here) found in Applications J-M on pp. 174-175 showing **the place of Christ, Church, and Israel at the 1st Advent, Rapture, and 2nd Advent**. Also, a summary of who/how Jesus Christ is revealed (by chapter) is found in Application G on pp. 204-206.*

iv. Abbreviations

Bible Book Abbreviations (Abr.)

OT Bible Book	Abr.	NT Bible Book	Abr.
OT Bible Book	**Abr.**	Nahum	**Nah.**
Genesis	**Gen.**	Habakkuk	**Hab.**
Exodus	**Exo.**	Zephaniah	**Zep.**
Leviticus	**Lev.**	Haggai	**Hag.**
Numbers	**Num.**	Zechariah	**Zec.**
Deuteronomy	**Deu.**	Malachi	**Mal.**
Joshua	**Jos.**	**NT Bible Book**	**Abr.**
Judges	*Jdg.*	Matthew	**Mat.**
Ruth	**Rut.**	Mark	**Mar.**
1 Samuel	**1Sa.**	Luke	**Luk.**
2 Samuel	**2Sa.**	John	**Joh.**
1 Kings	**1Ki.**	Acts	**Act.**
2 Kings	**2Ki.**	Romans	**Rom.**
1 Chronicles	**1Ch.**	1 Corinthians	**1Co.**
2 Chronicles	**2Ch.**	2 Corinthians	**2Co.**
Ezra	**Ezr.**	Galatians	**Gal.**
Nehemiah	**Neh.**	Ephesians	**Eph.**
Esther	**Est.**	Philippians	*Php.*
Job	**Job.**	Colossians	**Col.**
Psalms	**Psa.**	1 Thessalonians	**1Th.**
Proverbs	**Pro.**	2 Thessalonians	**2Th.**
Ecclesiastes	**Ecc.**	1 Timothy	**1Ti.**
Song of Solomon	**Son.**	2 Timothy	**2Ti.**
Isaiah	**Isa.**	Titus	**Tit.**
Jeremiah	**Jer.**	Philemon	*Phm.*
Lamentations	**Lam.**	Hebrews	**Heb.**
Ezekiel	**Eze.**	James	**Jam.**
Daniel	**Dan.**	1 Peter	**1Pe**
Hosea	**Hos.**	2 Peter	**2Pe.**
Joel	**Joe.**	1 John	**1Jo.**
Amos	**Amo.**	2 John	**2Jo.**
Obadiah	**Obo.**	3 John	**3Jo.**
Jonah	**Jon.**	Jude	**Jud.**
Micah	**Mic.**	Revelation	**Rev.**

- All Bible Books have the 1st 3 letters as the standard abbreviation, except for the 3 above in *Italics*

- Bible references are listed as Bible **_Book Abr. Chapter:Verse_** (e.g. **_Joh. 3:16_**)
- ";" refers to the same book unless another is noted (e.g. **_Joh. 3:16_**; **_6:47_**)
- Verses citing only **Chapter:Verse** are defaulting to **_Revelation_**
- "OT" means the Old Testament of the Bible
- "NT" means the New Testament of the Bible
- "e.g." means "Example Given" or "for example"
- "#" means number
- ">" means greater than
- "<" means less than
- "=" means equals
- "~" means approximately
- "FYI" means "For your information"
- "re:" means "regarding"
- "cf." means a Biblical Cross Reference is cited
- "hr." or "hrs." means "hour" or "hours"
- "Trib" means the 7-year Tribulation Period
- Numbers are frequently shown as numbers and not words, even in quoted Scriptures (especially helps on old English #s)
- All Biblical passages are from the King James Version (KJV) or the New King James Version (NKJV)

Revelation of Jesus Christ and Future from God by John to 7 Churches–Time is Near; Happy if Read, Heed, and Keep Prophecy.

Revelation of Jesus and Future to 7 Churches, The Time is Near

Introduction—*Revelation Revealed*
(Chapter 1 includes a Revelation 1-page overview and 1-page timeline chart, author, date, recipients, theme, tone, outline, key verse, and prophecy's and Revelation's purpose.}

A. What would you like to get out of **_Revelation_**? {Like to learn lots more about the future and what God wants me to know.}
B. Detailed Analysis Overview— {22 Chapters, 99 Paragraphs (depends how divided) averaging 4.5 paragraphs per chapter, 404 verses averaging 18 verses per chapter, and 12,016 words, averaging 546 words per chapter.}

Scripture (Observations/Interpretation/Commentary)
{Have someone read **_Revelation 1:1-8_** together.}

A. _1:1-3_— {Title: Revelation of Jesus and Future–Happy if Read, Understand, and this Keep Prophecy. **_1_**-"**_The Revelation of Jesus Christ_** (the most unique, influential, studied, quoted, discussed of all time, the only God-man, Who lived, died for our sin, resurrected, lives, is coming back soon, and is the only way to God His Father. John uses His full name "Jesus Christ" 7 times in Revelation, 5 as He is being introduced in this 1st chapter (**_1:1_**; **_1:2_**; **_1:5_**; **_1:9_**-twice), once in the summary of key persons in **_12:17_**, and once in the final verse of the final chapter, **_22:21_**, out of the 198 total times His full name "Jesus Christ" is found in the Bible, all in the NT; also shows my subtitle to *Revelation Revealed: of Jesus Christ and Things Soon to Come* as it reveals Jesus Christ), **_which_** (Revelation) **_God gave unto Him_** (Jesus), **_to show unto His_** (Jesus') **_servants_** (believers/saved) **_things which must shortly come to pass_** (future) **_; and He_** (Jesus) **_sent and signified it by His_** (Jesus') **_angel_** (messenger) **_unto His_** (Jesus') **_servant John_** (the Apostle)**_:"_** **_2_**-"**_Who_** (John) **_bare record_** (witness) **_of the Word of God, and of the testimony of Jesus Christ, and of all things that he_** (John) **_saw._**" (Can you imagine what John got to see being in Jesus' inner 3, raising people from the dead, making lame to walk, blind to see, deaf to hear, His death, burial, and resurrection, His teaching, and gospel preaching proving to John and the world that Jesus was the Son of God, the Creator of the universe, the Revealer of God, and the only Way to God-the-Father, cf. **Mat. 11:5**; _**John 1:13, 18**_; _**14:6**_; _**Heb. 1:1-3**_) _**3**_-"**Blessed is he that reads, and they that hear the Words of this prophecy, and keep those things which are written therein** (in it)**: for the time is at hand.**" (Soon; near; what a promise, what a blessing...).}

B. _**1:4-8**_— {Title: Greeting from Jesus and John to the 7 Churches. _**4**_- "**John to the 7 churches which are in Asia** (literal local churches in 1st century AD, that John personally impacted)**: Grace** (giving what isn't deserved) **be unto you** (believers)**, and peace, from Him** (God-the Father) **which is** (present)**, and which was** (past)**, and which is to come** (future)**; and from the 7 Spirits** (Holy Spirit in all His completeness; see _**3:1**_ note) **which are before His** (God-the Father's) **throne;**" _**5**_-"**And from Jesus Christ** (so includes all members in the Trinity or triune Godhead)**, Who** (Jesus) **is the faithful witness** (Words from the Word, Jesus is the most faithful)**, and the 1st begotten of the dead** (cf. _**1Co. 15:23**_; Jesus was raised 1st, to defeat death so that all believers of all time could later be resurrected)**, and the Prince of the kings of the earth** (Jesus is above all rulers)**. Unto Him** (Jesus) **that loved us** (Jesus loves the Church)**, and washed us** (believers) **from our sins** (Jesus paid for and cleansed us from our sin that once separated us from God) **in His** (Jesus') **own blood**" ("_the blood of Jesus Christ cleanses us from all sin,_" _**1Jo. 1:7**_), _**6**_-"**And** (Jesus) **hath made us** (Church) **kings and priests unto God and His** (Jesus') **Father; to Him** (Jesus) **be glory and dominion for ever and ever.** (His rule is forever). **Amen.**" _**7**_-"**Behold, He** (Jesus) **comes with clouds** (both Rapture, _**1Th. 4:13-17**_ and 2nd Coming, _**Acts 1:9-11**_; _**1Th. 3:13**_)**; and every eye shall see Him** (Jesus)**, and they** (Gentile and Jewish leaders crucifying Him; though Jesus laid down His life willingly to pay for all our sins, cf. _**John 10:17-18**_) **also which pierced Him** (Jesus)**: and all kindreds of the earth shall wail because of Him** (Jesus. Some wail saddened by His suffering and painful crucifixion, others wail in pain from the judgment He took in their place, and since they rejected Him will 1 day receive them self). **Even so, Amen.**" _**8**_-"**I** (Jesus) **am Alpha and Omega** (1st and last letters in Greek alphabet)**, the beginning and the ending** (only Jesus could be both beginning and end when there are more than 1)**, saith the Lord** (Master, Jesus)**, which is** (Jesus is presently)**, and which was** (Jesus was in the past)**, and which is to come** (Jesus will be in the future)**, the Almighty.**" (He always has, does, and will reign with all power, even if we are unaware).}

C. Background Overview and Review

1. Author (**1:1**)— {The Apostle John (**1:1, 4, 9**; **21:2**; **22:8**), who was the only living Apostle at this time. John was over the churches in Asia. John was imprisoned on the Isle of Patmos for his faith in Christ (**1:9**). John was credible, an apostle, close to, an eyewitness of Jesus, and living during the time Revelation was written. And of course, the ultimate source of this special Revelation is the triune God, the Father revealing His final plan in His final Book, through inspiration of the Holy Spirit, and Jesus' direct message to and through John. <u>Who better to receive the final and greatest Apocalyptic prophetic Book</u>?--The only living Apostle, who faithfully saw his fellow apostles all martyred for their faith, now aged, tortured, and exiled in prison needing a holy hug from His Savior and God. He was a direct eyewitness of Jesus, one who had already written 4 other Books in the Bible, one who did miracles himself, one who was with Peter and James in Jesus' closest mentoring, friendship, and discipleship inner circle. John was the disciple whom Jesus loved, the one Jesus entrusted with His earthly mom, Mary. Mary probably shared some of Jesus' greatest earthly stories, His unwritten childhood years, His unrecorded miracles, His wisdom, His imponderables, how she celebrated His birthdays (Christmas before others ever celebrated it), her favorite piece of furniture she still cherished from her Son, the Divine carpenter...God couldn't have chosen a better author.}

2. Date— {95 AD; the last of the 66 Books of Bible written.}

3. Recipients (**1:1**)— {"***unto His*** (Jesus') ***servants***" [Christians followers] (**1:1**), "***Brethren***"-5 times [Christians] (**1:9**; **6:11**; **12:10**; **19:10**; **22:9**); "***to the 7 churches which are in Asia***" [the local literal church gathering of Christians in the 1st century] (**1:4**). There are many who believe these 7 recipient churches are representative of the entire Church Age in 7 periods. Often are seen as 6 historical ages and the 7th age is current or the near future, with various representations easily found. Clearly, John says Revelation is written to each of these specific 7 local churches in Asia as referenced above. Clearly, John says this is to all the church throughout all the ages or to all the churches as he says it is, "***what the Spirit says unto all the churches***" (**2:7, 11, 17, 29**; **3:6, 13, 22**), He says "***all the churches shall know***" (**3:23**), and that Jesus sent His angel to testify to you "***in the churches***"

(**22:16**). So, He clearly says specific local Asia churches, He specifically says all the churches, and so that would imply all the churches throughout all of church ages and history, and one might infer even a 7-fold cycle that most churches go through. However, I would strongly disagree with anyone that only wants to see these Revelation churches as merely a historical period in church history and not also all churches (and Church Age believers), including those of John's day.}

4. Tone— {Apocalyptic/prophetic literature, many symbols, metaphors, many OT references to events and prophecies, transitions to and from divine heavenly scenes and human earthly worldwide events and timelines...cf. **1Pe. 1:12**; **2Pe. 1:19-21**. The more we study and apply, the clearer this becomes. Encouragement to the persecuted church, Jesus wins, so as a believer, we win too!}

5. Theme— {Jesus, Jesus, Jesus. Jesus "**was**," Jesus "**is**," Jesus "**is to come**" (**1:4**). Revealing the hidden and unknown of Jesus and His plan with actual occurrences of the final events of human history. Revelation is truly His-story (Jesus'). The story of God's sovereign justice through His only Son Jesus, Who lived, died for our sins, was buried, rose again, and is coming again. This is the Gospel. Please believe in Jesus now, if you have not, before it is too late...This time He's coming in judgment, power, and ultimate consummation of history and all things. The judicial evidence to believe: "**the testimony of Jesus**" (**1:2, 9**; **12:17**; **19:10**), "**Jesus Christ...the faithful witness**" (**1:5**); "*the faithful and true witness*" (**3:14**); "slain for the testimony" (**6:9**); "*144,000*" witnesses (**7:4**); "*2 witnesses*" "finished their testimony" (**11:3, 7**); Believers overcame by "*their testimony*" (**12:11, 17**); "*the testimony in Heaven*" (**15:5**); "*beheaded for the witness of Jesus*" (**20:4**); "*sent My angel to testify*" (**22:6, 16**); "*I testify*" (**22:18**)--What is your testimony of Jesus? You can believe in Him now and miss the judgment to come. Unlike the news today, which can sadden us because of the evil persecuting events of men, Christians are encouraged and promised that we will be happy if we read, understand, and apply Revelation as we trust our good and great coming Savior Jesus (**1:3**), and the unsaved are promised judgment on earth and for all eternity like they have never seen before in all of human history.}

6. Outline (**_1:19_**)— {A clear 3-fold outline or structure. 1) Past **_"things which thou has seen"_** (**_1:1-20_**)-these are all the things John has seen in **_Rev. 1_**, prior to addressing the 7 churches. 2) Present **_"things which are"_** (**_2:1-3:22_**)-the existing churches in John's time and the current/entire Church Age. 3) Future **_"things which shall be hereafter"_** (**_4:1-22:21_**)-things/events after the Church Age ends.}

7. Key Verses— {Prophecy's Purpose (**_19:10_**)—**_"the testimony of Jesus is the spirit of prophecy,"_** which is the setting that predicts/reveals Jesus, His plan, His involvement, and His purpose for man's future. Revelation's Purpose (**_1:1_**)—**_"...to show unto His servants things which must shortly come to pass..."_** Apocalypse is the disclosure of that which was previously hidden or unknown; only God truly knows so He can perfectly reveal the future. Revelation's Promise (**_1:3_**)— **_"Blessed is he that readeth...that hear the words of this prophecy, and keep those things that are written therein..."_**}

D. What does **_1:1-8_** reveal of Jesus? {Things to comfort and make us worship Jesus.}

1. Jesus gives hidden F_____ events and reveals them to us (**_1:1_**). {FUTURE}
2. Jesus is the Prince of, and Provides P_____ (**_1:4_**). {PEACE}
3. Jesus "is," "was," and "is to come" or E_____ P_____ (**_1:4, 8_**). {ETERNALLY PRESENT}
4. Jesus is the F_____ W_____ (**_1:5_**). {FAITHFUL WITNESS}
5. Jesus is the F_____ R_____ from the dead (**_1:5_**). {FIRST RAISED; implying Christians are next}
6. Jesus is the P_____ "of the kings of the earth" (**_1:5_**). {PRINCE; He is over all other rulers.}
7. Jesus demonstrated that He L_____ us (**_1:5_**). {LOVED; and always has and always will.}
8. Jesus W_____ us from our sins by His own B_____ (**_1:5_**). {WASHED / BLOOD; the greatest love demonstrated.}
9. Jesus made us K_____ and P_____ (**_1:5_**). {KINGS / PRIESTS; we have an elevated position in Christ.}
10. Jesus has G_____ and D_____ forever (**_1:6_**). {GLORY / DOMINION; see His glory revealed by John...}
11. Jesus is visibly C_____ again and all shall wail (**_1:7_**). {COMING; some with tears of joy, most with tears of terror.}

12. Jesus is the A_____ (*1:8*). {ALMIGHTY}

Application (Activity/Questions)
{Review Figure 1 on next page for these questions.}

A. What observations do you see on the Revelation Chart (on next page)? {Chapters, theme, key purposes, verses...}

B. Revelation of your heart—What excites you more, info on Jesus or the future? How can we shift more towards Him? {Returning to our 1st love; realizing Who/what's best; learning Him.}

C. How can Jesus'... radically transform/permeate your thinking, attitude, actions, motives...? {Focus on Him, Daily prayer and Bible reading, Scripture memory, Scripture meditation, seek and love Him...}

D. What coming is He referring to, the Rapture or 2nd Coming and why wailing? {2nd Coming as all eyes see Him; wailing because He is coming in Judgment, as they rejected and killed Him and are fighting against those whom He loves (Israel, believers).}

Figure 1 – 1.1 Revelation Overview

Author: John (the Apostle) — **Revelation** — **Date: 95 AD**

Top header (chapter references): 1:1-20 | 2:1-29 | 3:1-22 | 4:1-11 | 5:1-14 | 6:1-17 | 7:1-17 | 8:1-21 | 9:1-21 | 10:1-11 | 11:1-19 | 12:1-17 | 13:1-18 | 14:1-20 | 15:1-8 | 16:1-21 | 17:1-18 | 18:1-24 | 19:1-21 | 20:1-15 | 21:1-27 | 22:1-21

Past (1), Present (2-3) / **Future (4-22)**

1:19 "Write the things which thou" (1:1-20) "hast seen", "and the things which" (2:1-3:22) "are", "and the things which" (4:1-22:21) "shall be hereafter."

Timeline: Church Age (1-3) The Trib/Great Trib (4-18) 2nd Coming (19), Millennium (20:1-10), Eternal State (21-22)

Parenthetical & Satan (12): God's Throne & Judgment Book Worthy Lamb (4-5) Jesus, Remnant, & Everlasting Gospel (14:1-13) Armageddon Gathering (16:13-16) 4 Heavenly Hallelujahs (19:1-6) Angel, Little Book, & 2 Witnesses (10:1-11:14) Israel, Christ, & Satan (12) Jewish Remnant & 144K Saints (7:1-17)

Chapter-by-chapter narrative (right column)

1:1-20	Revelation of Jesus Christ & Future from God by John to 7 Churches–the Time is Near; Happy if Read, Understand, & Keep Prophecy
2:1-29	Jesus Christ encourages, warns, & gives promises to all churches & to the 1st 4 of 7 in Asia (Ephesus, Smyrna, Pergamos, & Thyatira)
3:1-22	Jesus Christ encourages, warns, & gives promises to all churches & to the last 3 of 7 in Asia (Sardis, Philadelphia, & Laodicea)
4:1-11	After Church Age, Elders & Seraphim worship God on His heavenly throne
5:1-14	Worthy Lion Lamb Reigning Redeemer (Jesus Christ) to Judge & be Worshipped
6:1-17	The Lamb opens 6/7 Seal Judgments beginning the 7-Year Tribulation Period
7:1-17	Who Can Stand? 144,000 Jews & Tribulation Saints Saved by the Lamb
8:1-21	The 7th Seal & the 1st 4 Trumpet Judgments (1-Hail Fire, 2-Fiery Mountain, 3-Meteor–Wormwood, 4-Darkness)
9:1-21	7th Seal & Trumpets 5 & 6 (1st & 2nd Woes)–Locusts with 5-Month Scorpion Stings & 200M Army Kill 1/3 Men; No Repentance
10:1-11	A Mighty Angel, a Secret Message, & Eating a Little Book
11:1-19	A Tale of 2 Witnesses & the 7th Trumpet-Christ's Judgment Reigning
12:1-17	The Dragon & his demons battle Christ, are cast out by Michael & his angels, & persecute Israel
13:1-18	The Anti-Christ, the Mark of the Beast (666) & the False Prophet
14:1-20	The Lamb, the 144K Choir, the 3 Angel Messages, & God's Judgment
15:1-8	The Final Plagues (7 Vials) Culminate God's Earthly Judgment–Heavenly Saints Praise God with Moses' & the Lamb's Song
16:1-21	The 7 Last Vial Plagues on the Wicked & Jesus is Coming Soon
17:1-18	Murderous Idolatrous Harlot Destroyed by Blasphemous "Babylonian" Beast, Conquered by Christ
18:1-24	Wicked Wail & Righteous Rejoice at God's Final Just Judgment on Babylon
19:1-21	Praise God; the Testimony of Jesus: His Wedding, Coming, & Wicked Defeated by Word of the Lamb
20:1-15	The Millennial Kingdom with Christ, Without Satan & The Great White Throne Judgment
21:1-27	New Heavens, New Earth, & New Heavenly City with God & the Lamb's Glory, Light, & Life
22:1-21	Keep God's Word & Be Blessed, Jesus is Coming Quickly, Please Come Lord Jesus

Left-column categorizations

7 Churches: 1-Ephesus (2:1-7) 2-Smyrna (2:8-11) 3-Pergamos (2:12-17) 4-Thyatira (2:18-29) 5-Sardis (3:1-6) 6-Philadelphia (3:7-13) 7-Laodicea (3:14-22)

7 Seals: 1-White Horse-Conquering (6:1-2) 2-Red Horse-Killing (6:3-4) 3-Black Horse-Famine (6:5-6) 4-Pale Horse-Death (6:7-8) 5-Martyrdom (6:9-11) 6-Earthquakes/Meteors (6:12-17) 7-Heavenly Silence-1/2 hr (8:1)

7 Trumpets: 1-Hail Fire-1/3 Land/Plants (8:7) 2-Fiery Mountain (8:8-9) 3-Meteor–Wormwood-1/3 Rivers/Lakes (8:10-11) 4-Darkness-1/3(8:12) 5-Demon Led Locusts-Sting(9:1-12) 6-200M Army-1/3 Killed(9:13-21) 7-Heavenly Voices/Christ's Wrath/Reign(11:15-19)

7 Vials or Bowls: 1-Boils (16:2) 2-Sea as Blood/Death (16:3) 3-Rivers/Lakes as Blood (16:4-7) 4-Scorching Sun (16:8-9) 5-Darkness (16:10-11) 6-Dried Euphrates (16:12-16) 7-Worst Earthquake & Hail (16:17-21)

7 "Seven": Spirits/Lamps (1:4 3:1 4:5 5:6) Churches/Candlesticks (1:4 11 12 13 20 2:1) Stars/Angels (1:16 20 2:1 3:1 8:2 6 15:1 6 7 8 16:1 17:1 21:9) Seals (5:1 5) Eyes (5:6) Horns (5:6) Trumpets (8:2 6) Thunders (10:3 4) Heads (12:3 13:1 17:3 7 9) Crowns (12:3) Plagues (15:6 8 21:9) Vials (15:7 17:1 21:9) Darkness

New Things: 1-Heaven (21:1) 2-Earth (21:1) 3-Jerusalem (21:2) 4... 5-All Things (21:4)

2nd Beast: The False Prophet [2 Lamb like Horns, miraculous power, deceives, makes living image of Anti-Christ & causes all to worship Anti-Christ to receive 666 in their right hand or forehead to buy or sell anything or kills those who don't] (13:11-18) &

1st Beast: The Anti-Christ [7 Heads, 10 Horns, 10 Crowns, "upon his heads the name of blasphemy", Jesus Christ-7, "Jesus Christ"-7, Who "Was ["Alpha", "the beginning", "the first", "was dead"]" healed, empowered by Satan] (13:1-10)

Jesus Christ—"Lamb" 29 times; 'the Lamb'-26, 'Jesus'-14, 'Christ'-11, 'Jesus Christ'-7, Who "Was ["Alpha", "the beginning", "the first", "was dead", "He that liveth"], & "Is To Come" ["Omega", "the ending", "the last", "am Alive Forevermore"] (1:4 8, 11, 17, 18, 28, 21:6, 22:13) &

Judicial Evidence: "the testimony of Jesus" (12:9, 12:17, 19:10) 2 Witnesses "finished their testimony" (11:3, 7) Believers overcome by "their testimony" (12:11, 17) "John for the testimony" (3:14) "144,000" Witnesses (7:4) "beheaded for the witness of Jesus" (20:4) "sent My Angel to testify" (22:6, 16) "I testify" (22:18) "the testimony in Heaven" (15:5)

Jesus Pictured As: "Almighty" "Faithful Witness" & Loving Resurrected Redeemer (1:5, 8) Bridegroom & Head of the Church (2:1-3:22, 19:7-9) "Lion of the tribe of Judah" (5:5) "Lamb that was slain" (5:6, 12) High Priest (8:3-6) Righteous Judge, King of kings & Lord or Lords (19:11-20:15)

Prophecy Purpose: "...the testimony of Jesus is the spirit of prophecy." (19:10)-the setting that predicts/ reveals Jesus & His plan & purpose for man's future

Revelation Purpose: "...to show unto His servants things which must shortly come to pass..." (1:1)-Apocalypse=disclosure of that previously hidden or unknown

Revelation Promise: "...Blessed is he that readeth...that hear the words of this prophecy, and keep those things that are written therein..." (1:3)

THEME/His-story: "The Revelation of Jesus Christ...," & "things which must shortly come to pass..." (1:1)

*Revelation of Jesus Christ and Future from God by John to 7 Churches—
the Time is Near; Happy if Read, Heed, and Keep Prophecy.*

Vision and Word of the Glorified Jesus to John and the Church

Introduction

{Chapter 2 begins the vision and Word of the glorified Jesus
to the Apostle John and Church, providing a time-sequenced outline
for the Book and the future of the church, nation of Israel,
and all the wicked.}

A. What do you think Jesus will look like when you see Him in Heaven?
{Awesome, Humbling, Overwhelming...John gets such a glimpse of
Jesus Christ.}
B. When you get to heaven, what age do you want your glorified body
to appear? {My best, mid-20s.}
C. Are you ever discouraged in your Christian walk? {Yes, when tired,
persecuted, or unsure of past, present, and future-Jesus has a treat for
you in Revelation.}

Scripture (Observations/Interpretation/Commentary)
{Read and Title Paragraphs and Fill in the Blanks}

A. **_1:9-11_**— {Title: Jesus, the Alpha and Omega, tells John to write to
the 7 Churches in Asia. **_9_**-**"_I John_** (the Apostle, known as he was exiled
in Patmos Prison), **_who also am your brother, and companion in
tribulation_** (Gr:thlipsis-"pressure, afflicted, anguish, burdened,
persecution, tribulation, trouble;" not The Tribulation or The Great
Tribulation, but persecuted and now imprisoned) **_and in the kingdom_**
(Gr:basileia-"royalty, rule, realm, kingdom, reign"-not the Millennial
Kingdom, which we'll see is still future and we'll explain the difference
further in **_Rev. 20_**, but this means John is like all dedicated Christians,
under the Lordship of Jesus Christ His Lord, Messiah, and King) **_and
patience_** (Gr:hupomone-cheerful, hopeful endurance, constancy,
enduring, patience, patient, continuance, waiting; as John must also
cheerfully wait for the coming of Christ) **_of Jesus Christ, was in the_**}
   1. Location: _____ **_called_** _____, {**_ISLE or ISLAND /
      PATMOS._** An Island off Turkey, like the prison, Alcatraz.}

2. Imprisonment Reasons: ***for the*** _____ ***of God, and for the*** _____ ***of Jesus Christ."*** {***WORD / WITNESS or TESTIMONY***} (The best reason to be persecuted, is for your testimony of Jesus. Just speak Jesus' name and watch the reaction of others) ***10-"I*** (John not in Church as he wanted, because in prison, but clearly worshiping, as he) ***was in the Spirit*** (the Spirit, is the Holy Spirit) ***on the Lord's day*** (Sunday, the day that Jesus was resurrected, the day the early church began to worship on. Under the Law, Jewish believers previously, and even some after the Law, and those unconverted unsaved Jews who rejected Christ, still worshiped on Saturday, the Sabbath), ***and heard behind me*** (John) ***a great voice*** (*Gr:Megas Phone-Great, Loud, Mighty, Strong...Voice, Sound, Tone*), ***as a trumpet,"*** (uses a literal simile "*as*" to describe Jesus' mighty voice) ***11-*** "***Saying, 'I am*** (the eternal present name of God, here of Jesus, cf. ***Exo. 3:14***) ***Alpha and Omega, the first and the last:*** (1st and last letter of Greek alphabet is alpha and omega, and Jesus is "*the*" 1st and last Person) ***and, What you see*** (are seeing),}

3. _____ ***tells John to*** _____ ***in a Book*** (Revelation), ***and send it unto the 7*** _____ ***which are in Asia, unto Ephesus, and unto Smyrna, and unto Pergamos, and unto Thyatira, and unto Sardis, and unto Philadelphia, and unto Laodicea.'"*** {JESUS / ***WRITE*** / ***CHURCHES***.}

B. ***1:12-16***— {Title: The Glorified Jesus with 7 Golden Candlesticks holding 7 Stars. ***12-"And I*** (John) ***turned to see the voice*** (Jesus' mighty trumpet like voice behind John) ***that spoke*** (was speaking) ***with me*** (John)***, and being turned, I*** (John) ***saw 7*** _____ _____;" {***GOLDEN LAMPSTANDS or CANDLESTICKS***-told to be Churches in ***1:20***; a picture that the church is supposed to be golden-valuable at holding forth the Light, Jesus, for themselves and the world to see Jesus, the Truth.}

1. ***13-"And in the middle of the 7 candlesticks*** (churches) ***One*** (Jesus) ***like the*** _____ ***of*** _____, {***SON / MAN***; "son of man" is 197 times in Bible; 85 times in Gospels, 12 times in ***John***-all by Jesus or people quoting Jesus, "Son of God" is 30 times in Bible, all in Gospels, except 2 in ***Acts***, ***John*** has the most. John primarily focuses on the Deity of Jesus in the Gospel of ***John***, but here in this heavenly scene, John emphasizes His humanity as Jesus is in the middle of the churches as a human being, man's substitute and church head, though is also God.}

9

2. Jesus' attire: *clothed* (arrayed) **with a garment down to the**
   _____, **and gird about the paps** (chest) **with a** _____
   girdle (or belt)." {**FOOT / GOLD** or **GOLDEN**; a picture of Jesus
   being modest and rich.}

3. <u>14</u>-"**His** (Jesus') **head and His hairs were white like** _____, **as**
   white as _____; **and His eyes were as a** _____ **of**
   _____; {**WOOL / SNOW**-see the similar description of God
   in <u>**Dan. 7:9-14**</u>; <u>**10:6**</u> re: "*the Ancient of Days*" and "*Son of Man;*"
   FLAME or **FLASH** / **FIRE** or **LIGHTNING**; white hair like snow for
   cool headed purity and wisdom; piercing eyes flashing lightning,
   quick to see any wrong-doing and all things. Notice again the 3
   uses of literal similes ("*like*" and "*as*") to describe and compare
   Jesus's appearance to something we can understand.}

4. <u>15</u>-"**And His** (Jesus') **feet like** _____ _____, **as if they**
   _____ **in a furnace; and His** (Jesus') **voice as the sound**
   of many _____." {**FINE** / **BRASS**-whiteness, brilliancy,
   can be brilliant luster of copper, silver, or gold; shows strength /
   BURNED or were **REFINED** -a perfect active participle "*having*
   been refined;" Jesus held His feet in the fire and they were
   beautifully refined / **WATERS**; brilliant strong feet and strong
   powerful voice speaking for all persecuted.}

5. <u>16</u>-"**And He** (Jesus) **had in His right hand** (picture of strength and
   security) **7** _____: **and out of His** (Jesus') **mouth went a**
   _____ _____-_____ **sword; and His countenance**
   (face) **was as the** _____ **shining in its strength** (power)."
   {**STARS**-told to be angels or messengers (<u>**1:20**</u>) / **SHARP** / **TWO** or
   DOUBLE / **EDGED**, cf. <u>**Heb. 4:12**</u>-"**the Word of God**" in Judgment-
   discerning thoughts/motives, and powerful bright face "*as*" the
   SUN; just as can't look into sun, can't look directly at Jesus' glory
   (cf. <u>**John 9:5**</u>, He is "*the light of the world;*" <u>**Rev. 21:23**</u>; <u>**22:5**</u> no
   sun as God is light). So, <u>**1:13-16**</u> shows Jesus modest clothes and
   belt, then His white head and hairs (for pure wisdom and Deity)
   and eyes of judgment to quickly see all, and a strong powerful
   voice like a trumpet and many waters-like crashing waves on
   Island of Patmos or Niagara Falls; holding Stars (either angels or
   pastoral messengers) in His right hand (action/strength) and
   speaking clear sharp (accurate) judgment with a powerful bright
   face. This prepares John's heart and should be all our responses
   to this coming Jesus.}

C. 1:17-20— {Title: .John Fearfully Worships and is Told by the Resurrected Jesus to Write.}

1. **17**-"*And when I* (John) *saw Him* (Jesus), *I* (John) *fell at His* (Jesus') *feet as* _____. *And He* {Jesus} *laid* (put) *His* _____ *hand on me* (John)*, {DEAD / RIGHT*-symbol of strength, security, authority, and honor} *saying unto me, 'Fear not; I am the first and the last:'*" {Same as verse **11**, "*I am*"- always here/eternally present (*Gr:protos-first in time, place, importance... Gr:eschatos-final, farthest, uttermost;* where we get eschatology or final things).}

2. **18**-*I am* (again the **Exo. 3:14** name for God that Jesus uses in **Joh. 8:58**, declaring His eternality and equality with God) *He that* _____, *and was* _____; *and Behold, I am* _____ *for evermore, Amen; and have the keys of* _____ *and* _____." {**18-LIVETH** (a present active participle-PAP showing He continually lives) / *DEAD*-gently reminding us bthat Jesus died for our sin, so we feel loved / *ALIVE* or *LIFE*-also PAP, forever (*Gr:Amen-Truly, trustworthy, so be it*); *HELL* or *HADES* / *DEATH*-Jesus has the keys or authority to open up/give life to us all if we will but by faith receive His death, burial, and resurrection in our place.}

3. **19**-"*Write the things which you have* _____, *and the things which* _____, *and the things which* _____ ____ _____." {*SEEN / ARE / SHALL BE HEREAFTER*- which is the Book of Revelation's outline: "*have seen*" (**Rev. 1**); "*are*" (**Rev. 2-3**); "*shall be hereafter*" (**Rev. 4-22**).}

4. **20**-"*The* _____ *of the 7 Stars, which you saw in My* (Jesus') *right hand, and the 7 Golden Candlesticks. The 7* _____ *are the* _____ *of the 7* _____: *and the 7 candlesticks which you saw are the 7* _____." {*MYSTERY / STARS / ANGELS* (*Gr:angelos-angel, messenger, to bring tidings, by implication pastor;* either real angels or pastoral messengers) to 7 *CHURCHES / CHURCHES*; Stars=Angels and Lampstands=Churches; the candlesticks or lampstands were golden-of great value and worth to Jesus; the church should be light to the world.}

A. Have you ever been persecuted for God's Word or Witnessing about Jesus? Why or Why not? {Yes; should happen more if speak up for Bible and Jesus' and the Gospel.}

B. What helps you be more patient when having to wait for something great? {Seeing someone you love and that loves you and knowing what's going to happen.}

C. How encouraged was John seeing the vision and inspired to write Revelation in prison? {Very encouraged to see Jesus and know His sovereign winning plan...}

D. What does it mean to be "*in the Spirit*" if the Spirit is in you always? {In sync with, feeling His presence, confessed up, in the Word, worshiping, in the heavenly here on earth...}

E. Do you get "*in the Spirit*" enough to see more of Jesus? If not, how can you more? {Not enough. By prayer, Bible reading, confession, fellowship, making my heart in tune with His heart...}

F. How was Jesus described in His 1st Coming and how is He described here? {1st-Meek, Lowly, Suffering, and Dying; 2nd-Strong, Bright, Judging, and Alive forevermore.}

G. Has God commissioned you to write or do anything important before He comes? What? {Yes, **_Mat. 28:18-20_**-The Great Commission-Go tell and teach about Jesus. God has specifically gifted me with the talent to.... will you go and obey?}

Figure 2 – 1.2 St. John's Vision of the Seven Candlesticks[1]

Jesus Christ encourages, warns, and gives promises to all churches and to the 1st 4 of 7 in Asia (Ephesus, Smyrna, Pergamos, Thyatira).

Ephesus-Return to 1st Love and Do 1st Works

Introduction

A. If Jesus was the guest speaker at your church, what do you think His message would be? {Gospel, repent from sin...}
B. Can anyone find on a map or draw the Mediterranean Sea? {Point out Egypt, Israel, Lebanon, Syria, <u>Turkey</u>, Greece, Italy, Isles of Sicily, Crete, Cyprus, and Patmos (in between Greece and Turkey—the candy cane of 7 churches starting on Turkey coast-Ephesus, Smyrna, Pergamos-at top, then Thyatira, Sardis, Philadelphia, and Laodicea.}

<u>Scripture</u> (Observations/Interpretation/Commentary)
{Let's read; Jesus' message to Ephesus and to all Churches; a 6 step outline for each of the 7 churches: 1:To x church, 2:From: Intro of Jesus, 3:Good of church, 4:Bad of church, 5:Warning, and 6:Promise; Have learners Read and Title Paragraph and Fill in Blanks}

A. **_2:1-7_**—Title: {Ephesus-Return to 1st Love and Do 1st Works.}
B. **_2:1-7_**—Verse Observations
1. To: **_1_-"Unto the angel of the church of** _____ **write; these things says He** {**_EPHESUS_**/Ephesian church; cf. **_Acts 20:17-38_**; the Apostle Paul's epistle to Ephesians on Body Building for Christians, Marriage, and the Church.}
2. From: (Jesus) **_that_** (Who) _____ **the 7** _____ **in His Right** _____, **Who walks in the midst** (middle) **_of the 7 golden_** _____-_____;**"** {**_2_-HOLDETH** (Gr: krateo-"use strength, seizes, retain, keep, hold;" we are safe in Jesus' hands) / **_STARS_** (Gr: Angelos-angels or messengers-angels or pastors delivering Revelation to church) / **_HAND_**-cf. **_John 10:27-28_**-"no one can pluck out of" / **_CANDLE-STICKS_** or **_LAMP-STANDS_**-**_1:20_** told us is the Church, which ironically, Jesus is holding the messengers and walking in the middle where the church is to hold forth "the Light of the World," Jesus, for the world to see.}
3. Good: **_2_-"I** (Jesus) **_know your_** _____, **and your** _____, **and your** _____, **and how you canst not bear** (don't put up with) **_them_** (unsaved), **_which are_** _____**: and you have**

tried them which (who) *say* (claim) *they are* _____ *and are not, and have found them* _____:" {*2-WORKS* (Gr:ergon-works, deeds) / *LABOR* (Gr:kopos-toil, pain, weariness) / *PATIENCE* / *EVIL* / *APOSTLES*-False, like Muslims, Mormons, and many other false religions or cults call their leaders Apostles or prophets (there were only 14 Apostles-12, Judas died, Matthias replaced Judas-*Acts 1:26*, Paul was the last-called directly by Jesus-*1Co. 15:7-10*-all called by God, all eyewitnesses of the risen Savior, and all had miraculous power that built the early NT church, and could pass on gifts) / *LIARS* or *FALSE.*} *3*-"*And have borne* (put up with), *and have* _____, *and for my* (Jesus') _____ *sake have* _____ *and has not* _____." {*3-PATIENCE* / *NAME'S* / *LABORED* / *FAINTED-Gal. 6:9*; Why do you think He repeats Patience and Labor again? -emphasizes He really appreciates their enduring persecution for Him. What type of service did they not faint from when it was hard, was Jesus commending? -Christian Service in the Church. **Going to *2:6*.} *6*-"*But this you* (Ephesian believers) *have, that you* _____ *the deeds* (works) *of the* _____, *which I* (Jesus) *also hate."* {*6*-Jesus uses the Kiss-Slap-Kiss method (Good-Bad-Good); *HATE* / *NICOLAITANS*-some say followers of Nicolas and others say from (Gr:Nicolah-"let us eat"), but both maintain it holds the doctrine (see *2:15*) that it is lawful to eat things sacrificed to idols and to commit sexual fornication contrary to the Apostles direction in *Acts 15:20, 29*, or what some call licentiousness-see Church Fathers. The Ephesians also hated the sinful works of the Nicolaitans and those choosing to live in sin, as Jesus hates their deeds, but loves them. **Now leave good and go back to *2:4*.}

4. Bad: *4*-"*Nevertheless* (But), *I* (Jesus) *have somewhat* (something) *against you* (Ephesian believers), *because you* (Ephesian church) *have* _____ *your* _____ _____." {*4-LEFT* (Gr:aphiemi-sent forth, forsake, lay aside) / *FIRST* (Gr:protos-foremost, best, first-time, place, priority) / *LOVE* (Gr:agape-unconditional love, God's love; they've stopped being loving, trusting, and obeying God above all else, and then also their brothers and others also. You can't begin loving until you've accepted God's love (cf. *1Jo. 4:7-8*), so you can have God's love live thru you-unconditionally. The church's 1st love is Jesus, their Bridegroom, their Savior...}

5. Warning: **5-"**_____ *therefore from where you are* _____, _____, *and do the* _____ *works; or else I* (Jesus) *will come unto you* _____, *and will remove your candle-stick* (lamp-stand; church) *out of his* (its) *place, except* (unless) *you* _____. {**5-REMEMBER / FALLEN / REPENT / FIRST** (Gr:protos-foremost, best, first-time, place, priority; these are the things all true believers do when they 1st get saved, they want to tell others, read God's Word, spend time at Church with other believers...) / **QUICKLY** / **REPENT**-change mind. Why do you think Jesus emphasizes remember and says *"Repent"* twice? --Recall and then change your mind, doubly pleading to please change their mind.}

6. Promise: **7-"He that has an ear** (even 1)**, let him hear what the Spirit** (interesting these are Jesus' Words, in red, in red letter editions, but Jesus said to be speaking the very Words of the Spirit, which is always the case, as Jesus is God) *says to the churches; To him that* _____, *will I* (Jesus) *give to eat of the* _____ *of* _____, *which is in the middle of the* _____ *of God."* {**7- OVERCOMETH** (Gr:Nicao-subdue, conquer, overcome, get the victory; cf. **1Jo. 2:13-14**; **5:4-5** says *"you have overcome"* and all that believe Jesus is the Son of God *"overcometh the world"*) / **TREE** (Gr:xulon-tree; used of cross, cf. **Acts 5:30**; **10:39**; **Gal. 3:13**..., that brought life through the death of Jesus, so all true Christians in the Church will overcome and won't undo what Christ's overcoming has already wrought). He will give us to eat freely, not like Adam and Eve who were prohibited from eating of this Tree in Paradise after they sinned / of **LIFE**-He also wants to give us *"abundant life"* now (**Joh. 10:10**) / in **PARADISE**-mentioned 3 times in the Bible (**2:7**; **Luk. 23:43**; **2Co. 12:4**-implying all believers will be with Him in Paradise to eat of the tree of life, as we'll see in heaven, cf. **Rev.22**.}

Application (Activity/Questions)

A. What are *"the first works"*? {Believe, Pray, Love, Read Bible, Tell others, Be filled with the Spirit, Obey Word, Serve in Church...}

B. Has anyone ever taught you that all believers are to use their abilities to love/serve God and others in Church? In what role do you think you should be serving? {Yes. Teaching; Praying.}

C. Who should be our *"first love,"* in importance and priority? {God/Jesus, and we should have *"no other"* *"before Him,"* in front of Him or in His place (***Exo. 20:3***; ***Deu. 5:7***).}

D. How do you return to your *"first love,"* once you've left? {Remember, quickly change your mind, *"do"* the first things in the relationship that rekindle that love...}

E. Has Jesus ever become your *"first love,"* and do you remember how you felt when 1st in love? {Yes, so excited I had to tell every-one, I wanted to be around others who loved Him, wanted to learn all I could about Him, wanted to talk to Him all the time, obey Him...}

F. Who overcomes sin, Satan, the world, the flesh, death, and Hell (***2:7***; ***1Jo. 2:13-14***; ***5:4-5***)? {Jesus, and all that believe Jesus is the Son of God.}

Jesus Christ encourages, warns, and gives promises to all churches and to the 1ˢᵗ 4 of 7 in Asia (Ephesus, Smyrna, Pergamos, Thyatira).

Smyrna-Don't Fear Suffering, Be Faithful.
{As 1-Day, Believers Will Rule & Wear a Crown.}

Introduction

A. Would you be willing to die for your faith in Jesus? {Yes; sometimes that is not as hard as living for Jesus as a _**"living sacrifice"**_ (cf. _**Rom. 12:1-2**_).}
B. How does one know whether you would be faithful to Christ when persecuted? {Going thru tests and the way you respond to lesser trials/tests.}
C. Does persecution usually make the Church and a Christian stronger or weaker in their faith? So, if you were God, would you sometimes allow Satan to persecute us? {Stronger; Sadly yes.}

Scripture (Observations/Interpretation/Commentary)
{Let's read Jesus' message to Smyrna and to all Churches; a 6 step outline for each of the 7 churches: 1:To x church, 2:From: Intro of Jesus, 3:Good of church, 4:Bad of church, 5:Warning, and 6:Promise; Have learners Read and Title Paragraph and Fill in Blanks}

A. _**2:8-11**_—Title: {Smyrna—Don't fear Suffering, Be Faithful.}
B. _**2:8-11**_—Verse Observations
   1. To: _**8**_-**"And unto the angel of the church in** _____ **write; these things says the** {_**8**_-**SMYRNA**; which is now Ismir, which is an important commercial city with a population of >120,000. Claims to be birthplace of Homer. Is a producer of wine. Some background on the famous and faithful Church elder Polycarp: when the governor said that he would spare his life if he would but deny Christ, Polycarp was martyred for his faith. He was quoted in a Smyrna letter saying, _"Eighty and six years have I served Christ, nor has He ever done me any harm. How, then, could I blaspheme my King who saved Me?....I bless Thee for deigning me worthy of this day and this hour that I may be among Thy martyrs and drink the cup of my Lord Jesus Christ..."_[2] When the governor persisted to try to get Polycarp to deny

Christ by threatening to burn him at the stake, Polycarp shared the gospel and warned him of eternal hell fire if the governor rejected Christ.}

2. From: (Jesus) **the _____ and the _____ Which** (Who) **was _____ and is _____;**" {*FIRST*-in priority, resurrection, beginning / *LAST*-end; *DEAD*; *ALIVE* or *LIFE*- emphasizing His resurrection and eternal state.}

3. Good: **9-"I know your _____ and _____ and _____ , (but you are _____)** {*9-WORKS / TRIBULATION / POVERTY*-worldly/outwardly/temporary; when persecuted, some were fired when converted and some had property taken away, and Jesus knows about it and promised heavenly property and wealth in **Heb. 10:34**; *RICH*- "are" now eternally/inwardly/character/God's approval, not just when a believer goes to heaven; many that have worldly riches are eternally poor and those eternally/inwardly rich (rich in faith, good works, in hope...) may also be worldly/ outwardly poor. God allows persecution of the church to purge and enrich its character and culture in its members.}

4. Bad: **and I** (Jesus) **know the _____ of them which** (who) **say they are _____ and are not; but are the _____ of _____.**" {*9-BLASPHEMY*- lying/speaking evil against (normally God, His Spirit, His gospel, or His true followers). *JEWS*-bigotry saying or pretending they are the chosen covenant-people with a special relationship with God and persecuting the church after Israel was blinded and set aside. Maybe they were even still trying to perform the sacrificial laws Jesus fulfilled, and they were attacking Christians who claimed Christ was the true Messiah and Savior (Who they rejected). Some "completed Jews" were ridiculed, but here these are not even true Jews. *SYNAGOGUE*-Jewish place of worship, assembly, congregation. *SATAN* is "*the accuser of the brethren,*" "*the great deceiver,*" the one who can appear as an "*angel of light,*" but is a "*liar,*" and a "*murderer,*" especially of those truly following Christ. God has the true Church and the deceiver has the false one. Satan's Synagogue or assembly always opposes the truth of the Gospel of faith in Jesus Christ and tries to lead men away from God into a false, works, traditions, ceremonies-based, false religion, which is always blasphemous.}

5. Warning: **10**-" _____ *none of those things which you* (Church) *shall suffer: behold, the Devil* _____ *cast* (throw) *some of you* (believers) *into prison,* _____ *you may be* _____ *; and you* _____ *have* _____ *10 days; be you* _____ *unto* (as far as) _____ ," {**10-FEAR; SHALL** (Gr:Mello-intends, purposes to, will) / **THAT** (Gr:hina-a purpose clause) / **TRIED** or **TESTED**-Satan wants to hurt, God sovereignly allows to purify/forge/prove your metal; **SHALL** (Gr:echo-will have). **TRIBULATION** or **PERSECUTION** 10 days. The 10-days warns and tells of 10 specific days of persecution coming. Some say 10 symbolizes the limited duration or completion of the persecution's purpose. Persecution often separates the wheat from the chaff, the sheep from the goats, the saved from unsaved. Christ isn't as concerned about circumstances, as He is for our spiritual state— So, He doesn't always remove the trial, misunderstanding, *"thorn in the flesh,"* illness, weakness, pain—His *"grace is sufficient"* and trials are sometimes the only time we see His strength and feel His presence like we need, cf. **2Co. 12:7-10**). **FAITHFUL-1Co. 4:2**-faithfulness is our duty; **2Ti. 2:13**-if we are faithless, God is still faithful / **DEATH**-physical, is only temporary for the true Church/saved, and is the farthest limit God will permit Satan's trial or touch.}

6. Promise: **10**b-"*And I will give you a* _____ *of life."* {**CROWN** (Gr:Stephanos-crown, badge of royalty, prize, a symbol of honor).} **11**-"*He that has an ear* (even 1)*, let him hear what the Spirit* (again are Jesus' Words speaking the very Words of the Spirit) *says to the churches; He that* _____ *, shall not be* _____ *of the* _____ *death."* {**11**-If you have ears, listen to what the Spirit says to the churches-all of us; **OVERCOMETH** (Gr:Nicao-subdue, conquer, overcome, get the victory; cf. **1Jo. 2:13-14**; **5:4-5** says *"you have overcome"* and all that believe Jesus is the Son of God *"overcometh the world"*); uses a double negative to emphatically encourage us that we will *"no never"* be **HURT** (Gr:adikeo-to be unjustly morally, socially, physically hurt, suffer, or done wrong); of the **2ⁿᵈ** / by *"the 2ⁿᵈ death"*-4 times in Bible (**2:11**; **20:6, 14**; **21:8**)-the spiritual death or Hell for the unsaved and Satan and His demons. Deep thought: **John 17:3**-says that eternal life is knowing the only true God and Jesus, those unsaved/hurt by the 2ⁿᵈ Death will not

experience daily knowing Him and will experience spiritual death (separation from God) in pain apart from Him forever.}

Application (Activity/Questions)

A. Do you fear suffering for your faith enough to be quiet about Jesus? {Sadly, sometimes.}

B. What is the worst Satan can do to you, if God allows it? {Physical Death.}

C. How can you obey Christ's command to not fear suffering and be faithful? {Just do it, think of rewards; know it makes you better / stronger in character and deeds like the Smyrna Church became; you can be like the Ephesian church-repent/return to make Jesus our 1st love and do the 1st works.}

D. How can you trust a loving rewarding God when going thru tough trials for your faith? {Know that it is only temporary, that Jesus knows and only permits it to make you stronger and have a stronger testimony; remember your eternal/spiritual riches.}

E. Can you share a story of being persecuted for Christ? Why or Why not? {Yes, witnessing; called names in school, told was religious, been laughed at, was actually fired for "testimony of Christ;" but not even close to imprisonment or death...If you can't, please don't fear man/Satan/world or God.}

F. Do you consider it a privilege to live or even die for Jesus? {Yes, that is how Jesus makes us more worthy and conforms us into His image. Sorry Lord, for wimping out, so many times.}

Jesus Christ encourages, warns, and gives promises to all churches and to the 1st 4 of 7 in Asia (Ephesus, Smyrna, Pergamos, Thyatira).

Pergamos-Repent, Separate from Worldly and Licentious Doctrine.
{And Christ Will Give Believers a Special Name.}

Introduction

A. What are some of the things _"the world"_ focuses on? {Pleasure, eating, dollars, drugs, drinking, sex, idols, fame, power...}

B. Read **Pilgrim's Progress** (free/downloadable on web; paragraphs 37, 53-56 and 58). {Written as an allegory of the Christian life; 404 total paragraphs, with Scripture and references; one of the best books ever written; uses old English. These 6 paragraphs give you just a little regarding: Christian's experience with Evangelist helping Christian regarding Mr. Worldly Wisdom's counsel.}

Scripture (Observations/Interpretation/Commentary)

{Let's read; Jesus' message to Pergamos and to all Churches; a 6 step outline for each of the 7 churches: 1:To x church, 2:From: Intro of Jesus, 3:Good of church, 4:Bad of church, 5:Warning, and 6:Promise; Have learners Read and Title Paragraph and Fill in Blanks}

A. _2:12-17_—Title: {Pergamos-Repent and Separate from Worldly and Licentious Doctrine.}

B. **_2:12-17_**—Verse Observations

1. To: **_12_-"And to the angel of the church in _____ write; these things says He** {**_12_-PERGAMOS**; in Greek means _"fortified."_}

2. From: (Jesus) **_Which_** (Who): **has the _____ _____ with _____-_____;"** {**SHARP**; **SWORD**; **TWO** or **DOUBLE**; **EDGES**; a metaphor for the Word of God/Truth emanating from the Word-Jesus (**_1:16_**; **_Heb. 4:12_**), that cuts both extreme right and left sides with absolute truth and accuracy.}

3. Good: **_13_-"I** (Jesus) **know your _____ and where you _____, even where Satan's _____ is: and you hold fast My _____, and have not _____ My faith** ("faith of Me," Jesus; faith in Jesus), **_even in those days wherein_** (when) **_Antipas was My faithful _____, who was slain_** (murdered) **_among you, where Satan _____."_** {**WORKS**

(*Gr:ergon-works, deed, occupation*); **DWELL** (*Gr:katoikeo-to house permanently, dwell*); **SEAT** (*Gr:thronos-seat, throne-place of power*; God is everywhere, Satan can only be 1 place at a time and Pergamos is ground zero for Satan's throne. John calls Satan *"the prince of this world"*-**John 12:31**; **14:30**; **16:11**-and that we should not be part of that world-system, thinking, politically correctness-cf. **Eph. 2:2-6**; **1Jo. 2:15-17**), which is Biblical incorrectness; **NAME**-implies authority or character, the only way to cast out Satan is by Christ's name and power (cf. **Mat. 7:22**; **Mar. 16:17**); **DENIED** faith in Jesus (My faith); **MARTYR** (*Gr:martus- martyr, witness, record; the* witness of Jesus); **DWELLS**-don't allow Satan to dwell in your Church, *"resist the devil and he will flee from you"* (**James 4:7**).}

4. Bad: **14**-**"But I have a few things against you because, you have there them that** (who) **hold the_____ of _____, who taught _____ to cast** (put) **a _____-_____ before the _____ of Israel, to _____ things offered unto idols, and to commit _____."** {**DOCTRINE** or teaching; **BALAAM** (cf. **Num. 22-24**), *"who loved the wages of unrighteousness"* (**2Pe. 2:15**) so much that (even though he knew God wouldn't curse His people, Israel), Balaam counseled Israel's enemies, **BALAK**-King of Moab, to intermingle with Israel and so Israel would *"commit trespass against the LORD in the matter of Peor"* (**Num. 31:16**), by putting a **STUMBLING-BLOCK** before the **CHILDREN** (see warning of hurting children **Mat. 18:6**) of Israel, to **EAT** (see gray areas re: eating in **Rom. 14:1-23**; summary in **14:21**, *"it is good neither to eat flesh, nor to drink wine, or anything whereby thy brother stumbleth, or is offended, or is made weak"*); and to practice **FORNICATION** (clearly sinful, and the most intimate a believer can be with the unsaved world, which **1Co. 6:15-19** tells us we are spiritually Christ's bride and soon to be spouse, so don't commit physical and emotional fornication by our body, Christ's temple).} **15**-**"So have you** (Pergamos saved Church) **also them** (false teachers) **that hold the _____ of the _____, which thing I** (Jesus) **_____."** {**DOCTRINE** of the **NICOLAITANS**- remember **2:6** where the *"deeds of"* here it is the *"doctrine of"* or teaching of, that taught licentiousness; eating things offered to idols and sexual

fornication. Jesus **HATES** this doctrine/sin (because it destroys and hurts sinners that He died for and loves.}

5. Warning: **16**-"_____; *or else I* (Jesus) *will come unto you* (Church) _____, *and will fight against them* (wicked/unsaved) *with the* _____ *of my mouth.*" {**16**-**REPENT**-change your mind so the results of your action and direction can change; **QUICKLY**; **SWORD**-again a picture of God's judging correcting Word, where Jesus's "*mouth*" is not used to eat cheap meat offered to idols (a sinful or questionable use of a Christians mouth at best), but to judge those not worshiping and testifying of the true God.}

6. Promise: **17**-"*He that has an ear* (even 1), *let him hear what the Spirit* (again are Jesus' Words speaking the very Words of the Spirit of God as He is God) *says to the churches* (all); *To him that* _____, *will I* (Jesus) *give to* _____ *of the* _____ *manna, and will give him* (believer) *a white* _____ *and in the stone* (engraved in it), *a* _____ *name, which no man* (no one) *knows saving* (except) *he* (the one) *that receives it.*" {**17**-OVERCOMETH-(Gr:Nicao-subdue, conquer, overcome, get the victory; cf. *1Jo. 2:13-14*; *5:4-5* says "*you have overcome*" and all that believe Jesus is the Son of God "*overcometh the world*"). **EAT**-not temporary meat to false idols; **HIDDEN** (*Gr: krupto-concealed. hidden, secret*; manna in Hebrew-" what *is it,*" but made a sweet honey bread; where Jesus is the true, spiritual, or hidden "*bread of life*" that forever fills our hungry soul, cf. *Joh. 6:35, 48*). STONE-(*Gr:psephos-"a pebble (as worn smooth by handling),*" "*a verdict (of acquittal), a ticket (of admission).*" Jesus here emphasizes Christians don't have to sneak around to buy something bad, but He will give both this heavenly food and a **NEW** name, possibly this stone is like a ticket into heaven, worn smooth by being carried in the hand of the Father, cf. *Joh. 10:28-28*, a spiritual name that only God uses for you. Please receive Jesus today if you don't know Him so you can have hidden or secret sustaining food, a most precious stone or ticket to heaven, and a special new name that only Jesus and you know...}

Application (Activity/Questions)
A. Why is it hard for Christians/the Church to live separate from "*the world?*" {Our fleshly physical desires, we live in "*the world,*" but try to

go contrary to it and its philosophies; we try to love unsaved and it is hard to also hate the world's sin, but love them, and be different from it when in it...}

B. Who overcomes "*the world*" and how do they do so (*1Jo. 2:13-14; 5:4-5*)? {All believers/all eternally saved, by our faith.}

C. Does doctrine in the Church matter? Why? {Yes; we are to teach God's Word and gospel, and false doctrine can bring us and the Church under judgment; doctrine determines how we think/live and the gospel or good news is teaching about Jesus' death, burial, and resurrection, and our response to it is the only way to be forever saved...}

D. Why is it easy to let gray areas become doctrines that cause Christians to stumble? {Because we try to justify what our flesh wants to do and the world tells us to do, especially if we can't find a clear verse to forbid it; once we start doing wrong, we want company, so start teaching people what they want to hear...}

E. How can you help purify/purge the Church of false teachers and doctrine? {Love enough to exhort and confront sin and sinners humbly in love following *Mat. 18:15-18* (Church Discipline), even up to kicking false teachers out of the Church; Accurately teach God's Word/Truth/Doctrine; Teach or require teachers to pass a competency test.}

F. What would you like your new special spiritual name to be that Jesus gives you? {I don't know but can't wait to see and hope to become worthy of it now. I'll never forget the posted nickname my elementary teacher gave me, Ravishing Ron. I had to look it up, it made me want to live up to it, be better. How much more by a new name given by our Lord and Savior Jesus Christ...}

Jesus Christ encourages, warns, and gives promises to all churches and to the 1st 4 of 7 in Asia (Ephesus, Smyrna, Pergamos, Thyatira).

Thyatira-"Hold Fast Until Jesus Comes."
{Don't Get Spiritually Discouraged & Stop Doing Right.}

Introduction

A. Do you ever get discouraged and want to give up (doing the right thing, loving your spouse or kids, going to church...)? Why? {Yes, because it is sometimes hard, folks tell you it is not worth it or you should do something different, sometimes feel alone.}

B. What spiritually encourages you the most? {God's presence and promises; when someone notices, appreciates, and says something about how hard they see I'm working; God's Word, Prayer, Family, and Friends being there; thinking about Heaven and our Future.}

C. What is something that was hard to hold onto? {My 1st son said, "_tubing_," the other said, "_the last pull-up_," my daughter said, "_a great GPA or good cardio shape._"}

Scripture (Observations/Interpretation/Commentary)

{Let's read; Jesus' message to Thyatira and to all Churches; a 6 step outline for each of the 7 churches: 1:To x church, 2:From: Intro of Jesus, 3:Good of church, 4:Bad of church, 5:Warning, and 6:Promise; Have learners Read and Title Paragraph and Fill in Blanks}

A. _2:18-29_—Title: {Thyatira-"_Hold Fast Til I Come._"}

B. _2:18-29_—Verse Observations {As we step thru: please pay close attention to "_you_," "_her_," and "_they_" addressees.}

1. To: **_18-"And unto the angel of the church in _____ write; these things says_** {**_18_**-THYATIRA; between Pergamos and Sardis; they worshiped Apollo, which many believed was the sun god.}

2. From: **"the (1 and only, not a) _____ of God** (Jesus)**, Who has His eyes like unto a _____ of _____, and His feet are like _____ _____;"** {**_18_**-SON, not sun; eyes (Gr:ophthalmos-"eyes, vision, sight;" figuratively a jealous side glance; **FLAME**; **FIRE**, like a consuming piercing look; **FINE**; **BRASS**; powerfully strong stance. So Jesus' fiery glance and firm stance shows him polished and ready.}

3. Good: **_19_-"I** (Jesus) _____ **your** _____, **and** _____, **and** _____, **and** _____, **and your** _____, **and your** _____; **and the** _____ **to be more than the** _____." {**_19_-KNOW** (Gr:eido-see or know) "your" (is personal to Church) **WORKS**, and **CHARITY** (Gr:agape-God's love, unconditional love), and **SERVICE**, and **FAITH**; and "your" **PATIENCE**, and "your" **WORKS**; and the **LAST** (Gr:eschatos-final, last, end; where we get Eschatology-Final Events; > the **FIRST**. Meaning they were maturing, doing greater works than they did at 1st.}

4. Bad: **_20_-"Notwithstanding** (But), **I have a few things against you** (Thyatira, believers)**, because you sufferest** (permit) **that** _____ _____ **which** (who) **calls herself a** _____, **to** _____ **and to** _____ **my servants to commit** _____ **and to eat things offered to** _____." {**WOMAN**; **JEZEBEL**-found 23 times in Bible (**_1Ki. 16-21_**; **_2Ki. 9_**; **_Rev. 2:20_**), who intermarried an Israelite King, brought in idolatrous, sexual, infanticide, Baal worship, and even killed prophets and followers of the true God. **PROPHETESS**-8 times in Bible, clearly a false prophetess here. To **TEACH** (cf. **_1Ti. 2:12_**; **_1Co. 14:34-35_**) and to **SEDUCE** (cf. **_Mar. 13:22_**-"For false Christs and false prophets shall rise, and shall shew signs and wonders, to seduce, if it were possible, even the elect." How much more when we let them in to teach false doctrine in the church). To continually do **FORNICATION** (Gr:porneuo-fornication, practice idolatry) eating things offered to **IDOLS**.} **_21_-"And I** (Jesus) **gave her** (Jezebel) **space** (time) **to** _____ **of her fornication; and** (but) **she** _____ **not."** {**_21_-REPENT; REPENTED**; this "woman Jezebel" is a consistent metaphor with both Israel and the church of the False Church with false prophets that seduce, teach, and commit adultery with Christ's True Church and Bride and this adulteress will be judged as we'll see later in **_Rev. 17-18_**.}

5. Warning: **_22_-"Behold, I will cast** (throw) **her into a** _____ **and them that commit** _____ **with her into** _____ **tribulation, except** (if they don't) _____ **of their** _____." {**BED**-instead of "you've made your bed, now you have to sleep in it," it is "she's unmade her bed and all who get in it with her will have them self and their children judged." And those committing **ADULTERY**-a married person being the most

intimate possible with someone other than their spouse, not just sex outside of marriage. Will result in **GREAT**-this is throughout history, but also points to the False Church not being Raptured, but going into *"the Great Tribulation,"* which is a technical term used of the last 3 and ½ years of The 7 Year-Tribulation period. If they don't **REPENT**, God is patient. From their **DEEDS** or **WORKS**; you will see Jesus speaking to 3 audiences: *"you"*-True Church/Saved, *"her"*-False Church/Unsaved, and *"them"*-which are unsaved, but still could choose to be saved if they repent (change their mind by faith, which also results in a corresponding change in actions/works).} ***23***-"*And I* (Jesus) *will _____ her _____ with _____; and _____ the churches shall _____ that I am He* (Jesus) *Which* (Who) *_____ the reins and _____: and I will give unto to every one of you according to your _____.*" {**KILL**-God is serious about not leading people to hell. **CHILDREN**-those pulled back and forth prodigy will also suffer physically and get to choose spiritually. Kill with **DEATH**-not kindness, like Jesus' normal, patient, turning of the cheek, cf. **Mat. 5:39**; **Luk. 6:29**. Jesus emphasizes this, though killing always produces death. **ALL**-includes true churches will **KNOW** (*Gr:ginosko-experiential knowledge*) it is Jesus **SEARCHETH** (*Gr:ereunao-seeks, investigates, searches*; Jesus seeks our minds (*Gr:nephros-kidneys, reins, inmost mind*) and **HEARTS**-is just like the Word (Jesus) discerns *"thoughts and intents of the heart,"* cf. **Heb. 4:12**); **WORKS**; Jesus will reward— be patient if good, repent if evil.} ***24***-"*But, unto you I* (Jesus) *say, and unto the rest in _____, as many as have not this _____, and which* (who) *have not _____ the depths of _____, as they speak, I will put upon you none* (no) *other _____.*" {Changes from *"them"* back to *"you"*-Christians/church/ saved, and specifically **THYATIRA**-this local church; you who don't have this **DOCTRINE**-false teaching and worship; and haven't **KNOWN**-again the Greek word for experiential knowledge; the depths of **SATAN**-deep dark deceived devilish debauchery that started with blindness to *"the glorious gospel of Christ"* (**2Co. 4:4**); as *"they"* again unsaved false teachers/prophets; Christ sees the church's struggle so won't add any other **BURDEN** (*Gr:bara-heavy burden*, not *Gr: phortion-light burden/normal responsibility*).} ***25***-"*But that which you have already, _____ fast until I* (Jesus)

_____." {**HOLD** (*Gr:krateo-use strength to hold, retain*; keep the right teachers and doctrine and works/love/faith/ service /patience (**2:19**); until I **COME**-the Rapture (**1Th. 4:13-18**)-Jesus meets the church in the air and takes us to heaven, it is imminent, or could happen at any moment, it will be like a *"thief in the night"* (**1Th. 5:2**) when Jesus takes His church home to be with Him forever in heaven. Hold on for Jesus}

6. Promise: **26**-"**And He that** _____, and _____ **my** _____ **unto the end, to him will I give** _____ **over the nations:"** {OVERCOMETH (*Gr:Nicao-subdue, conquer, overcome, get the victory*; cf. **1Jo. 2:13-14**; **5:4-5** says *"you have overcome"* and all that believe Jesus is the Son of God *"overcometh the world"*), and **KEEPETH** (*Gr: tereo-watches, guards*; not my words-doctrine, not *"your"* works-human effort, but *"my"* **WORKS**, Jesus' finished work, the gospel and the things He is doing. Be a part of protecting what Jesus is doing. He will accomplish His will and works with or without you. This is consistent with what **James 2:18** says, *"I will show you my faith by my works"* and **Gal. 2:20**, *"Christ lives in me"* and works thru me. When your works become Christ's works, you are working on all cylinders. These next 3 promises are given to believers (Israel and Church, but here specifically says us/the Church-yea) in the 1,000-year Millennium, which we'll study more in **Rev. 20**. Christ will give 1) **POWER** (*Gr:exousia-privilege, mastery, power, authority*; we'll see that the Church Age believers get to rule and reign with Christ in the Millennial Kingdom over the nations, cf. **Rev. 20**).} **27**-"**And he** (Christ and believers) **shall** _____ **them with a** _____ **of** _____; **as the vessels of a potter shall they** (wicked nations) **be broken to** _____: **even as I** (Jesus) **received of My** (Jesus') _____." {2) **RULE** (*Gr:poimaino-tend as a shepherd, feed, rule*; which we should be shepherding the sheep in the church now; but also get to do with Christ with a; **ROD**; of **IRON**; a *"rod of iron,"* found 4 times (**Psa. 2:9**; **Rev. 2:27**; **12:5**; **19:15**; then **Isa. 11:1, 4** calls Jesus *"a rod out of the stem of Jesse"* and says He will fairly judge the poor and meek, but smite the wicked with *"the rod of His mouth"* another metaphor for the absolute truth of the Word of God using the Shepherd's 1 end of the staff for protecting/saving sheep and the other for protection from/judging unsaved attackers. **SHIVERS**-or into pieces; literally

as Jesus received from "my" **FATHER**-the greatest and ultimate source of authority and power, He will share with us during His rule.} **28**-"**And I will give him** (believers; **the _____ _____**.**" {3) God's greatest gift to believers is the **MORNING STAR** (cf. **22:16**; **2Pe. 1:19**)-what a sweet metaphor for Jesus, the morning star is the brightest as can be seen even when the sun is out, or during the day. It is contrasted with the idol Apollo, the mythical sun-god who was distant and terrorizing. Jesus is true, close, and giving. Jesus even gives us Himself, the best gift anyone can give, especially when you are perfect. How intimate, how wonderful. It will be the dawning of a new day when we see Jesus brightly shinning in and for us for ever and ever.} **29**-"**He that has an ear** (even 1)**, let him hear what the Spirit says unto the churches.**" {If you have ears, listen to what the Spirit (from Jesus Himself) says to the churches-all of us.}

Application (Activity/Questions)

A. How can you better "*Hold Fast until I* [Jesus] *come*[s]"? {Read Bible More (>), Pray >, Separate from World >, Help Cleanse church from false teachers/teaching >; Serve Christ >, Share Gospel >, Love >, Trust Him >...}

B. How can you guard Jesus' works in your life? {Guarding your heart and mind by who and what you let influence it. Doing things Jesus would do; WWJD (What Would Jesus Do?).}

C. What are some reasons to look forward to ruling and reigning with Christ one day with a perfect ruler? {Peace, love, long life, learning, beauty, evil restrained and quickly dealt with...}

D. How bright is your future with Jesus? Why? {The brightest! He is perfect, loving, wonderful, Prince of Peace, Giving, Protecting, the bright and Morning Star...}

Jesus Christ encourages, warns, and gives promises to all churches and to the last 3 of 7 in Asia (Sardis, Philadelphia, and Laodicea).

Sardis-Only a Few Saved; Remember, Repent, Guard, and Watch.
(Or Jesus Will Come Like A Thief.)

Introduction

A. How do you know if you are in a dying church? {Few saved and getting saved; numbers dropping or only increasing unsaved and worldly; immature, few growing and obeying God.}
B. Is Jesus most like your father, best friend, enemy, or acquaintance, and how would you like it? {Father; Best Friend.}

Scripture (Observations/Interpretation/Commentary)

{Let's read; Jesus' message to Sardis and to all Churches; a 6 step outline for each of the 7 churches: 1:To x church, 2:From: Intro of Jesus, 3:Good of church, 4:Bad of church, 5:Warning, and 6:Promise; Have learners Read and Title Paragraph and Fill in Blanks}

A. _3:1-6_—Title: {*Sardis-Only a Few Saved; Remember, Repent, Guard, and Watch.*}
B. **_3:1-6_**—Verse Observations
 1. To: **_1_-"And unto the angel of the church in** _____ **write; these things says"** {**_1_-SARDIS**; ancient city of Lydia; 1 of the 1st cities converted by John's witness; was a chief city in Asia minor; left Christianity and was laid and still lays in ruins.}
 2. From: "**He** (Jesus) **that has the** _____ **Spirits of God, and the 7** _____; GOTO #4 {**_1_-SEVEN** (Spirits of God. Clearly this is not a redefinition of the Trinity, which is 1-God, eternally existing in 3-Persons, Father, Son, and Holy Spirit. And is not a redefinition of the 1 Holy Spirit, into 7 Persons or individual Spirits. The Greek word for "Spirits" is *pneuma*, which means breath, spirit, soul, life, mind, mental disposition, and can even mean angel. So some say this is 7 angels as are talked about repeatedly in Revelation, some say it is Christ's mind or mental disposition consistent with the Spirit's working in the 7 churches. I rule out angel, as John consistently uses *Gr:angelos* for "*angel*" or "*messenger*." One could hold the mind or mental disposition and be consistent in the context of this passage. It is found only

4 times in all of Scripture, all in Revelation, where the number 7 is consistently and repeatedly used for perfection. The first occurrence is In *1:4*, where these 7 Spirits are *"before His [God's] throne."* Next, here in *3:1*, Jesus *"has"* or holds them as Jesus is completely/perfectly God, as the number 7 represents perfection and completed purpose or maturity. Most understand these 7 Spirits as the working of the Holy Spirit and His various ministries, operations, and graces showing His complete involvement and commitment to each of the 7 churches. If you will, a complete working of the Spirit in each church. Just as we would not say there are 1,000 Spirits of God that indwell 1,000 Christians in a church, but we do know He works in many different ways in those 1,000 specific individuals. So, most hold the *"7 Spirits of God"* to mean 7 different ministries or 7 different specific ways in which the Holy Spirit worked with the specific issues of each of the 7 specific churches. In *4:5*, they are *"7 lamps of fire burning before the throne."* The final occurrence is in *5:6*, where they are *"7 horns and 7 eyes,"* which we will learn later are kings/kingdoms and perfect vision for judgment. So the 7 Spirits metaphor as *"lamps"* or light, showing the truth revealed by the Spirit, *"of fire burning before the throne"* pictures the Spirit's work in holy judgment coming from God's throne, the 7 horns we're told in *17:12* shows the Spirit's involvement in the government and their leaders rule, and finally the 7 eyes, shows the Spirit of God seeing with perfect vision what is happening in the world and each church to best enable believers by the complete working of the Spirit to overcome), **STARS**-(*1:20* told us they were *"the angels of the 7 churches"* in His right hand) and no one can pluck them out of His or His Father's hand (cf. *John 10:28-29*) GOTO #4.}

3. Good: *4*-*"You have a few _____, even in Sardis, which have not _____ their garments, and"* Go to #6 {*NAMES*-representing people or the character of faithful Christians, the remnant; that have not **DEFILED** (*Gr:moluno-defiled or soiled their pants or outfit*). Go to #6 for Promise: section.}

4. Bad: *1*-*"I (Jesus) know your _____, that you have a _____ that you live, and are _____."* {1st church where Jesus starts with bad/not good (as He later does with Laodicea); **WORKS.** You have a **NAME** (*Gr:onoma-name, character*; people think they have a name/reputation for really living, but Jesus

knows their works and who they really are). But are **DEAD** (*Gr:nekros-dead-spiritually*; unsaved think they are really living when religious, getting drunk, but God says they are dead and have dead useless works.} **2-"Be** _____ **and strengthen the things** (good works) **which** _____, **that are ready to** _____: **for I have not found your works** _____ **before** _____." {Be **WATCHFUL** (*Gr:gregoreuo-awake, watchful, vigilant*); **REMAIN**-whatever is left that are good works; as they are ready to **DIE** (*Gr:apothnesko-die off, die, be dying*; this church is apathetically dying out without enough godly saved and growing members); because Jesus hasn't found their works **PERFECT** (*Gr:pleroo-finished, complete, leveled up, perfect, filled up*); before **GOD**-the ultimate judge, it doesn't matter what is right in our eyes, only what God thinks and sees...}

5. Warning: **3-"**_____ **therefore, how you have** _____ **and** _____, **and** _____ **fast, and** _____. **If therefore, you will not** _____, **I will** _____ **on you as a** _____ **and you shall not know what** (the) _____ **I will come upon you."** Go to #3 {**REMEMBER**; how or in what way; you have **RECEIVED** and **HEARD**-how did you 1st grow and start doing good works, works of life and faith?- By asking God to speak to you, receiving His commands, hearing and obeying Him; and **HOLD** (*Gr:tereo-guard from loss, keep from escaping, implies a full military fortress*; hold-fast); and **REPENT**-change your mind from your current apathy and disobedience and dead works. If you "*will not,*" doesn't say if you do not, it is a choice of the will, if you won't **WATCH**-same word as before, for wake up, be vigilant; Jesus will **COME** "*on*" or Jesus is going to get "*on your case.*" If rejecting His merciful presence, you will get His coming in judgment; like a **THIEF**-*Gr:kleptes-stealer, thief*; where we get the root for kleptomaniac, someone who can't resist the urge to steal. It will seem if Jesus sneaked in and Raptured the church and found the spiritually dead members in the church napping and unprepared (cf. *1Th. 5:2*); and you will (*Gr:ou me-"no never" "not at all"*) know the **HOUR**-Jesus will come upon you. You may not get another warning to be prepared—so please receive Jesus now so you are prepared. Go to #3 for the "Good:" in *3:4*.}

6. Promise: __4__-"*And they shall* _____ _____ *Me* (Jesus) *in* _____: *for they are* _____." {Christians shall 4-Ws: 1) **WALK**-all around on pleasant prepared paths in paradise; 2) **WITH** me/Jesus (what a privilege); in 3) **WHITE** (no soiled, only pure clean outfits); for they are 4) **WORTHY** (Gr:axios-deserving, due a reward, worthy).} __5__-"*He that* _____, *the same shall be* _____ *in* _____ *raiment; and I will not* _____-_____ *his* (saved; each believer) *name out of the* _____ *of* _____, *but I will* _____ *his* (believer's) *name* _____ *My* (Jesus') _____ *and before His* (God's) _____." {He that **OVERCOMETH** (Gr:Nicao-subdue, conquer, overcome, get the victory; cf. __1Jo. 2:13-14__; __5:4-5__ says "you have overcome" and all that believe Jesus is the Son of God "overcometh the world;" **CLOTHED** (Gr:periballo-arrayed, clothed; invested in by Christ); in **WHITE**-purity, like a bride's wedding garment of virtuous worthiness by Jesus giving us righteousness, His perfect, which perfect matches the perfection of the Father; and I will not **BLOT-OUT** (Gr: exaleipho-smear out, obliterate, blot out, take away; his name out of) the **BOOK** of **LIFE**-[believers names were written in "*The Lamb's Book of Life*" (__Rev. 13:8; 21:27__, when they believed in Jesus, and no one's name can be blotted out of the Lamb's Book of Life. "*The Book of Life*"-TBoL (__Php. 4:3__; __Rev. 3:5__; __17:8__; __20:12, 15__; __22:19__) has everyone's name written in it of all who were conceived. A person's name gets blotted out of TBoL when they blaspheme the Holy Spirit (or reject the Spirit's drawing to Christ/refuse to believe in Jesus). Either a different book, or TBoL is the book that contains all the works that a person has performed]. But Jesus will **CONFESS** (Gr:exomologeo-acknowledge, agree fully, profess, promise); **BEFORE** (Gr: enopion-in the face of, before, in the presence of); My/Jesus' **FATHER**-highest person in universe; and before His **ANGELS**-all of God's other non-human created creatures. Wow, not only does Jesus give us a wedding garment, but also gives us eternal life, and even promises before the righteous judge of all the universe-His Dad, that we are now worthy.} __6__-"*He that has an ear* (even 1)*, let him hear what the Spirit* (again are Jesus' Words speaking the very Words of the Spirit) *says unto the churches.*" {If you have ears. Listen to what The Spirit says to the churches-all of us.}

Application (Activity/Questions)

A. Do the mature or immature Christians watch more for Christ's coming? {Mature watch for Christ most in faith, keeping their eyes on *"Jesus, the author and finisher of our faith"* (**Heb. 12:1-2**).}

B. Who and why will people be most surprised when Jesus comes? {Immature/unsaved will be most surprised, because the > they don't trust God, the > they get deceived that He is not true/real, and they always hope there will be more time before judgment.}

C. Is it sometimes hard to stay strong in the Lord when the church seems cold and dead? Why? {Yes. Because unsaved or weak Christians pull you down, discourage you, don't help you focus, and enable us to be double minded and hearted.}

D. How can you be more watchful and strengthen the good ones/things in the church? {Look to Jesus daily, talk to and about Him; do more good works; encourage/exhort; pray and ask God to strengthen your walk with Him and church/fellow Christians its leaders.}

E. What can you do to help keep your church from dying out? {Witness to add believers; build up fellow Christians, pray for them; serve more using your gifts in the church...}

F. Do you look forward to walking with Jesus in Heaven one day? What about daily now? {Yes. Not as much as I want and should.}

G. Can a Christian get their name blotted out of *"the Book of Life"*? Why (cf. **John 10:28-29**; **John 6:47**; **1Jo. 5:13**; **1Pe. 1:2-5**...)? {No. Because they have already overcome through Christ (**1Jo. 2:13-14**; **5:4-5**). Jesus promises them to be with Him in Heaven and that **John 10:28**-*"they shall never perish;"* (**John 6:47**-*"He that believeth on me hath everlasting life."* **1Jo. 5:13**-*"These things have I written unto you that believe on the name of the Son of God; that ye may know that ye have eternal life."* **1Pe. 1:2-5**-believers have *"an inheritance incorruptible, and undefiled, and that fadeth not away, reserved in heaven for you, Who are kept by the power of God."*}

Jesus Christ encourages, warns, and gives promises to all churches and to the last 3 of 7 in Asia (Sardis, Philadelphia, and Laodicea).

Philadelphia-Jesus Loves and Delivers the Faithful Patient Church.
{Jesus Will Keep the Church Out of the 7-Year Trib Period.}

Introduction

A. The world looks down on the Church spiritually, why do we want their love so? {Since we live in world, we often feel excluded and want to be included.}

B. Are you Pre-Trib, Mid-Trib, Partial-Trib, or Post-Trib (Christ's Coming in Air in relation to the Tribulation)? {4 main Rapture views below.}

Figure 3 – 8.1 Main Rapture Views

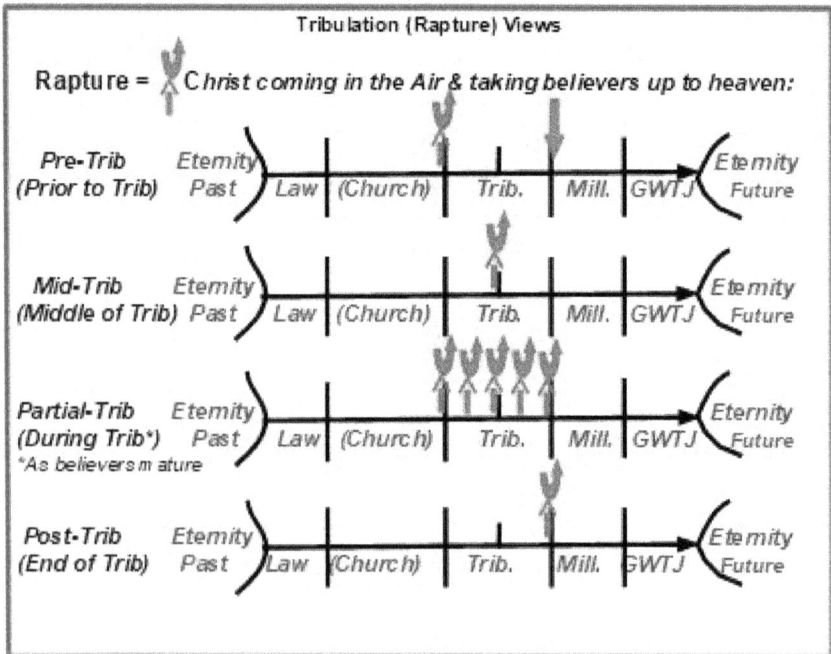

{Quickly draw views on board or reference chart above. Briefly here are 7 top reasons most are Pre-Trib. 1) Literal interpretation of Scripture requires it (e.g. **_3:10_**-Church will be kept _"from,"_ out of the Trib, not _"through"_ it-we'll look at today. **_1Th. 5:9_**-talking about the Church and the Trib _"God hath not appointed us to wrath;"_ **_1The. 5:2_**-Christ's coming is as a _"thief in the night;"_ 1 of the places we get... 2) The doctrine of Imminence-Christ could come at any moment. He could not come right away if we know of many of the specific years of judgment, we'll soon see in **_Rev. 6-18_**. 3) Enough Time to have enough saved to populate the Millennium (7 years). 4) The Holy Spirit's indwelling presence removed as the Church is Raptured (**_2Th. 2:1-12_**). 5) **_Dan. 9:24-27_** literal fulfillment of last 7 years of Israel's 490 prophesied years, where 483 years have already been fulfilled. 6) Trib called "*a time of Jacob's* [Israel's] *trouble,*" not the Churches' trouble (cf. **_Jer. 30:7_**; **_Dan. 12:1_**). 7) The Church is found on earth in **_Rev. 1-3_**, the Church is in heaven in **_Rev. 4-5_**, and the Church is not found in the Trib (**_Rev. 6-18_**), because the Church was Raptured prior to the Trib.}

<u>Scripture</u> (Observations/Interpretation/Commentary)
{Let's read; Jesus' message to Philadelphia and to all Churches; a 6 step outline for each of the 7 churches: 1:To x church, 2:From: Intro of Jesus, 3:Good of church, 4:Bad of church, 5:Warning, and 6:Promise; Have learners Read and Title Paragraph and Fill in Blanks}

A. **_3:7-13_**—Title: {Philadelphia-Jesus Loves and Delivers the Faithful Patient Church.}
B. **_3:7-13_**—Verse Observations
   1. To: **_7_-"And to the angel of the church in** _____
      write; these things says" {**_7_-PHILADELPHIA**; Gr:phileo-friendship love; Gr:adelphos-brother; "*city of brotherly love;*" a center of wine trade; a dozen churches. Jews flocked there after 70AD when their temple was destroyed; many earthquakes; taken over by Turks in 1300s-named Allah Shehr: "*the city of God.*"}
   2. From: **_7_-"He** (Jesus) **_that is_** _____, **_He that is_** _____ (cf. **_6:10_**), **_He that has the_** _____ **_of_** _____, **_He that openeth and no man_** _____; **_He that closes and no man_** _____;" {**_7_-HOLY**-an attribute only God (Father, Son, and Holy Spirit) perfectly is. He that is **_TRUE_**-or truthful (cf. **_Joh. 14:6_**, where Jesus is "*the truth*"), Jesus has the "**_KEY_** (sg) of **_DAVID_**"-an initial quote of lowly Eliakim, a type of Christ, who was promoted and strengthened to rule Israel with the same opened door opportunity in the royal house of David (**_Isa. 22:20-22_**), and then ultimately the Davidic Covenant (**_2Sa. 7:12_**f) will be fulfilled by Christ the Messiah in His Millennial/Kingdom reign (**_Isa. 9:6-7_**). In **_1:18_**, Jesus has the keys of Hell and Death and here positively

the Key to the Kingdom. Jesus opens and no one **SHUTTETH**; and closes and no one **OPENETH**. It is the holy, true Jesus Who has the authority and key of the kingdom of David (which Jesus promised to the Jews) and to the church in **2:26-27**; where no one can open or close, but Jesus who will let in and out (by His holiness and truth alone).}

3. Good: **8**-"*I know your* _____, *behold, I* (Jesus) *have set before before you an* _____ *door, and no man* (one) *can* _____ *it; for you have a little* _____, *and have* _____ *My* (Jesus') _____, *and have not denied My* (Jesus') _____." {**8-WORKS** (Gr:ergos-works/deeds); **OPEN**-an "*open door*" of blessing and eternal opportunities (cf. *1Co. 16:9*; *2Co. 2:12*); **SHUT** or close; **STRENGTH** (Gr: dunamis-force, power, strength, ability; since our strength is small and Jesus' strength is omnipotent, Jesus has the door already opened for us to come in); **KEPT** (Gr:tereo-kept, guarded), My Jesus' **WORD** (obedient and protected from false teachers) and have not denied My **NAME**.}

4. Bad: **9**-"*Behold, I* (Jesus) *will* _____ *them* (wicked impostors) *of the synagogue of* _____, *which* _____ *they* (wicked) *are* _____, *and are not, but do* _____; *behold, I* (Jesus) *will* _____ *them to come and* _____, *before your* _____, *and to know that I* (Jesus) *have* _____ *you.*" Go to #6 {**MAKE** (Gr:didomi- give, bestow); those of the SoS-Synagogue of **SATAN** (only twice in Bible, both in Revelation, both by John, here and **2:9**). They are going to have a real SoS if they are getting what Satan and his demons get, Hell (cf. **20:10, 15**). **SAY** they are **JEWS**, and are NOT, but do **LIE** (Gr:pseudomai-falsely, lie, attempt to deceive by falsehood; these were religious hypocritical persecutors). Warning/Promise: Again "*Behold*" I will "**MAKE**"-though different than 1st word for make or give as a result, in first part of verse, this one is (Gr:poieo-make, do, cause, execute) is to cause them to come and **WORSHIP** (Gr:proskuneo-to kiss, like a dog licking/kissing his master's hand, to prostrate oneself in homage, to worship); before your **FEET** (this could be fulfilled in a Millennial Kingdom rule reference of saints in **2:26-27**, or when the wicked bow at the Great White Throne Judgment in **20:11-15**, the saved could stand in Christ and have the wicked at their feet) and they'll know that I, Jesus have **LOVED** (Gr:agapao-love, in a social or moral sense; socially saints

will finally be completely powerfully politically correct) you. Go to #6.}

5. Warning: **_11_-"Behold, I** (Jesus) _____ **quickly: Hold fast that which you** (believers) _____, **that no man** (one) **take your** _____." Go to: #6b {**COME**-this is the Rapture-where Jesus is coming for us as Bridegroom, not the 2nd Coming as Judge. We (Church) are coming with Him, preceded by the testing/judgment time of the 7-year Trib. Strongly hold that which you **HAVE** (*Gr:echo-possess, hold, have*; present tense, active voice, indicative mood; you now have it in possession; their testimony; good works); (*Gr:hina-that, purpose clause*); no one saved or unsaved, or no thing take away your **CROWN** (*Gr:stephanos-crown, public prize, badge of royalty, reward, symbol of honor*). Go to: #6b.}

6. Promise: **_10_-"Because you** (believers) **have** _____ **the Word of My** (Jesus') _____, **I also will** _____ **you** _____ **the** _____ **of temptation** (or Tribulation)**, which shall come upon** ____ **the world to** _____ **them that dwell upon the** _____." {**KEPT**; "the Word"-Jesus' Word, of My-Jesus' **PATIENCE** (that which Jesus asks us to endure); Jesus will **KEEP** (*Gr:tereo-watch, guard, keep, detain [in custody]*; same word as "kept"); you (believers); **FROM** (*Gr: ek-out of, or from, that place or time*); the **HOUR** (*Gr:hora-hour, season, or time*); of temptation (*Gr:peiramos-a putting to proof [by experiment of good], experience [of evil], solicitation, discipline, provocation, adversity, temptation, try*; infers strong Tribulation for purpose), which will come (future from 1st century AD) upon **ALL** the world/earth (this can only be the world-wide 7-Year Tribulation period coming), to **TRY** or test (purpose) them (unsaved, including Jews) that reside upon the **EARTH**. An incredible promise, that because the Church is faithful (because of Jesus), keeping Jesus' Word patiently that Jesus will keep the Church "*out of*" the 7-year Trib (Pre-Trib) designed to test Israel and the world/not the Church.} Go to: #5/#6b **_12_-"Him that** _____, **will I** (Jesus) **make a** _____ **in the** _____ **of My** (Jesus') **God, and he** (saved) **shall go no more** _____: **and I will** _____ **upon him** (saved) **the** _____ **of My** (Jesus') **God, and the name of the** _____ **of My** (Jesus') **God, which is** _____ **Jerusalem, which comes down out of** _____ **from My** (Jesus') **God: and I** (Jesus) **will**

write upon him (saved) *My* (Jesus) _____ *name.*" {After #5 *12*-
The saved person that **OVERCOMETH** (*Gr:Nicao-subdue,
conquer, overcome, get the victory*; cf. *1Jo. 2:13-14*; *5:4-5* says
"*you have overcome*" and all that believe Jesus is the Son of God
"*overcometh the world*"); Jesus will make a **PILLAR** (*Gr:stulos-
support, pillar*; Jews only allowed Christians in the Court of the
Gentiles of their Temple). Jesus says that believers are now
God's temple and building, cf. *1Co. 3:15-17*; *Eph. 2:6, 19-22*; *1Pe.
2:4-10*, and here promises Christians will have pillars erected
engraved with their name in the **TEMPLE** (cf. *2Ch. 3:17*-the 2
pillars named Jachin and Boaz; *Jer. 1:18*; *Gal. 2:9*-all metaphors
of strength and endurance, particularly applicable for
Philadelphia's earthquakes weakening their buildings). And that
we will (*Gr:ou me-"no never"*) be put **OUT** and I will **WRITE**
(*Gr:grapho-describe, write*); upon him (saved) the **NAME** of God
(where many Jews wouldn't even write God's name, now
believers will have it written upon them); and the name of the
CITY of God (Jerusalem); and the **NEW** Jerusalem (even better
than the old one); which comes down from **HEAVEN** from My
God; and I will write upon you (believers) My **NEW** name (Jesus
will have a new name, which is also given us like God's name
was). So Jesus promises the Church to safely keep them out of
the 7-year Tribulation period (by Rapturing believers out), and
will let us permanently support the heavenly temple, never have
to leave, have God's and Jesus' new name written on us (like
people call us Christians today, what will God's new name for us
be?), and the name/authority/character of God's new heavenly
city, prepared for us (cf. *John 14:2-3*).} *13*-"*He that has an ear*
(even 1)*, let him hear what the Spirit* (again are Jesus' Words
speaking the very Words of the Spirit) *says unto the churches.*"
{If you have ears. Listen to what the Spirit says to the churches-
all of us.}

Application (Activity/Questions)

A. How can you help our church be known as a loving church (a caring
place)? {By loving members, caring enough to invite and help meet
needs of non-members, giving, showing God's love, telling them about
heaven, and how to get there through Jesus...}
B. Have you ever been asked to deny Jesus or not use His name yet?
{Yes; the more you speak up for Him the more likely you will be.}

C. How can you patiently stand strong in a pagan society? {Pray, read, study, obey, speak up, and seek God's praise above other's...}

D. What spiritual good things are you doing each week and how can you keep doing them? {Bible Reading, Prayer, Witnessing, Church/Life Group attendance...Hold fast, endure, plan/schedule/ commit to do them, have an accountability partner, pray to be faithful, give, serve...}

E. How can you best keep Jesus' Word during persecution? {Read, study, decide to obey, plan, endure, ask others to check you, expect persecution to come (cf. *2Ti. 3:12*)...}

F. Does it help to know Jesus knows every good work you do for Him? {Yes, it is comforting.}

G. How do you see God testing and maturing you at this phase in your life? {Trials, learning to trust Him during them, daily dependence...}

H. How does it encourage you knowing you will miss the worst Tribulation ever coming on the world? {Very glad to miss. Makes me feel loved/blessed and that God sees my trials now and will reward me later.}

Jesus Christ encourages, warns, and gives promises to all churches and
to the last 3 of 7 in Asia (Sardis, Philadelphia, and Laodicea).

Laodicea-Repent, Desire, and Dine with Jesus-Lukewarm Christians.
{Subtitle: Spiritually Blind and Naked and Don't Know or Care or
The Christian Who Has No Clothes (not by Hans Christian Andersen)}

Introduction
{My 1ˢᵗ week as a new college Professor I wanted to get to know my
students and so asked what they thought was the biggest problem in
the Church today, ignorance or apathy? A guy in the back quickly
responded with "I don't know, and I don't care." I knew then they both
were true, and it would be a fun year. We'll see today that was also the
case in Laodicea.}

A. What is worse when your zipper has been down all day, 1) to know
it's down and not care, or 2) to NOT know it's down and care greatly?
{1-cause then you are immoral and apathetic, not just ignorant, but
still caring.}
B. Are you 1) Cold as Ice, 2) Hot and Passionate, or 3) Somewhere in
Between? How about spiritually? {Hot and Passionate; Spiritually
2/3ʳᵈ but wanting to be only Hot and Passionate for Christ.}
C. How clearly do you see with an eternal perspective or do worldly
lenses cloud your view? {Pretty good eternal perspective, but don't
always best follow the eternal path.}

Scripture (Observations/Interpretation/Commentary)
{Let's read Jesus' message to Laodicea and to all Churches; a 6 step
outline for each of the 7 churches: 1:To x church, 2:From: Intro of Jesus,
3:Good of church, 4:Bad of church, 5:Warning, and 6:Promise; Have
learners Read and Title Paragraph and Fill in Blanks}

A. **_3:14-22_**—Title: {_Laodicea-Repent, Desire, and Dine with Jesus-_
Lukewarm Christians.}
B. **_3:14-22_**—Verse Observations
  1. To: **_14_-"And unto the angel of the church of the** _____
     write; these things says" {**_14_-LAODICEANS**; founded about 260
     BC, named after King Antiochus II's wife Laodice, a very
     prosperous trade route (lots of travelers from Rome, Egypt,

Europe...), including a Port (large imports/ exports), a Colosseum (athletic, music, drama, and cultural events), in the Lycus River Valley (sheep exporting high quality black wool clothes-fashion), Hierapolis (hot water-6 miles away) and Colossae (cold water-10 miles; cf. *Col. 4:16*) also in valley, 40 miles southeast of Philadelphia (loving), vs lukewarm rich due to much gold with a main banking center for Asia Minor (finances and currency exchange), a medical center world famous for their eye and ear salve (medical and pharmaceuticals). The city lacked water so built elaborate stone aqueducts to pipe in cold and hot water where often received lousy lukewarm water due to distance and would slow and clog needing artery-like cleaning from mineral and sediment build-up.}

2. From: __14__-"the _____ (Jesus), *the _____ and _____ witness, the _____ of the creation of God;"* {*14-AMEN* (*Gr:amen-trustworthy, true, truly*); *FAITHFUL*, and *TRUE* (repeated from amen) witness (*Gr: martus-witness, martyr, record*). Jesus was truly the One Who gave His life for us, so we ought to be passionately living for Him; the *BEGINNING* (*Gr:arche-commencement, chief, beginning, power, rule*). Cult groups try to say this means Jesus was created by God, but this is clearly saying that Jesus is the creator Who commenced, powered, is chief, is the ruler of God's creation...cf. *Col. 1:15-19*.}

3. Good: {Sadly, no good is mentioned about Laodicea, because they thought they were so good.}

4. Bad: __15__-"*I* (Jesus) *know your _____, that you are neither _____ nor _____; I* (Jesus) _____ *you were cold or hot*." {*WORKS* or deeds; *COLD* (*Gr:psuchros-chilly, cold*); *HOT* (*Gr:zestos-boiled, hot. fervent*); *WOULD* (*Gr:ophelon-wish, would, interjection-"oh that," "would to God"*) you were cold or hot. GOTO: #5} #4b: __17__-"*Because you say, 'I am _____, and increased in _____, and have need of _____; and know not that you are _____, and _____, and _____, and _____, and _____:*" {*17-RICH*-and they were worldly/temporarily rich; *GOODS*-earthly/materialism, and have need of *NOTHING* or no one; but really you don't even know you are *WRETCHED*, and *MISERABLE*, or pitiable, and *POOR* (*Gr:ptockos-to crouch, beggar, or poor*; contrary to their high headed nose lifted demeanor), and *BLIND* (physically or mentally/clearly spiritually), and *NAKED*: though wearing

wealthy wool, were clearly not living like His sheep, following the Good Shepherd), but stripped bare. Shows a 5-fold deception of their eternal reality. GOTO: #6.}

5. Warning: *16*-"*So then, because you are* _____, *and neither cold nor hot, I* (Jesus) *will* _____ *you out of My* (Jesus') *mouth.*" GOTO #4B {*LUKEWARM; SPEW* (Gr: emeo-vomit, spew; lukewarm Christians out of My mouth. You never want to leave a bad taste in Jesus' mouth. GOTO: #4b.}

6. Promise: *18*-"*I* (Jesus) _____ *you to* _____ *of Me* (Jesus) *gold* _____ *in the fire, that you may be* _____, *and white raiment, that you may be* _____, *and that the shame of your nakedness do not* _____; *and anoint your eyes with eye salve, that you may* _____." {*COUNSEL*-Jesus is our advocate/attorney/counselor (*1Jo. 2:1*; *Isa. 9:6*) and He recommends to us to *BUY* (Gr:agorazo-purchase, redeem, buy; of Jesus gold-gold survives all currency exchanges); especially the type that is *TRIED* (Gr: puroo-kindle, refined, tried by fire, cf. *1Co. 3:9-15* shows our works will be tried by fire including all that we are investing our time, talents, hearts and minds); "*that*" (here 4 times is Gr:hina-purpose, result, intent) you may be *RICH*-true, lasting, eternal riches; and white-for purity, raiment, that you may be *CLOTHED*, and that the shame of your nakedness not *APPEAR* (Gr:phaneroo-render apparent, manifest; these worldly rich were concerned about appearances; looking refined) more than having truly refined character; and anoint your eyes with eye salve that you may *SEE*-with a true, eternal perspective. They were well-known for their eye salve, but need spiritual eye salve to see what is eternally valuable and best.} *19*-"*As many as I* (Jesus) _____, *I* (Jesus) *rebuke and chasten: be* _____ *therefore, and* _____. {As many as I *LOVE* (Gr:phileo-friendship love; unusual for God/Jesus, normally Gr:agape-unconditional love). But clearly showing Jesus acting as a true friend, like everyone that is truly your friend will love you enough to tell you what you don't see clearly about you and your life, cf. *Pro. 27:6*). As many as Jesus loves, He rebukes and disciplines: "*therefore*" (Almost sounds like a parent's love, "because I love you, do..." 2 things; both commands] be *ZEALOUS* (Gr:zeloo-hot feeling for or against, desire, be zealous over; not lukewarm); and *REPENT* (Gr:metanoeo-think differently, reconsider, repent).} *20*-"*Behold, I* (Jesus) *stand at*

the _____, and _____: if any man (one) _____ ***My*** (Jesus') ***voice, and*** _____ ***the door, I will*** _____ ***in*** _____ ***him, and will*** _____ ***with him, and he with Me*** (Jesus)***.***" {Behold/see Jesus standing at the ***DOOR***, and I ***KNOCK***, He could easily enter, but only does when invited. If anyone ***HEAR***-listens to Jesus' voice (His sheep do, "*My sheep hear my voice...and follow Me*," cf. ***Joh. 10:16, 27***); and ***OPEN*** the door, Jesus will ***COME***-he wants your invitation into your heart and life (even after you're engaged to Him); ***TO*** (*Gr:pros-toward, to, near*). "*Draw near to God and He will draw near to you,*" ***Jam. 4:8***. It is Jesus that asks for an invitation and it is Jesus Who moves towards/ near you, it is He that says, "*if I be lifted up from the earth* [on the cross]*, will draw all men unto me,*" ***Joh. 12:32***. And I (Jesus, personal) will ***SUP*** (*Gr:deipneo-dine, sup [at the main meal]*) with you; and He emphasizes again, you get to dine "*with*" Jesus. What a promise. Say yes, to His daily dinner knocking.} ***21-To him that*** _____ ***will I*** (Jesus) ***grant to*** _____ ***with Me*** (Jesus) ***in My*** (Jesus') _____, ***even as I*** (Jesus) ***also overcame, and am*** _____ ***down with My*** (Jesus') ***Father in His*** (God's) _____." {To him that ***OVERCOMETH*** (*Gr:Nicao-subdue, conquer, overcome, get the victory*; cf. ***1Jo. 2:13-14***; ***5:4-5*** says "*you have overcome*" and all that believe Jesus is the Son of God "*overcometh the world*"). Jesus will give you the privilege to ***SIT*** (*Gr:kathizo- seat, set, sit, settle, dwell*; denotes rest and honor at the main throne, and later wedding table); "*with Jesus*" in My ***THRONE***, He doesn't say thrones, He says "*throne,*" like we are sitting in His lap, and lap of luxury, and ruling place; wow! And you can say that backwards, wow! And we can overcome, just like Jesus overcame (not by His will, but the Father's (***Luk. 22:42***); and am ***SAT*** (same Greek word as above for sit, resting and honored); with Jesus' Father in His Father's ***THRONE***-wow, what oneness Jesus has with the Father and He has promised for us (cf. ***Joh. 17***; ***Eph. 4:3-6***).} ***22-***"***He that has an ear*** (even 1)***, let him hear what the Spirit*** (again are Jesus' Words speaking the very Words of the Spirit) ***says unto the churches.***" {If you have even 1 ear, listen to what the Spirit says to the churches-all of us.}

Application (Activity/Questions)
{Can do in groups to save time}

A. How can you take off world-tinted glasses and anoint your eyes with spiritual salve? {Don't buy into lukewarm political correctness, prepare your heart, mind, and commitment to see things Biblically, the way God says is unchangingly true. Abortion is murder/not a choice, Homosexuality is an abominable sin/not a way a person is born or preferred choice, Truth and Ethics are absolute/not relative or situational...}

B. Are you satisfied with or pursuing temporary worldly riches? Why/why not? {No, but sometimes start focusing that way as if I would be.}

C. How does a Christians now *"buy of Me gold"* from Jesus for eternal riches later (**_3:18_**)? {Serving in church, loving others-especially Christians, tithing/giving, doing good/walking in the Spirit, earning persecution by speaking up for and living for Jesus, not just living for ourselves or the world—these riches last.}

D. How do you keep the white outfit Christ gave you at the cross, when you wear it daily? {Refrain from sinning, don't hang around in the mud/the World, quick confession when sin... (By the way, Christ promised to give us the whitest wedding outfit for heaven, cf. **_3:4-5_**).}

E. What type of brother helps you see and remove stains in your spiritual outfit now, 1) Loving/Spiritual, 2) Hateful/Non-spiritual, or 3) Lukewarm/Baby Christian)? {1. Most Loving and Spiritual-**_3:19_**; cf. **_Gal. 6:1_**f.}

F. What makes God the sickest to His stomach and why, 1) Unsaved living for Satan, 2) Saved living for Christ and them self, or 3) Saved living for Christ only? {2. Since such a waste, the most painful for person to know the Truth and live hypocritically, pulled back and forth, up and down, not fruitful or ever really experiencing the joy of the Lord's abundant life by totally following Jesus as Lord.}

G. Who repents quickest when they sin: 1) One who is closest, most intimate relationship with Christ, or 2) One distant, or lukewarm, and why? {1; Because they care and are motivated by the relationship and miss the daily joy of Christ in their life.}

H. Most apply **_3:19-20_** of Christ's knocking at the door of their heart to unsaved; who is the real audience and context? {Saved to repent and return with their full heart to be "hot" or on fire for Christ and not to be spiritually blind and naked, but to pursue Christ/eternity and be truly rich. Though clearly Christ seeks or knocks on the hearts of the lost too, cf. ***Luk. 19:10***.}

I. How can you best get and keep an eternal spiritual perspective? {Same answers as C and D + prayer, which aligns our will with God's, Bible reading, study, and application to renew our minds, refocus our perspective on Christ, and committing our life to an eternal service/vocation/purpose...}

J. What does it mean to be spiritually Lukewarm? {Part cold and part hot, apathetic, neither on fire for Christ, nor the devil, complacent, double-minded, double-hearted, one who tries to blend in with the world and with Christians, Christian politicians in the world, one who lives around a dark cold world (not enough to be frozen), but to have their fiery light dimmed and hot living water lukewarm...}

K. Are you Lukewarm and if so, will you repent? {Sometimes, yes, Lord please forgive me and help me to return to my 1st love, to see with your eternal perspective by trusting you today...}

L. How do you listen to the Spirit speaking through Jesus most effectively? {Pray for Him to; commit your heart to obey what He says in His Word, read, re-read, meditate, memorize, tell it to others, live it!}

After Church Age, Elders and Seraphims Worship God
on His Heavenly Throne

God Worshiped on His Heavenly Throne.
{Chapter includes Chart with Definitions of 7 Key Prophet Events.}

Introduction
A. What will you do when you get to heaven and see God on His
throne? {I can only imagine, but I know I will fall on my face and thank
Him for His Love, Mercy, Grace, His Worthiness, Holiness, His Glory,
Honor, and Power...that is what Jesus' church and Angels do.}
B. Would you like to be one of the top 24 church believers, why? {Yes,
demonstrates gratitude and faithfulness.}
C. Do you think there will be some surprises as to who the top
believers are, why? {Yes, maybe a closet prayer warrior, someone
faithful behind the scenes walking in the Spirit.}

Scripture (Observations/Interpretation/Commentary)
A. Read **4:1-11** {Note the continued action, only 3/11 verses don't
begin with _"and;"_ the whole chapter is 1 big paragraph.}
B. **4:1-11** Commentary {Verse-by-verse Exposition.}
   1. **4:1**— {_"**After this**_ (after _**Rev. 2-3**_ where Jesus addressed all the
   churches and the things which _"are,"_ cf. _**1:19**_ showing the Book
   outline; the present; the Church Age; clearly ended} _I_ (John)
   **looked, and a door was** (being) _**opened in heaven**_ (good picture
   of Jesus' open door policy for _"all who believe,"_ cf. _**3:20**_; _**Joh.**_
   _**3:16**_; _**6:40, 47**_..., but this gave John visibility into heaven): _**and**_
   **the 1st voice** (implying more angel voices to come) _**which I**_ (John)
   **heard was as it were** (like) _**a trumpet**_ (used for announcements,
   alarms, majestic events) _**talking with me**_ (John); _**which said,**_
   **'Come up hither** (here; a picture of the Church Rapture that
   culminates the Church Age), _**& I**_ (an angel) _**will show you**_ (So
   John, in this 3-D vision, is told to go up through the door into
   heaven to see more. Sure John longed for heaven in the middle
   of his suffering in prison; and the 1st angelic voice told John he
   would show him) _**things which must be hereafter.**_" (Again
   showing a quote from _**1:19**_ on the last part of Rev. outline; things
   "hereafter" the Church Age, which is the Tribulation Period and
   things following it.}

2. ***4:2***— {"***And immediately*** (no time delay, action; as the Rapture is "*in the twinkling of an eye,*" cf. ***1Co. 15:52***) *I* (John) ***was*** (became) ***in the spirit*** (does not tell us if this was John's spirit, like Paul says "*whether in the body, or out of the body*" when he went to heaven in a vision, cf. ***2Co. 12:2-3***, or whether this is in the Holy Spirit, as in fully filled with and controlled by the Spirit enough to be carried up to heaven): ***and, behold, a throne was set in heaven, and 1*** (God) ***sat*** (sitting; continuously) ***on the throne.*** " (We'll find out that this is God-the-Father as made clear in ***5:7*** that He is not the Son.}

3. ***4:3***— {"***And He*** (God) ***that sat*** (was sitting; on the throne) ***was to look upon*** (Gr:horasis-the act of gazing, an inspired appearance; John is wowed) ***like a jasper and a sardine stone*** (precious gemstones; jasper-opaque variety of chalcedony-multicolored with many unique patterns, bands, speckles; 7 times in Bible, twice re: high priest breastplate gemstone in gold representing the last tribe of Israel, cf. ***Exo. 28:20***; ***39:13***; once of Satan's beautiful and counterfeiting covering, cf. ***Eze. 28:13***; once of God, cf. ***4:3***; and the final three of the light, wall, and the wall's 1st foundation of the New Jerusalem in Heaven, cf. ***Rev. 21:11, 18-19***; sardius or sardine-is red or some call blood-colored, better known today as carnelian; 5 times in Bible; twice re: high priest breastplate gemstone representing 1st tribe, cf. ***Exo. 28:17***; ***39:10***; once of Satan's covering and counterfeiting God, cf. ***Eze. 28:13***; once of God, cf. ***Rev. 4:3***; and the 6th foundation of New Jerusalem, cf. ***Rev. 21:20***): ***and there was a rainbow*** ("*rainbow,*" 5 times in Bible; ***Gen. 9:13-14, 16***; ***Rev. 4:3***; ***10:1***; always found in a cloud; representing the multifaceted beauty of God's merciful everlasting promise to all living creatures that He would never again completely destroy all flesh by flood) ***round about*** (all around) ***the throne, in sight like*** (similar) ***unto an emerald.*** " (An emerald is another precious stone found 5 times in Bible; twice re: high priest's breastplate gemstone representing the 4th tribe, cf. ***Exo. 28:18***; ***39:11***; once again of Satan's covering, cf. ***Eze. 28:13***; once of God, cf. ***Rev. 4:3***; and the 4th foundation of New Jerusalem, cf. ***Rev. 21:19***). So God on His throne with glorious gemstones (one that looks like blood that was shed for sin), two like the 1st and last tribes, some say alpha and omega, the beginning and the end; a rainbow as a sign of God's merciful promise to not completely destroy the world (which He died for)

and also prismatic beauty reflecting rays of hope; and the emerald green hews as signs of new life and growth arising from judgment.}

4. ___4:4___— {"***And round about*** (all around) ***the throne*** (God's) ***were 24 seats*** (*Gr:thronos-thrones, or stately seats, implies power; same Greek word as God's throne, but KJV translates seats to show under God's all powerful throne*): ***and upon the seats*** (thrones) ***I*** (John) ***saw 24 elders sitting*** (denotes rest, rule, or judgment)***, clothed in*** (wearing) ***white raiment*** (showing honor and purity, like at a wedding)***; and they*** (24 elders) ***had on their heads crowns*** (*Gr:stephanos-a badge of royalty, prize, or symbol of honor*) ***of gold.*** " (Not just the normal plant wreathe crown, but costly gold. So who are these 24 elders closest to God and His throne? The white clothes and gold crowns were specifically promised to the churches, cf. ___2:10___; ___3:5, 11___; "*Elder*" was a specific office of Pastor/Overseer commanded in the church, "*elders*" is found 12 times in ___Revelation___, and John, the apostle, was an elder over multiple churches and referred to himself as "*the elder*" in 2nd and 3rd John; these 24 elders sound like top church believers in God's inner circle; which may have been the 12 apostles, cf. ___Mat. 19:28___, Paul, and 11 others, but could be top believers of all time, where some have speculated the 12 apostles and 12 tribes of Israel or not tribes, but Abraham, Moses, David, Paul, and 8 others; God doesn't tell us, but we'll see, and they are all worshiping God.}

5. ___4:5___— {"***And out of the Throne, proceeded*** (discharged) ***lightnings and thunderings and voices*** (all 3 are plural and feminine-like our storms used to be; all picturing God's throne of power): ***and there were 7 lamps of fire burning before the throne, which are the 7 Spirits of God.*** " (A clear picture of perfect judgment with the 7 lamps of burning fire [to clearly see] before the throne, "*which are the 7 spirits of God*" [another unexplained mystery of our eternal incomprehensible God, and the full working of His Spirit(s). In ___1:4___-they are "*before God's throne;*" in ___3:1___-Jesus "*has*" the complete working of these 7 Spirits as He is completely, perfectly, and 100% God-7 is the number of perfection. Many understand these 7 Spirits as the Holy Spirit and His various ministries, workings, operations, and graces, showing His complete involvement and commitment to each of the 7 churches. In ___4:5___-these 7 Spirits of God are "*seven*

lamps of fire burning before the throne" [perfect judgment about to be unleashed from the rule of God's holy throne]. In **5:6**-they are *"seven horns and seven eyes"* [which we will see later are kings/kingdoms for God's complete Spirit's involvement and perfect vision for judgment in the world governments and affairs of men]).}

6. **4:6**— {**"And before the throne** (not the 24 other surrounding supportive subordinate thrones, but God's, the 1 in the center of the universe and heaven) **there was a sea of glass like unto a crystal** (cf. **15:2**)**: and in the midst of** (or among) **the throne** (God's)**, and round about the throne** (God's; emphasized for the 3rd time in this verse alone of His rightful ruling place)**; were 4 beasts** (living creatures; good angels)**, full of eyes before** (in front) **and behind."** (Clearly seeing sin in need of judgment— these Seraphims, Angels that **Isa. 6:2, 6**; **Rev. 4:8** tell us have 6 wings and many eyes; they use 2 wings to cover their face, 2 to cover their feet, and 2 to fly; they worship God, speak, and minister at God's throne and altar. He continues now re: their appearance or character.}

7. **4:7**— {**"And the 1st beast** (living creature; Seraphim) **was like** (similar in appearance or character to) **a lion, and the 2nd beast** (living creature) **was like** (similar to) **a calf** (young bull)**, and the 3rd beast** (living creature) **had a face as** (similar to) **a man, and the 4th beast** (living creature) **was like** (similar to) **a flying eagle."**}

8. **4:8**— {**"And the 4 beasts** (angelic living creatures) **had each of them 6 wings about** (Gr:kuklothen-all around) **him** (not in Greek, but KJV supplies *"him"* to help understand that each angel had 6 wings around the individual angel)**; and they were full of eyes within** (they see the truth about God and others)**: and they** (Seraphim angels) **rest not day and night, saying, 'Holy, Holy, Holy** (Trinity of holiness-Father, Son, and Holy Spirit, perfection, separateness)**, Lord** (supreme authority)**, God** (1 supreme being)**, Almighty** (universal sovereign, God, omnipotent)**, Who was, is, and is to come."** (An expression of the only eternal ruling One).}

9. **4:9**— {**"And when** (whenever, as long as) **those beasts** (living creatures, special angels) **give Glory** (Gr:doxa-dignity, glory, honor, praise, worship; cf. **1Ch. 16:29**; **Psa. 29:2**; **96:8**) **and honor** (Gr:time-value, money, esteem, dignity, honor) **and thanks** (Gr:eucharistia-gratitude, grateful language, thanks,

thanksgiving) *to Him* (God) *that sat upon the throne, Who lives forever and ever,"*}

10. **4:10**— {*The 24 elders fall down before Him That* (Who; God) *sat on the throne* (what will you do before God's throne?-same)*, and worship* (Gr:proskuneo-to kiss, like a dog licking/ kissing his master's hand, to prostrate oneself in homage, to worship) *Him* (God) *That* (Who) *lives forever and ever, and cast their crowns* (good worship group name; next verse will tell us why they do this; these are the same crowns Jesus had given them, *2Ti. 4:8*; *1Pe. 5:4*; *Rev. 2:10*; *3:11*) *before the throne* (God's), *saying,"*}

11. **4:11**— {*"'You* (God) *are worthy* (Gr:axios-deserving, due, worthy), *O Lord, to receive glory and honor and power: for You have created all things* (not just some and the rest evolved, but God created all), *and for Your pleasure* (Gr:thelema-determination, choice, purpose, decree, inclination, desire, pleasure, will) *they are* (imperfect active; shows that God is continuing, actively creating) *and were created."* (The inalienable right of the One that created something is to be able to do whatever they want with their creation. And the creation, if made so well as to be able to choose, should clearly desire to give, and also give, glory, honor, and power, that He's given them, back to Him).}

Figure 4 – 10.1 St. John Kneeling Before Christ & the 24 Elders[3]

Application (Activity/Questions)

A. *"After this,"* what happened in ***Rev. 2-3*** that this is after? {Jesus addressing all the churches and the things which *"are"* (the present Church Age) clearly ended.}

B. What imminent prophetic event does ***Rev. 4:1-2***'s trumpet/voice, invitation to come up, and immediately being in heaven sound like (cf. ***1Th. 4:16-17***; ***1Co. 15:52***; ***2Co. 5:8***)? {The Rapture of the Church.}

C. ***Rev. 4:3, 5*** picture holy God on *"the throne"* prepared mainly for coming _____? {Judgment.}

D. Who do you think the 24 elders are and why? {12 Apostles, 1 Paul, and 11 other top Christians, as they have church promised rewards of white garments, gold crowns, thrones to rule and reign with Christ.}

E. What are the fierce 4 living creatures each with 6 wings and many eyes (cf. ***Isa. 6:2, 6***; ***Rev. 4:8***)? {Seraphims; Great angels; 2 wings to cover their face, 2 to cover their feet, and 2 to fly; they worship God, speak, and minister at God's altar.}

F. What do these top men and angels in God's inner circle do *"day and night"*? {Worship God.}

G. Why do you think God shows us this heavenly throne-room prior to world judgment? {So we understand how He is on His throne and requires judgment as His holiness to protect the good from evil and show truth and justice, holding evil accountable.}

H. Why should worship be enjoyable? {It is fitting; there is joy in the truth; shows we see the truth; we were created to...}

I. What type of people will we and should we surround our self now? {Worshipers of God.}

J. What are 3 reasons God deserves all glory, honor, thanks, power, and worship? {1-Because He created it all for His pleasure, 2-Because He has all power, 3-Because He has given us so much and promised us even more, 4-Because He is holy and so worthy of more than we can give or express.}

K. What makes you worship more? How can you encourage others to worship more? {See God's hand, creation. Start worshiping.}

L. Can you still worship even during what feels like horrible circumstances (cf. ***Job 1:20-22***)? {That is when it is most valued.}

M. Can you draw a timeline and define 7 major prophetic events (e.g. the Church Age, Rapture, Tribulation Period, 2nd Coming, Millennium, The Great White Throne Judgment, Heaven...)? {See Figure 5 below. This may mentally prepare you as we see them in the various chapters of the Book of Revelation.}

Figure 5 – 10.2 Revelation Timeline of 7 Key Events Defined[1]

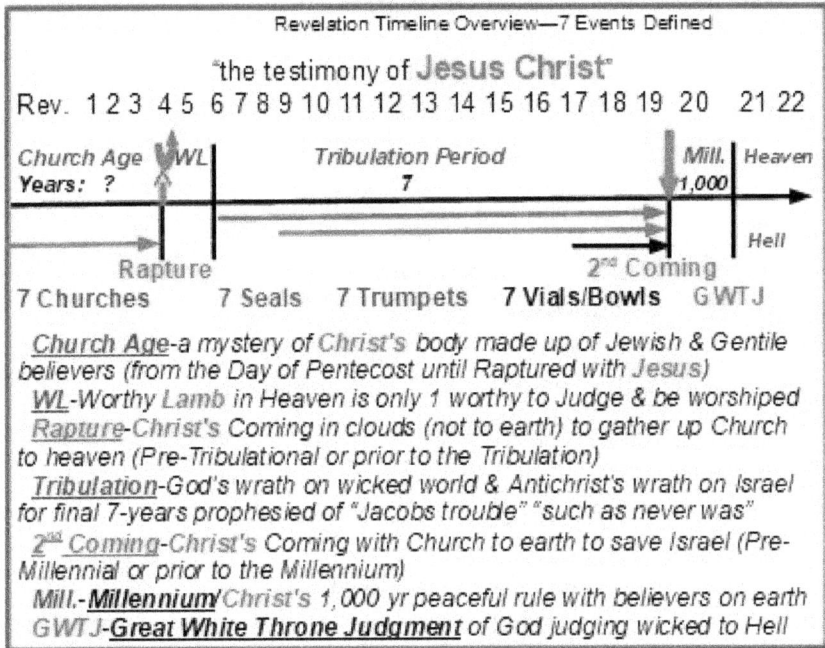

Revelation Timeline Overview—7 Events Defined

"the testimony of Jesus Christ"

Rev. 1 2 3 4 5 6 7 8 9 10 11 12 13 14 15 16 17 18 19 20   21 22

| Church Age | WL | Tribulation Period | | Mill. | Heaven |

Years: ?   7   1,000

Rapture   2nd Coming

7 Churches   7 Seals   7 Trumpets   7 Vials/Bowls   GWTJ

Hell

Church Age-a mystery of Christ's body made up of Jewish & Gentile believers (from the Day of Pentecost until Raptured with Jesus)

WL-Worthy Lamb in Heaven is only 1 worthy to Judge & be worshiped

Rapture-Christ's Coming in clouds (not to earth) to gather up Church to heaven (Pre-Tribulational or prior to the Tribulation)

Tribulation-God's wrath on wicked world & Antichrist's wrath on Israel for final 7-years prophesied of "Jacobs trouble" "such as never was"

2nd Coming-Christ's Coming with Church to earth to save Israel (Pre-Millennial or prior to the Millennium)

Mill.-Millennium Christ's 1,000 yr peaceful rule with believers on earth

GWTJ-Great White Throne Judgment of God judging wicked to Hell

Worthy Lion Lamb, Sacrifice and Savior (Jesus Christ) is the only one
Worthy to Judge and be Worshiped.

Jesus is Worthy and Worshiped as Judge.
{Believers Sing a New Song, are Promised to Reign with Christ.}

Introduction
A. Which heavenly choir will be best, all angels or all believers from
every nation and era? {I can only imagine. Both together. I plan to sing
my best, with my glorified vocal cords...}
B. https://www.youtube.com/watch?v=qdOOBO9tKdo {Play on laptop
or phone...best with projector-2:47; KJV with images.[4] Or
https://www.youtube.com/watch?v=B-OADLF5xmE 3:22 KJV with
animation.[5] Or https://www.youtube.com/watch?v=4L2_KCiOQEM
3:27 KJV with animation.[6] All read **5:1-14.**}

Scripture (Observations/Interpretation/Commentary)
{Divide into 3 Groups for them to write paragraph and verse Titles and
any questions. Each assign timekeeper to only allow 2 minutes/verse;
Group A: **5:1-5**; Group B: **5:6-10**; Group C: **5:11-14.**}

A. _5:1-5_ {Group A-Paragraph Title—Only Jesus is Worthy to Judge.
The "—" section at end of each paragraph or verse is my Title; Notice
all verses begin with "_and_" showing continued action.}
1. **_5:1_**— {"**_And I_** (John; consistently uses the personal 1st person)
   saw in the right hand (the hand of authority/judgment/ action)
   of Him (God-the-Father) **_that sat_** (sitting; present participle
   showing He continues to rule) **_on the throne_** (of judgment/rule)
   a book written within and on the backside (on the inside and
   outside), **_sealed_** (closely/tightly) **_with 7_** (# of
   perfection/completion) **_seals._**" (Sealed for protection/
   privacy/genuineness)—God's 7 sealed book of judgment.}
2. **_5:2_**— {"**_And I_** (John) **_saw a strong_** (mighty/powerful/forceful)
   angel (messenger) **_proclaiming with a loud_** (Gr:megas-loud,
   exceedingly, wide, strong, mighty) **_voice, 'Who is worthy to open_**
   the book, and to loose (break) **_the seals thereof?'_**"—Who is
   worthy to judge?}
3. **_5:3_**— {"**_And no man_** (Gr:oudeis-not even one, none, nobody,
   nothing) **_in heaven_** (most likely place if someone was holy or

worthy), ***nor*** (*Gr:oude-neither, nor, not even*) ***in earth*** (2nd mostly likely place)***, nor*** (*Gr:oude*) ***under the earth*** (down under for you Australians; most likely pointing to those who have died and were buried)***, was able to open the book*** (of judgment)***, neither*** (not even) ***to look thereon.***" (At it; much less look inside it; at this holy book of judgment. Many gossip when hear what is causing judgment or when see deserved judgments coming on others and don't have pure enough hearts or eyes to see or understand God's judgment; cf. ***Hab. 1:13-14***–"*Thou are of purer eyes than to behold evil.*")—Nobody/nothing worthy anywhere to Judge.}

4. ***5:4***— {"***And I*** (John) ***wept*** (sobbed/wailed) ***much*** (a lot)***, because no man*** (no one, nothing) ***was found*** (all looked for someone) ***worthy*** (righteous/deserving enough) ***to open and to read*** (*Gr:anaginosko-upward knowing, read, to know again-from person writing*)***, neither to look thereon.***" (At It.—much sorrow as no one found worthy to judge.}

5. ***5:5*** (cf. ***Gen. 49:8-10***; ***Heb. 7:14***; ***Mat. 1:2-3***; ***2Sa. 7:13, 16***; ***Isa. 11:1, 10***; ***Jer. 33:14-21***; ***Zec. 3:8-10***; ***Rom. 15:12***; ***Rev. 22:16***)— {"***And 1 of the Elders*** (representing the Church or believers in heaven; maybe even one of the martyred Apostles he knew so well) ***said to me, 'Don't weep: Behold, the Lion of the tribe of Judah*** (a judging reigning title and human Jewish lineage of Jesus Christ; cf. ***Gen. 49:8-10***; ***Heb. 7:14***; ***Mat. 1:2-3***; irony, weeping when Judah means "*praise.*" I'd rather face Jesus' sacrifice as Lamb than His judgment as Lion), ***the Root of David*** (the kingly human Jewish lineage prophesied of Jesus Christ; cf. ***2Sa. 7:13, 16***; ***Isa. 11:1, 10***; ***Jer. 33:14-21***; ***Zec. 3:8-10***; ***Rom. 15:12***; ***Rev. 22:16***; many believe "*the root*" implies divinely created heritage and "*branch*" shows His incarnated humanity, so the God-Man was able and)***, has prevailed*** (*Gr:nikao-conquered, overcome, gotten the victory, prevailed*; an Aorist Active Indicative; Aorist Tense-completed action, completed at one-point-in-time, "*on the cross;*" Active Voice-"*Jesus*" was the performer of the action, the work; Indicative Mood-this is a statement of fact) ***to open the book*** (of judgment)***, and to loose*** (break) ***the 7 seals thereof.***" (Of it; to unleash all judgments).—The prophesied pedigreed Jesus is the only One that overcame and is worthy to judge all wicked rejectors of His mercy.}

B. **5:6-10** {Group B-Title—Jesus takes judgment book, sends His Spirit, redeems, receives a new worship song, and makes us ready to reign with Him. Again, all verses begin with "*and.*"}

1. **5:6** (cf. **13:8**; **Isa. 53:6-8**; **Acts 8:32-35**; **Joh. 1:29, 36, 41**; **1Pe. 1:18-21**; **Rev. 17:12**; **Joh. 16:7-14**; **Joh. 12:32**; **Acts 5:30-32**)— {"*And I* (John) **beheld, and, lo, in the midst** (middle) **of the throne** (God's) **of the the 4 beasts** (living creatures/Seraphim angels) **and the midst of the Elders** (center stage of God's throne room), **stood** (not laying down His life now) **a Lamb** (**13:8**; **Isa. 53:6-8**; **Acts 8:32-35**; **Joh. 1:29, 36, 41**; **1Pe. 1:18-21**; without blemish, the perfect Passover sacrifice, Who shed His blood in our place), **as it had been slain** (Gr:sphazo- butchered, sacrificed, killed; reminding us here of His love for "*the whole world,*" even those He's preparing to judge), **having 7 horns and 7 eyes, which are the 7 Spirits of God sent forth into all the earth.**" (Obviously Jesus isn't a literal lamb nor do literal lambs have 7 horns or 7 eyes and there is only 1 Holy Spirit. So God's Word is not talking about physical "*horns*" of a bull, ram or altar. He frequently shows beasts or animals with horns that He states specifically are a metaphor for rulers or kingdoms, cf. **17:12**. So, 7 horns mean a complete or perfect rule. 7 eyes show He sees perfectly all things including sin, so with that perfect vision is also worthy to judge sin and sinners. Christ's reign is accomplished by the work of "*the 7 Spirits of God*" or the perfect working of God's Spirit sent forth into all the earth. So, God's Spirit especially works in convicting all the world of sin, righteousness, and judgment, He comforts and guides believers into all truth, cf. **Joh. 16:7-14**, and the Spirit testifies and especially draws all to Christ with the gospel, cf. **Joh. 12:32**; **Acts 5:30-32**, through Jesus death, burial, and resurrection, as the successfully sacrificed Lamb now standing in the middle of God's throne).—Jesus, the sacrificed Lamb is standing at God's throne sending out His Spirit.}

2. **5:7**— {"*And He* (Jesus) **came and took** (took or received; as is His right as He is the only one holy and worthy) **the book** (of judgment) **out of the right hand of God** (the-Father; "*right hand of God*" is called anthropomorphism or ascribing human characteristics or behavior to God to aid our finite attempt to understand the Infinite and His workings. So God-the-Father "*is Spirit,*" cf. **John 4:24**, and doesn't have hands. So this is

conveying to us that this book is being taken by Jesus out of God's strong possession, that no unworthy person could ever remove, as *"no man can pluck them out of My Father's hand,"* cf. **John 10:28-29**) *That* (Who) *sat* (is sitting; residing; in His rightful ruling place) *upon the throne."* —Jesus takes God's book of judgment.}

3. **5:8**— {*"And when He* (Jesus) *had taken the book* (of judgment)*, the 4 beasts* (amazing Seraphim angels guarding and worshiping God's holiness and right to judge) *and 24 Elders* (key believers) *fell down* (a humble position of worship) *before the Lamb* (surely the only Lamb ever worshiped or deserving as the God-man humbly substituted Himself, in our place, to die and to pay for all God's righteous demands of death as a wage of our sin, fulfilling all the legal requirements to satisfy God's holiness, justice, and love), *having every one of them harps* (a worshipful orchestral scene by key angels and men), *and golden vials* (containers made for pouring or drinking) *full of odors* (*Gr:thumiama- aroma, odor, incense*; a perfume for God's nose out of expensive containers), *which are the prayers of saints."* (Saved, believers; pictures martyrs and other persecution petitioning prayers for justice to the throne of God and Jesus Who also suffered and was slain).—Jesus worshiped by Angels and Elders/fragrant prayers in His name for judgment.}

4. **5:9**— {*"And they* (angels and Elders) *sung a new song* (as Tribulation is about to come to all the earth, while saints are in heaven. Words probably that most were singing prior was either: who can judge, or please don't be so patient, judge them now. So this new song of worship was to Jesus)*, saying, 'You are worthy to take the book* (of judgment)*, and to open the seals thereof* (Jesus is holy enough for all 7 seals or God's final, complete judgment)*: for* (because) *You* (Jesus) *were slain* (killed)*, and* (You) *have redeemed* (*Gr:agorazo- purchased, redeemed, bought*) *us* (some ancient manuscripts make *"us"* *"they"* or some translate *"people,"* but *"us"* is accurate. If you are a believer, and that still means all of us saved whether 1st person or 3rd person plural) *to God* (the Father)*, by Your* (Jesus') *blood* (the only way anyone has ever been redeemed/saved in OT or NT) *out of every* (*Gr:pas-all or every*) *kindred, and tongue, and people, and nation;"* (God uses 4 things to cover His desired diversity from every possible race, tribe, clan, or however one

refers to any group. He even says every tongue or language will be in Heaven because of Jesus' sacrificial death, burial, and resurrection. This answers one of the toughest questions always asked. What about a person in the darkest most remote tribe that never heard the gospel? Clearly God says that not only will they hear the gospel, but that some will be saved from every people everywhere);—Jesus's death, blood, and redemption is a new song showing His worthiness to judge.}

5. **_5:10_**— {**_"And_** (Jesus) **_has made us_** (Church believers; not just originally created us) **_unto our God_** (but in Christ, He made us "*a new creature*," cf. **_2Co. 5:17_**, as He redeemed us to God, and made us) **_kings and priests_** (not just over or with people, but to God)**_: and we will reign_** (rule) **_on the earth.'"_** (Those in heaven will get to come back with Jesus to earth. There will be a Millennium, a Theocracy, a Christocracy, and a "Believeracracy" under Jesus. This clearly shows praise or thanks as part of the new song).—Jesus made us kings and priests and we get to rule with Him on earth.}

C. **_5:11-14_** {Group C-Title—All creation sings and worships God and praises Jesus' worthiness forever. All verses except **_5:12_** begin with "and" showing continued action.}

1. **_5:11_**— {**_"And I_** (John) **_saw, and heard the voice of many angels_** (not just 4 key ones) **_round about_** (all around) **_the throne_** (God's) **_and the beasts_** (4 Seraphims) **_and the Elders: and the number_** (*Gr:arithmos-number*; where we get arithmetic; don't worry, you'll see John wasn't a math major as he starts counting) **_of them was ten thousand times ten thousand, and thousands of thousands;"_** (*Gr:murias murias- myriad or indefinite number, countless number, and thousands of thousands*; it is like he keeps looking around and sees more nations);—Innumerable angels and believers sing about Jesus.}

2. **_5:12_**— {**_"Saying_** (Present Active Participle-PAP-continuing; not the word for singing, but may also be a song) **_with a loud voice, 'Worthy is the Lamb_** (those in heaven focused on what He was for them, our perfect Passover Lamb) **_That_** (Who) **_was slain_** (and Jesus died for them) **_to receive_** (of course 7 things as Jesus is perfect and they want to be complete and thorough in their praise to our substituting Savior; *Gr:kai- "and, even, also;"* builds and continues) **_power, and riches, and wisdom, and strength,_**

and honor, and glory, and blessing.'"—All in heaven are praising the worthiness of Jesus.}

3. **5:13**— {"*And every creature, which is in heaven, and on the earth, and under the earth, and such as are* (those) *in the sea, and all that are in them* (everything everywhere)*, heard I* (John) *saying,* (PAP-continuing; that either means the creatures on earth and in the sea will be able to talk in order to praise God or they'll praise God in the ways He made them to communicate), '**Blessing** (*Gr:eulogia-fine speaking, eulogy, commendation, adoration, benediction, blessing*), *and honor, and glory, and power* (dominion)*, be unto Him* (God-the Father) *That* (Who) *sits* (is sitting) *upon the throne, and unto the Lamb* (Jesus; shown here to be forever worshiped with God by all) *forever and ever*.—John heard all creation praising God and Jesus forever.}

4. **5:14**— {"*And the 4 beasts* (key angelic Seraphims) *said, 'Amen.' And the 24 Elders* (believers) *fell down and worshiped Him* (God-unity of Godhead) *that lives forever and ever."*—Angels and Elders amen and worship the eternal God.}

Figure 6 – 11.1 The Hymn in Adoration of the Lamb[7]

Application (Activity/Questions)

A. Why is Jesus worthy to judge the wicked? {He is righteous; the only one that didn't sin, so is worthy; He died for everyone's sin, but they rejected Him; He is the perfect holy standard.}

B. What should be the reaction of every righteous person when God/Jesus judges the wicked? {Soberness/sorrow; recognizing Jesus' right to judge; silence or praise; that He was merciful; that we have a part to play trying to keep the wicked from judgment by sharing the gospel, praying, showing a loving life and lips now...}

C. What are 3 main reasons God/Jesus is waiting to pour out judgment on the world? {His patient mercy; so, more will be saved; and His perfect timing (prophecy) to accomplish the best.}

D. What is your 1st reaction when you see such sin in need of judgment and justice? {Righteous indignation, but not as much sorrow for time to repent as I should demonstrate.}

E. How do you think the wicked feels about God bringing justice and judging them? {Anger; sometimes fear; sorry known/caught.}

F. How do you feel about God bringing justice and judging the wicked? {Sad for wicked, and happy for justice and righteous.}

G. How will the righteous feel about God bringing justice and judging the wicket? {Thankful and worshipful.}

H. How do you think God feels about judging the wicked? {Sad and happy, but with a more perfect understanding and acceptance that it is best and brings God the most glory.}

I. What observations do you see from the Revelation Timeline Overview chart on the next page? What terrible event is primarily described in chapters 6-18? {Church Age, Rapture, Tribulation, 2nd Coming, Millennium, The Great White Throne Judgment. The Tribulation Period.}

Figure 7 – 11.2 Revelation Timeline Overview

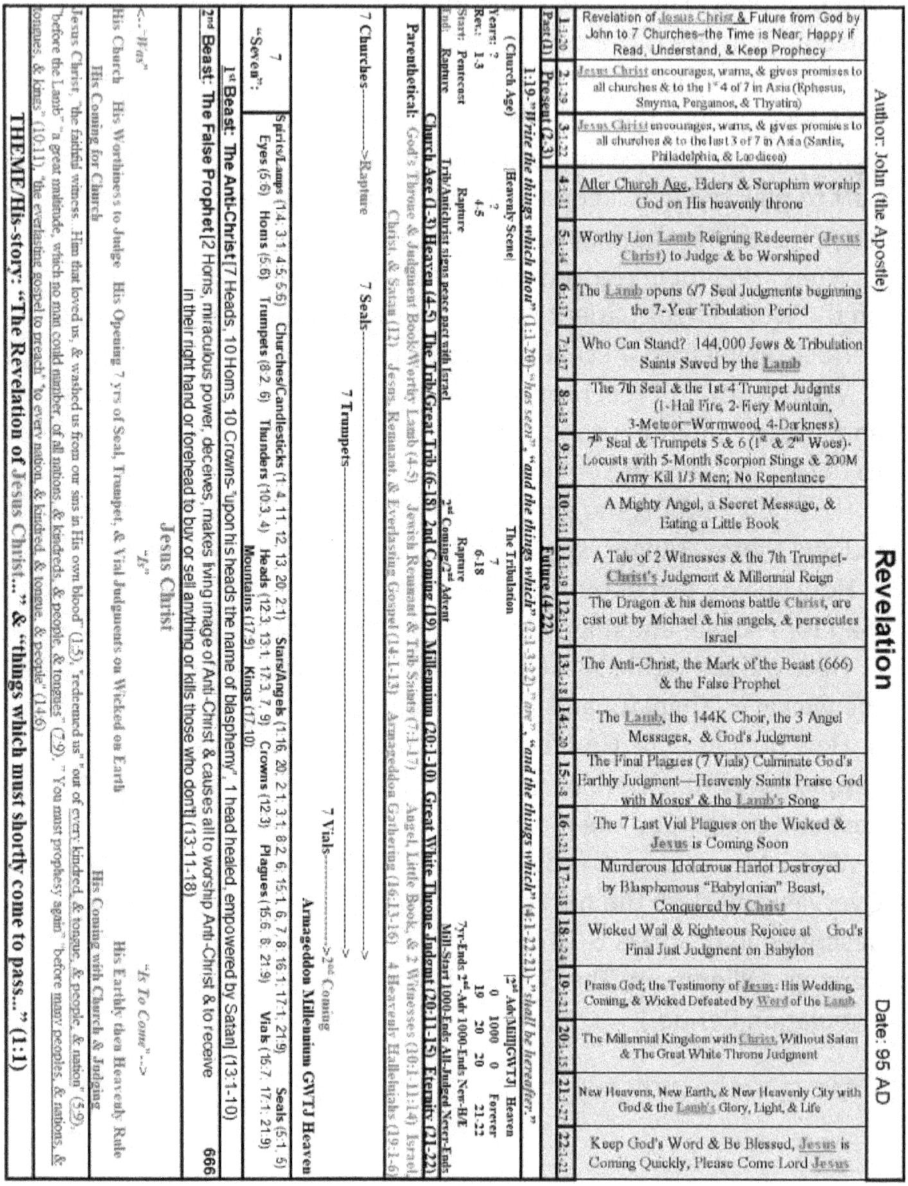

Author: John (the Apostle) | **Revelation** | **Date: 95 AD**

1:1-20	Revelation of Jesus Christ & Future from God by John to 7 Churches–the Time is Near; Happy if Read, Understand, & Keep Prophecy
2:1-29	Jesus Christ encourages, warns, & gives promises to all churches & to the 1st 4 of 7 in Asia (Ephesus, Smyrna, Pergamos, & Thyatira)
3:1-22	Jesus Christ encourages, warns, & gives promises to all churches & to the last 3 of 7 in Asia (Sardis, Philadelphia, & Laodicea)
4:1-11	After Church Age, Elders & Seraphim worship God on His heavenly throne
5:1-14	Worthy Lion Lamb Reigning Redeemer (Jesus Christ) to Judge & be Worshiped
6:1-17	The Lamb opens 6/7 Seal Judgments beginning the 7-Year Tribulation Period
7:1-17	Who Can Stand? 144,000 Jews & Tribulation Saints Saved by the Lamb
8:1-13	The 7th Seal & the 1st 4 Trumpet Judgments (1-Hail Fire, 2-Fiery Mountain, 3-Meteor-Wormwood, 4-Darkness)
9:1-21	7th Seal & Trumpets 5 & 6 (1st & 2nd Woes)-Locusts with 5-Month Scorpion Stings & 200M Army Kill 1/3 Men; No Repentance
10:1-11	A Mighty Angel, a Secret Message, & Eating a Little Book
11:1-19	A Tale of 2 Witnesses & the 7th Trumpet-Christ's Judgment & Millennial Reign
12:1-17	The Dragon & his demons battle Christ, are cast out by Michael & his angels, & persecutes Israel
13:1-18	The Anti-Christ, the Mark of the Beast (666) & the False Prophet
14:1-20	The Lamb, the 144K Choir, the 3 Angel Messages, & God's Judgment
15:1-8	The Final Plagues (7 Vials) Culminate God's Earthly Judgment—Heavenly Saints Praise God with Moses' & the Lamb's Song
16:1-21	The 7 Last Vial Plagues on the Wicked & Jesus is Coming Soon
17:1-18	Murderous Idolatrous Harlot Destroyed by Blasphemous "Babylonian" Beast, Conquered by Christ
18:1-24	Wicked Wail & Righteous Rejoice at God's Final Just Judgment on Babylon
19:1-21	Praise God; the Testimony of Jesus: His Wedding, Coming, & Wicked Defeated by Word of the Lamb
20:1-15	The Millennial Kingdom with Christ, Without Satan & The Great White Throne Judgment
21:1-27	New Heavens, New Earth, & New Heavenly City with God & the Lamb's Glory, Light, & Life
22:1-21	Keep God's Word & Be Blessed, Jesus is Coming Quickly, Please Come Lord Jesus

Part(1): Present (2-3) — 1:19-"Write the things which thou" (1:1-20)-"has seen", "and the things which" (2:1-3:22)-"are", "and the things which" (4:1-22:21)-"shall be hereafter." **Future (4-22)**

(Church Age) — [Heavenly Scene] — The Tribulation — "Is" — Jesus Christ — "Is To Come" — "... Was"

Years: ? | Start: Pentecost | End: Rapture | Trib/Antichrist signs peace pact with Israel | Rapture 4-5 | 6-18 | 7 | 1st Coming/2nd Advent | 2nd Coming/2nd Advent

1st Adv/MJ/GWTJ Heaven: 0 / 1000 / 0 / Forever; 19 / 20 / 20 / 21-22; Mill Start 1000-Ends/New-B/E; 7yr-Ends 2nd-Adv 1000-Ends All-Judged Never-Ends

Parenthetical: God's Throne & Judgment Book/Worthy Lamb (4-5) Jewish Remnant & Trib Saints (7:1-17) Millennium (20:1-10) Great White Throne Judgment (20:11-15) Eternity (21-22)

Church Age (1-3) The Trib/Great Trib (6-18) 2nd Coming (19) Armageddon Gathering (16:13-16) 4 Heavenly Hallelujahs (19:1-6) Israel, Christ, & Satan (12) Jesus, Remnant, & Everlasting Gospel (14:1-13) Angel, Little Book, & 2 Witnesses (10:1-11:14) Israel

7 Churches -------->Rapture | 7 Seals------- 7 Trumpets------- 7 Vials------------->2nd Coming | Armageddon Millennium GWTJ Heaven

"Seven": 7 — Spirits/Lamps (1,4,3) Eyes (5,6) Horns (5,6) | Lamps (1,4) Horns (5,6) Trumpets (8,2,6) | Churches/Candlesticks (1,4,11,12,13,20,21) Thunders (10,3,4) | Stars/Angels (1,16,20,21,3,1,8,2,6,15,16,2,8,16,1,17,1,21,9) Heads (12,3,13,1,17,3,7,9) Crowns (12,3) Mountains (17,9) Kings (17,10) | Seals (5,1,5) Plagues (15,6,8,21,9) Vials (16,7,17,1,21,9)

2nd Beast: The False Prophet [2 Horns, miraculous power, deceives, "upon his heads the name of blasphemy", 1 head healed, empowered by Anti-Christ & to receive in their right hand or forehead to buy or sell anything or kills those who don't] (13:11-18) — 666

1st Beast: The Anti-Christ [7 Heads, 10 Horns, 10 Crowns: deceives, makes living image of Anti-Christ & causes all to worship Anti-Christ & to receive in their right hand or forehead to buy or sell anything or kills those who don't] (13:11-18)

His Church — His Worthiness to Judge. His Opening 7 yrs of Seal, Trumpet, & Vial Judgments on Wicked on Earth — His Coming with Church & Judging — His Earthly then Heavenly Rule

His Coming for Church

Jesus Christ, "the faithful witness, Him that loved us, & washed us from our sins in His own blood" (1,5), "redeemed us" "out of every kindred, & tongue, & people, & nation" (5,9). "You must prophesy again" "before many peoples, & nations, & tongues, & kings" (10,11) "the everlasting gospel" "to preach" "to every nation, & kindred, & tongue, & people" (14,6). Jesus Christ, "the Lamb" "a great multitude, which no man could number, of all nations, & kindreds, & people, & tongues" (7,9); before the Lamb"

THEME/His-story: "The Revelation of Jesus Christ...," & "things which must shortly come to pass..." (1:1)

The Lamb Opens 6/7 Seal Judgments
Beginning the 7-Year Tribulation Period.

6/7 Seal Judgments of the Tribulation.
(Includes the 4 Riders of the Apocalypse, and All Hide.}

Introduction
A. Are all 4 riders of the Apocalypse doing terrible things on earth?
{Yes, dreadful things.}
B. Even though we (the Church) are NOT going to be in the 7-year
Tribulation period, do you want to know what will happen on earth,
while we are in heaven? {Yes, definitely so.}

Scripture (Observations/Interpretation/Commentary)
{Read **_6:1-17_** together; notice 1st 16 verses begin with _"and"_ showing-
continuous action, **_6:17_** begins with _"For"_;
Divide into Groups to answer Who does What and Its Impact.}

A. **_6:1-2_**—**Seal 1-White Horse-Conquering** {**_6:1_**-"**_And_** (after the
heavenly scene of all worshiping God and the God-Lamb for His
worthiness to Judge) **_I_** (John) **_saw when the Lamb_** (Jesus) **_opened 1 of_**
the seals (the 1st Seal of Judgment; some see these as past history
fulfilled by kings, generals, or apostles, others as a present history of a
spiritual warfare of the gospel throughout the Church Age, but these
seals are prophetic/future, after the true Church, cf. **_Rev. 2-3_**, _"after_
this," and **_4:1_**, _"things which must be hereafter."_ So the _"when"_ is
during the 1st part of the 7-year Tribulation period), **_and I_** (John) **_heard_**
as it were the voice of thunder (an angelic <u>trumpet voice</u> was heard
before for a good announcement in **_4:1_**, and now an angelic
<u>thundering voice</u> for this bad one), **_1 of the 4 beasts_** (living creatures; a
Seraphim angel), **_saying, 'Come and see.'_** (So, glad as the Church we
are watching with Jesus from heaven and not participating on earth).
_6:2_-"**_And I_** (John) **_saw, and behold a white horse_** (white, a color
consistent with a person masquerading as the righteous
Christ/Messiah. _"Horse/horses/horseman/ horsemen,"_ found 215
times in the Bible, often picture war/battle or strong/quick
conveyance); **_and the one sitting on it_** (white horse) **_had a bow_** (not a
Sword like Christ, but a 1st century weapon for distant sometimes
secret attacks); **_and a crown was given to him_** (he is given a kingdom,

rule, or "*power*," cf. **_Dan. 8:24_**; Christ is already ruling on a throne so it is not Jesus getting crowned here): **_and he went forth_** (*Gr:exerchomai-issue out, proceed, escape*; this is the Antichrist. This language is consistent with the Holy Spirit's restraining influence on the Antichrist being removed as the Church was Raptured, now the Antichrist is released, cf. **_2Th. 2:1-10_**) **_conquering_** (present active participle denoting continuous conquering), **_and to_** (*Gr:hina-"in order that, for the purpose, or result to"*) **_conquer_**." (So the Antichrist's purpose is to conquer; some think this is Jesus sending Himself to judge as later He is described in His 2nd Coming as coming in judgment sitting on a white horse, cf. **_19:11, 19, 21_**, but Jesus here is in Heaven, cf. **_Rev. 5_**, with His Bride, the Church, later called His wife in **_21:9_**, and our wedding and wedding supper in **_19:6-10_**, and we are with Him in heaven and He is sending this Judgment from heaven. Jesus' purpose for His 1st Coming was not to conquer, but "*to seek and to save that which is lost*," cf. **_Luk. 19:10_**, His 2nd Coming will be to judge the wicked and deliver the righteous, after this 7-year Tribulation period. So, this conqueror on a white horse is one of the first main characters in the Trib. Some believe this rider is/are false prophets preaching a false gospel, others a combination of all that is the spirit of antichrist, but an individual rider makes most sense to be the actual "*Antichrist*," cf. **_13:1-10_**. Interesting, he is intentionally not named or introduced in detail here. This rider is consistent with the role of the other riders, so is clearly not Jesus. The Antichrist deceives as if he is the Christ/the Messiah, he may look like Christ, and he signs a peace pact with Israel, but he is empowered by Satan, he is a false Christ and false Messiah, he wars with true believers, blasphemes God, and is worshiped, as we'll see later when God is ready to introduce the true antagonist and his top minions in **_Rev. 12_** and **_13_**).}

Figure 8 – 12.1 The Four Horsemen of the Apocalypse[8]

B. 6:3-4—Seal 2-Red Horse-Killing {**6:3-"And when He** (the Lamb, Jesus) **had opened the 2nd Seal** (again, containing the next judgment), **I** (John) **heard the 2nd beast** (living creature; a seraphim angel), **saying 'Come and see.'"** (The seraphim quoting to John what Jesus had said in **John 1:39**, when Jesus was calling the disciples). **6:4-"And there went out another horse, that was red** (Gr:purrhos-"fire like, flame colored, red;" a color consistent with bloodshed/killing): **and was given to him that sat** (the one sitting) **thereon** (on it; red horse) **to take peace from the earth** (strong strife; even more proof the 1st rider is not "the Prince of Peace," cf. **Isa. 9:6**; **Dan. 8:25**), **and that** (Gr:hina-for the purpose/result/intent that) **they should kill one another; and there was given unto him a great** (Gr:mega-great, mighty, large, strong) **sword."** (Gr:machaira-knife, sword, figuratively war or judicial punishment).}

C. 6:5-6—Seal 3-Black Horse-Famine {**6:5-"And when He** (the Lamb, Jesus) **had opened the 3rd Seal, I** (John) **heard the 3rd beast** (living creature; a Seraphim angel), **saying 'Come and see.' And I** (John) **beheld, and lo a black horse** (consistent with dark days of famine); **and he that sat** (the one sitting) **on him** (black horse) **had a pair of balances** (scale) **in his hand."** (Consistent practice to measure in times of scarcity). **6:6-"And I** (John) **heard a voice in the middle of the 4 beasts** (living creatures; Seraphim angels), **saying, 'A measure of wheat for a denarius; and 3 measures of barley for a denarius;'"** (A measure-Gr:choinix-dry measure; said to be the minimum daily amount for a person, 2 times this word is in the Bible out of 108 total for the word measure(s)-both found here. Gr:denarius was a Roman silver coin for a day's labor. Wheat is more expensive and widely used for human food, barley less expensive and used more in animal feed and malt for alcohol. This seems to be saying that this famine is causing paychecks to go almost entirely just for minimal bread/drink for themselves and/or feed for their animals; so food rationing); **"and see that you hurt not the oil and wine.'"** (Some attach symbolism to oil as the working of the Holy Spirit and the wine as a symbol of Christ's blood still being unfettered to all that believe, but it clearly shows that Jesus' mercy didn't allow the famine to destroy all crops, and shows some inequity of the rich and poor, as the rich can still afford oil and wine, while the poor cannot. Emphasizes rich and poor and not the middle class, as economies get strained).}

D. 6:7-8—Seal 4-Pale Horse-Death {**6:7-"And when He** (Jesus) **had opened the 4th Seal** (again of next judgment), **I** (John) **heard the 4th**

beast (living creature; a Seraphim angel), **saying, 'Come and see.'"**
6:8-**"And I** (John) **looked and beheld a pale** (Gr:chloros-greenish,
green, pale; a color consistent with dead or rotting flesh) **horse: and
his name that sat** (the one sitting) **on him** (it; pale horse) **was Death,
and Hell** (Gr:hades-hades, grave, hell, place of departed spirits)
followed with him (Death). **and power** (Gr:exousia-priviledge,
delegated influence, jurisdiction, authority, power, strength) **was given**
(by God Who is still and always sovereign and in control implementing
His will) **unto them** (1st 3 riders-see context to follow) **over the fourth
of the earth** (25%), **to kill with the sword, and with hunger** (famine)**,
and with death, and with the beasts** (dangerous animals) **of the
earth."** (As a result of Death, even the animals run wild killing and
feeding on the dead. We've always had war and death, but nowhere
to the extent that will happen during the Tribulation. A time of *"great
tribulation, such as was not since the beginning of the world to this
time, no, nor ever shall be,"* cf. **Mat. 24:21; Mar. 13:19, Dan. 12:1**).}
E. 6:9-11—**Seal 5-Martyrdom** {**6:9**-**"And when He** (the Lamb, Jesus)
had opened the 5th Seal, I (John) **saw under the altar** (the true altar in
heaven; an altar is a place of sacrifice) **the souls of them that were
slain for the Word of God, and for the testimony** (Gr: marturia-record,
report, testimony, witness; a root of martyr) **which they** (martyrs)
held:" (Gr:echo-have, hold, kept; even through martyrdom)**: 6:10**-
"And they cried (Gr:krazo-to "croak," as a raven, to scream, to call
aloud, shriek, entreat, to cry out) **with a loud voice saying, 'How long**
(martyrs don't want God's mercy and patience in judging the wicked),
O Lord (Gr:despotes-absolute rule, "despot," Lord, master), **holy** (after
calling God a despot, recognizes He is perfect) **and true** (aligned with
reality, even in judgment), **do** (will) **You not judge and avenge**
(Gr:ekdikeo-vindicate, retaliate, punish, avenge; God has promised
about 40 times in the Bible that He will righteously vindicate the
righteous, so they shouldn't seek revenge, but can rejoice because
though patient and merciful, He promises He will avenge, cf. **Deu.
32:43; Rom. 12:19**) **our blood** (pictures their blood poured out as an
offering on the true heavenly altar to God; cf. **Heb. 12:4**-most have not
resisted sin *"unto blood,"* but these had) **on them who dwell upon the
earth?'** (We know you'll judge the wicked dead in Hell one day, but
when will you judge those still living on earth?) **6:11**-**"And white robes**
(Gr:stole-stoles or long fitting gowns, as a mark of dignity) **were given
unto every one of them** (all rewarded); **and it was said unto them,
that** (Gr:hina-purpose, intent, the result) **they should rest** (Gr:anapauo-

69

take ease, refresh, rest), **yet a little** (Gr:mikros-small, least, less, little; even a little time seems long to those awaiting justice or going through trials, but God sees and accepts their sacrifice and will judge in due) **season** (time)**, until their fellow-servants** (Gr:sundoulos-co-slave, servant of the same master) **also and** (or even also) **their brothers, that should** (will) **be killed, as they were, should be fulfilled."** (Gr:pleroo-made replete, satisfied, accomplished, filled, fulfilled, be perfect. Here we see even Tribulation believers praying and partially rewarded but having to be patient for God's eternal justice).}

F. **6:12-17**—Seal 6-Earthquakes/Meteors {**6:12**-"**And I** (John) **beheld** (saw) **when He** (the Lamb) **had opened the 6th Seal** (again opening another judgment)**, and lo** (behold)**, there was** (came to be) **a great earthquake** (Gr:seismos-commotion-of the air, earthquake-of the land, tempest-of the water); **and the sun became black as sackcloth of hair; and the moon became as blood;**" (2 similes-"as" for the darkness on sun and moon); **6:13**-"**And the stars of heaven fell unto the earth, even as a fig tree casts** (drops) **her untimely** (unripe) **figs, when she is shaken of a mighty wind.**" (This fig metaphor was used by Jesus in answering the disciples' question of Israel's tribulation and temple destruction as a sign prior to His 2nd Coming in **Mat. 24:32-35** and **Mar. 13:28-31**. This earthquake has seismological events that even dimmed the light of the sun, moon, and stars. Another simile and personification-giving personality to inanimate objects, where stars fall like a fig tree's rotted fruit falls in a storm. This seal is very challenging and interesting listening to those who believe this happened in history and not the future). **6:14**-"**And the heaven departed** (rent apart) **as a scroll when it is rolled together; and every mountain and island moved out of their places.**" (Pictures nature kneeling and falling prostrate, and shows a big God, where big issues or big things to us are little in His hands, like a small scroll). **6:15**-"**And the kings of the earth, and the great men, and the rich men, and the chief captains** (of a thousand)**, and the mighty men, and every bondman** (slave)**, and every free man** (everybody from high to low that was free too)**, hid themselves in the dens** (caves)**, and in the rocks of the mountains.**" (All afraid and hide, just like Adam and Even in the Garden when they sinned and knew God was coming and were guilty and afraid of His promised judgment, cf. **Gen. 3**); **6:16**-"**And said to the mountains and rocks, 'Fall on us, and hide us from the face** (wicked feel guilty and don't even want God to see them, but He does, and so does His Seraphim) **of Him** (God) **That** (Who) **sits** (is sitting; residing in His rightful place of judgment) **on the throne** (God's; of the throne of the universe and all judgment), **and from the wrath of the Lamb;"** (Jesus pictured as a paradox of being a judging God, yet meek and mild Lamb. It's been noted that the wicked would rather have death, than face the reality and truth of God and His right to judge); **6:17**-"**For** (because) **the great day of His** (God-the Father and Son's) **wrath is come; and who is able to stand?'"** (*"Day of the Lord"* is found 31 times in the Bible, 27 times *"the"* precedes it and it refers to God's coming judgment, frequently ultimately to His final judgments. Many times, the prophets referred to both a near term deliverance by the Lord for the righteous, judgment for the wicked, and then both ultimate righteous deliverance and final judgments detailed in **Revelation**. The answer to His question is that no one shall stand before God. All will ultimately kneel and confess Jesus' Lordship to God-the-Father's glory, cf. **Php. 2:10-11**, even those blaspheming and rejecting Him on earth. Before the 7th Seal is opened in **Rev. 8**, there is a hint of the only ones who can stand, shown in parenthetical **Rev. 7**. They are those that *"stand fast in the Lord,"* **Php. 4:1**, so are made righteous by Christ's grace and gospel, cf. **Rom. 5:1-2**; **1Co. 15:1**; **1Pe. 5:12**, so can stand *"strong in the Lord and in the power of His might,"* cf. **Eph. 6:10**).}

Figure 9 – 12.2 The Opening of the fifth and Sixth Seals[9]

Application (Activity/Questions)

A. When do the Seal Judgments occur (Historically past, historically present, or future Tribulation Period)? {Future Tribulation Period; cf. **4:1**.}

B. Who do you believe is the rider on the white horse conquering? {Antichrist, counterfeiting Christ's ministry, acting like the Messiah signing a peace-pact with Israel, but then tries to conquer and destroy them and other believers and witnesses for God.}

C. State several reasons why the rider on the white horse isn't Jesus? {1-Jesus is sending this rider. 2-Jesus is already on the throne. 3-Jesus is in heaven, not on earth. 4-Jesus is not being crowned; He is already King with all authority. 5-This rider has a bow, not a Sword like Jesus. 6-Not consistent with other 3 evil horsemen and 6 seals. 7-Jesus doesn't have a ministry of continual conquering, Christ's rule brings true lasting eternal peace.}

D. Are there some in the Tribulation who are faithful to God's Word and to witness (**6:9**)? {Yes.}

E. What is the prayer content of the Tribulation martyrs? {Please hurry and judge wicked persecutors more and now.}

F. How do the wicked unsaved respond in the Tribulation (**6:15-17**)? {Few get saved; most fear, hide, ask nature (not God) for death, and don't turn in prayer to God in repentance for mercy.}

G. Why do you think God-the-Father has God-the-Son release all these terrible judgments? {To show He is without spot or blemish, holy, worthy, powerful, and in perfect unity and harmony with the will of the Father.}

H. Was there ever a time in world history that 25% of the population died? {No. So we aren't in the Tribulation yet...}

Who Can Stand? 144,000 Jews and Trib Saints Saved by the Lamb.

God Grants a Judgment Interlude, Protects Witnesses & Saints.
{Discusses Jewish Tribe Dilemma, God Wipes Away Tears.}

Introduction

A. Have you ever watched a scary adrenaline pumping action movie where you wanted an interlude to relax, recover, and prepare for the next action scene? Why do shows change scenes? {Yes. It relaxes you to make the next scare more of a surprise. It can introduce another key character, plot, or complexity. It truly makes it more enjoyable and interesting.}

B. What just happened in *Rev. 6*? {Jesus opens the 1st 6 Tribulation Seals of Judgment.}

Scripture (Observations/Interpretation/Commentary)

A. 7:1-8— {Title: Delayed Judgment until 144,000 Jewish Witnesses Sealed. **1**-"**And after these things** (What things?-6 Judgment Seals; but before 7th and final Seal, somewhat of an interlude when everyone is hiding from the face of God as they don't want God to see them and judge them and they're hiding from the Lamb's wrath. John answers his own **6:17** question of "who shall be able to stand" in "the day of His wrath" or during this 7-year Trib. We'll see later at His 2nd Coming, also after the Millennium, and then at the Great White Throne Judgment, the answer is the same. *Rev. 7* provides this answer before the final 7th Seal begins in **8:1** and also unleashes Trumpet and Vial Judgments. So after the 6 Seal Judgments,) "**I** (John) **saw 4 angels** (messengers and ministers) **standing** (ready) **on the 4 corners** (quarters; like North, East, South, and West) **of the earth, holding** (strongly retaining) **the 4 winds of the earth, that** (Gr:hina-in order *that, purpose, result*) **the wind should not blow on the earth, nor on the sea, nor on any tree." 2**-"**And I** (John) **saw another** (different) **angel ascending** (rising) **from the east** (*Gr:anatole helios-rising of light, dawn, east, sun, light*), **having the seal of the living** (not dead or false) **God: and he cried** (the angel screamed or exclaimed) **with a loud voice to the 4 angels, to whom had been given to hurt the earth and the sea," 3**-"**Saying, 'Hurt** (*Gr:adikeo-hurt, be unjust, wrong; word conveying the idea that it would be unjust to be judging the righteous with the wicked*) **not the earth, neither the sea, nor the trees, until we**

74

have sealed ("sealed"-15/36 times found in Bible are in **_Rev. 7_**; doesn't tell us whether this is an invisible Holy Spirit seal only or a visible mark that others can see in direct contrast with the Antichrist's mark-of-the-beast. **_14:1_** does tell us that God-the-Father's "name [is] written in their foreheads;" the *Gr:sphragizo-seal, stamp with signet or private mark for security or preservation*; same word where believers are sealed by the Holy Spirit in **_2Co. 1:22_**; **_Eph. 1:13-14_**; **_4:30_**. But clearly God and the judging angels can see it. So the angels are not to judge until God has sealed) **the servants of God** (144,000, seen in next verse) **in their foreheads.**" (A gracious protecting seal from the Lamb that protects them from the wrath of the Lamb in the Trib and forever. **_Deu. 11:18_**-"*Therefore shall ye lay up these my words in your heart and in your soul, and bind them for a sign upon your hand, that they may be as frontlets between your eyes.*" Frontlets or phylacteries were strips of parchment, on which Jews wrote 4 passages of Scripture that reminded the Israelites that the Lord brought them out of Egypt using signs and wonders and with a mighty hand, cf. **_Deu. 6:21-22_**; exactly what God was going to do in bringing a faithful remnant of Jews out of the Tribulation). **_4_**-"**And I** (John) **heard the number that were sealed** (*Gr:Perfect Passive Participle-PAP= completed past action with continuing present results*), **and there were sealed** (*Gr:PAP*), **144,000 of all tribes of the children** (*Gr:uihos-sons, children*; we'll see these are all virgin men in **_14:4_**; sons in the sense of responsible inheritors and children in the sense of innocent believers/ followers of God with His special protection, cf. **_Mat. 18:1-6_**) **of Israel.**" **_5_**- (Then God repeats 12 times "of the tribe of_____were sealed 12,000," instead of just saying 12,000 were sealed from each of these tribes once and listing them; he repeats it 12 times for emphasis and clearly showing the inclusion of each of the tribes and each are given an equal number of witnesses). "**Of the tribe of Judah were sealed 12,000.**" (God starts with Judah, Israel's 4th born son, of 1st wife Leah, but listed 1st as this is Jesus' human Jewish tribal lineage; cf. **_Gen. 29:32-30:24_**; **_35:16-18_** for births of 12 sons of Israel), "**Of the tribe of Reuben were sealed 12,000.**" (Reuben, Israel's true 1st born son, also of Leah), "**Of the tribe of Gad were sealed 12,000.**" (Gad, Israel's 7th born son, of Leah's handmaid a concubine named Zilpah). **_6_**-"**Of the tribe of Asher were sealed 12,000.**" (Asher, Israel's 8th born son, also of Zilpah), "**Of the tribe of Naphtali were sealed 12,000.**" (Naphtali, Israel's 6th born son, of Rachel's handmaid a concubine named Bilhah), "**Of the tribe of Manasseh were sealed 12,000.**" (Manasseh, 1st son of Joseph-Israel's

11th born). _7-"Of the tribe of Simeon were sealed 12,000."_ (Simeon, Israel's 2nd born son, of Leah), _"Of the tribe of Levi were sealed 12,000."_ (Levi, Israel's 3rd born son, of Leah), _"Of the tribe of Issachar were sealed 12,000."_ (Issachar, Israel's 9th born, of Leah). _8-"Of the tribe of Zebulun were sealed 12,000."_ (Zebulun, Israel's 10th born, of Leah-her 6th and last son), _"Of the tribe of Joseph were sealed 12,000."_ (Joseph, Israel's 11th born, 1st of Rachel), _"Of the tribe of Benjamin were sealed 12,000."_ (Benjamin, Israel's 12th born, 12th in the list, last, but not least, in fact, was the 2nd loved of Jacob/Israel as 2nd/last of Rachel. So, _**Rev. 7:4**_ says "_all_" tribes were sealed, but Dan, Israel's 5th son, of Bilhah, seems missing, Manasseh is really redundantly listed, since his dad, Joseph is there, though Manasseh's brother, Ephraim is not listed. Joseph never got territory, but Manasseh and Ephraim did. Though _**Rev. 7**_ is not about territory, it is about tribal descendants. So why was Manasseh included and Ephraim not and Joseph their father, redundantly included? 3 main views of why some think Dan is intentionally excluded. 1) Danites were the 1st tribe in large scale idolatry in the territory of Ephraim and continued in idolatry for centuries, cf. _**Judges 18:14-31**_; _**1Ki. 12:25-33**_; _**Hos. 4:17**_; _**Amos 8:14**_; _**Deu. 29:18-21**_. 2) The Antichrist is believed by some to come from the Danites, cf. "_serpent_" reference in _**Gen. 49:17**_. 3) The tribes listed could provide a hidden meaning or a Hebrew "remez," by the message in the order of the meaning of the tribe's names. Judah: Praise the Lord, Reuben: He has looked on my affliction, Gad: good fortune comes, Asher: happy and blessed am I, Naphtali: my wrestling, Manasseh: has made me forget my sorrow, Simeon: God hears me, Levi: has joined me, Issachar: rewarded me, Zebulun: exalted me, Joseph: adding to me, Benjamin: the Son of His right hand. So putting it all together would read this encouraging message to Israel (with the tribal names excluded): "Praise the Lord, He has looked on my affliction, good fortune comes, happy and blessed am I, my wrestling, has made me forget my sorrow, God hears me, has joined me, rewarded me, exalted me, adding to me, the Son of His right hand." Some think Dan was unintentionally left out due to a scribal error and they cite that a couple manuscripts show DAN / MAN, Greek letter Delta, 1st letter of Dan looks like "M" making MAN, an abbreviation of Manasseh. If this is the case, then all tribes are clearly included. To me scribal errors become a slippery slope, so I currently lean towards, that all tribes are included, including Dan/Ephraim, but silently called out as they are becoming strong witnesses and Dan and Ephraim were for centuries, the opposite of witnesses by intentionally pulling people away from God into idolatry. Dan did abandon its tribal territory and shared some of Ephraim's territory, cf. *Jdg. 17-21*. Ephraim was contained in Joseph where Dan was also a part of Ephraim's territory. So, this does provide rationale to explain that Dan is tacitly included in those 12 tribes and provides a reason why both Dan and Ephraim are kind of silently called out for their sin, but also included with the 12 tribes. By the way, if you study God's listing of the 12 tribes of Israel in depth you will see that many times the tribes are listed differently in number and in order for the purpose of the listing, cf. *Gen 35:23-28* shows tribes/sons listed by mother; *Num. 1* includes some sons of tribes, including Joseph's sons Manasseh and Ephraim, but excludes the Levites as they were not to go to war; *Gen. 46* shows those coming out of Egypt; *Gen. 48:4-6* shows Israel promising Joseph's two son's Manasseh and Ephraim an everlasting portion/possession with the other 11 tribes; *Gen. 49:3-27* provides Israel's prophetic blessing on all 12 tribes; *Eze. 48* shows all 12 tribes of Israel (including and starting with Dan), inheriting their promised land in the Millennium. The main point of this section is that 144,000 of all 12 tribes of Israel, 12,000 from each tribe, are Jewish in nature and witnesses that God gives a seal of protection and identification in their foreheads.}

B. 7:9-12— {Title: Angels, Creatures, and Saved Multitude in Heaven Worshiping God and Jesus from Every Nation and Tongue} **9**-"*After this* (What event is this referring? The Sealing of the 144,000 Jewish believers/witnesses. You'll see the heavenly response. Some consider this parenthetical to take place later) *I* (John) **beheld, and lo, a great multitude, which no man** (one; *Gr: oudeis-no one, none, nothing, no body, no man, no woman...*) **could number** (there will ultimately be many saved, a great revival in the Trib), **of all** (exciting God is bringing the gospel and saving people from all) **nations, and kindreds, and people, and tongues** (*5:9*; *11:9*; *14:6*; shows this massive diverse heavenly inclusion), **stood** (based on Jesus' imputed righteousness they have the ability to stand "complete in Him," *Col. 2:10*; *4:12*) **before the throne** (of God-the-Father), **and before the Lamb** (God-the-Son; the God-Man), **clothed with white robes** (a picture of imputed or given righteousness and reward), **and with palms in their hands;"** (Not palms of their hands, but palm trees/branches in their hands, which were even carved in the temple, symbolizing homage and a royal restful oasis. Jews worshiping King Jesus' at His triumphal entry in *Joh. 12:13*, "took branches of palm trees, and went forth to meet Him, and cried, 'Hosanna: Blessed is the King of Israel that cometh in the name of the Lord.'"); *10*-"*And cried with a loud voice saying, 'Salvation to our God Which* (Who) *sits* (is sitting) *upon the throne, and unto the Lamb.*" (Another acknowledgment that God-the-Father through the blood of the Lamb is saving the 144,000 witnesses. He is about to save many through the 144,000 witnesses in the Trib and He has saved the heavenly worshipers. Both are shown as patiently and mercifully "sitting upon the throne," on the place of judgment, "not willing that any should perish, but that all should come to repentance" *2Pe. 3:9*). *11*-"*And all the angels stood* (I picture a massive standing ovation with hands and wings clapping and flapping) *round about* (encircling) *the throne* (God's)*, and around the elders* (Church leaders)*, and the 4 beasts* (living creatures; special Seraphim angels)*, and they fell down* (this was not accidental tripping, but purposeful humble worship, none will stand long, before showing by body the truth of God's exalted presence) *before the throne* (again, "the" throne above all thrones; the place of exalted judgment) *on their faces* (can't even look up so overwhelmed by God and His glory)*, and worshiped God.*" (Worship in truth, how?), *12*-"*Saying, 'Amen: Blessing, and glory, and wisdom, and thanksgiving, and honor, and power, and might, be unto our God for ever and ever. Amen.'*" (Started and ended with Amen-truly, surely, trustworthy; and says 7 things that try to embody what they are thinking, feeling, and experiencing of God. Oh, that we might worship our God like that even now...}

C. *7:13-17*— {Title: A Church Elder Describes those Trib Saints Serving God and Being Fed, Led, and De-Teared by Jesus in Heaven. *13*-"*And 1 of the elders* (Church leaders) *answered* (began to speak) *saying unto me* (John)*, 'Who are these arrayed in white robes? And whence came they* (from where have they come)*?'*" (So after seeing and hearing people and angels crying out in worship, a Church elder asks John who are the people and where did they come from?). *14*-"*And* (showing continued action and dialog again) *I* (John) *said to him* (elder)*, 'Sir* (Gr:kurios-Lord, master, Mr., Sir)*, you have known.' And he* (elder) *said to me, 'These are they which* (ones who) *came out of the Great Tribulation* (a technical term for "the final 3 ½ years" of the 7-year Trib period, cf. *2:22*; *7:14*; *Mat. 24:21*)*, and have washed their* (Trib saints) *robes, and made them* (robes) *white* (called out 4 times in *Rev. 6:11*; *7:9, 13, 14*)*, in the blood of the Lamb.'*" (The only way anyone ever got or gets saved or righteous, even in the Trib, as was also promised by Jesus to the church in *3:4*). *15*-"*Therefore* (because they were saved by the blood of Jesus) *are they* (these saved Trib saints) *before* (in the presence of) *the throne of God* (the Father), *and serve* (worship) *Him* (God) *day and night in His* (God's) *temple* (the true Heavenly temple, not the earthly one that is patterned after the true one, cf. *Heb. 8:1-5*; *9:22-28*): *and* (as if that wasn't enough to be saved, be in God's presence, and be able to always worship God) *He that sits* (is sitting/residing) *on the throne* (God-the-Father, ruler of all; He) *shall dwell* (reside) *among* (with) *them."* (The Trib saints). *16-* (1 might think by the period this was all, but wait there is more); *"They* (Trib saints) *shall hunger* (Gr:peinao-toil, pine, famish, hunger, crave) *no more, neither thirst* (literally or figuratively; there are going to be so many unfulfilled longings and cravings of the unsaved, all who reject Jesus, the Passover Lamb, the "bread." and the "water of Life") *any more; neither shall the sun* (Gr:helios-ray, light, sun) *light* (Gr: pipto-fall, fail, light) *on them, nor any heat."* (Gr:kauma-burn, glow, heat; which we'll see, happens a lot to all in the Trib). *17-*(How is all this going to happen for the Trib saints?) *"For the Lamb Which* (Who) *is in* (Gr:ana-up, in) *the midst of the throne* (God's) *shall feed* (Gr:poimaino-tend as a shepherd, feed; a paradox, the Lamb shall shepherd as "the Great Shepherd," cf. *Heb. 13:20*) *them* (saved Trib saints)*, and* (Jesus) *shall lead* (Gr:hodegeo-show them the way, guide, lead) *them* (Trib saints) *unto living fountains* (Gr:pege-gushing plumply, fount, supply, enjoyment, fountain, well) *of waters* (still the best drink for you): *and* (wait there's more) *God shall wipe away* (blot out/erase) *all tears from their* (those saints coming out of the Trib and promised to all believers, cf. *7:17*; *21:4*; *Isa. 25:8*) *eyes."*}

Application (Activity/Questions)

A. Who will be able to stand after the Trib and go into the Millennium and Heaven? {Jews and every nation/person that is saved by the blood of Jesus, the Lamb.}

B. Who will be eternally saved during the 7-year Tribulation period? {Jews and Gentiles that believe in God.}

C. With demonic miracles, Satanic deception, government persecution, and strong delusion (*13:13-15*; *Mat. 24:24*; *2Th. 2:11-12*), why do you believe many will be saved during the Trib period (*7:9, 14*) and what does that reveal about the God you know? {God says a great innumerable multitude will be saved; because He is sovereign, loving, gracious, and merciful--even in judgment; before a person dies or Christ's 2nd Coming.}

D. How will people be saved in the Tribulation period (**7:14**)? {The same way people have always been saved: By grace through faith, by the blood of the Lamb; and we'll see later that they will NOT worship the Antichrist or take the mark of the beast.}

E. What do you experience of God in your worship now, and how will that differ in heaven? {Too much of eyes on world and my flesh so distracted by "cares of this world." In heaven, we will have our eyes focused more on our big glorious God and His eternal will and purposes.}

The 7th Seal and the 1st 4 Trumpet Judgments (1-Hail Fire, 2-Fiery Mountain, 3-Meteor=Wormwood, 4-Darkness).

The 7th Seal and the 1st 4 Trumpet Judgments.

Introduction

A. When Jesus opens the final book's seal of the final wicked judgment on earth, what should the reaction be by those of us eternally saved who are with Him in heaven? {Silence; since none is worthy to speak, but God is worthy to judge. Let's praise God for His mercy to us.}

B. Do you think there will be millions, billions, or trillions of prayers for justice (God to judge the wicked) over the millennia? {Trillions, assuming numerous from each saved, especially persecuted or tortured people.}

C. What is the Book Outline (**_1:19_**) and Final Event Timeline so far?

1. **_1:19_** (**_Rev. 1_**)—   {**_"things you have seen"_**}
2. **_1:19_** (**_Rev. 2-3_**)— {**_"things that are"_**--the Church Age}
3. **_1:19_** (**_Rev. 4-22_**)— {**_"things to come"_**--Mostly the 7-Year Tribulation Period, and summary of thereafter}

 ➢ **_Rev. 4-5_**— {Heavenly Throne; Who is worthy to judge and open the Seals?--Only Jesus}
 ➢ **_Rev. 6-7_**— {Trib: 6/7 Seals}
 ➢ **_Rev. 7_**—   {Sealing 144K and Trib Saints Worship}
 ➢ **_Rev. 8_**—   {Trib: 7th Seal: 1st 4/7 Trumpet Judgments and later Bowl Judgments; in this chapter}

{Write timeline on board with images or names of Creation, Law, Cross, Tomb, Ascension, Church Age (Pentecost to Rapture), Rapture, 7-Year Trib (Seals/Trumpets/Vial judgments), 2nd Coming, 1000-year Millennium, and Great White Throne Judgment.}

Scripture (Observations/Interpretation/Commentary)
{Every verse, except **_8:7_** begins with "and" for continued action; have Groups Title Paragraphs and Answer Questions A-H.}

A. **_8:1-2_**— {Title: The 7th Seal Brings Silence and 7 Trumpets to 7 Angels before God}

1. Who is the only 1 worthy to judge? (**_4:11_**; **_5:12_**; **_6:1_**; **_7:17_**)? {Ask each Group to give answers to their Group questions when you

get to Questions=Q, Answers=A; <u>Q1-4</u> and <u>A1-4</u> in the commentary below}

2. Why do you think there was shushing/silence?
3. What did God give the 7 angels?
4. What are trumpets used for by angelic messengers?

{**8:1**-"***And when He*** (<u>Q1: Who is the only 1 worthy to judge, **4:11**; **5:12**; **6:1**; **7:17**</u>)?-A1: "the Lamb," Jesus Christ, the only 1 worthy, the only 1 Who opened the 1st 6 Seals of Judgment) ***had opened the 7***^{***th***} ***Seal*** (the final 1, the perfect #), ***there was silence*** (*Gr:sige-from sizo-to hiss, hush, shhhh, silence;* <u>Q2: Why do you think there was shushing/silence?-A2: Sobering Silence/Holy Hush (cf. **Hab. 2:20**)-fear and looking for God's justice without full understanding of what must be</u>); ***in heaven*** (the Godly are silent in heaven, the ungodly are crying/screaming on earth) ***about the space of*** (like) ***half an hour.*** " **8:2**-"***And I*** (John) ***saw the 7 angels which stood before God; and to them*** (angels) ***were given 7 trumpets.*** " (<u>Q3: What did God give the 7 angels? -A3: Trumpets. Q4: What are trumpets used for by angelic messengers? -A4: Heralding, warning, announcing judgment</u>).}

B. **8:3-5**— {Title: Angel Offers Incense and Prayers of Saints up to God and Casts Fire from Altar to Earth}

1. What was given to this different angel?
2. What does the fire always do on the altar?
3. Any guess as to what the voices may have been uttering, while judging the earth?

{**8:3**-"***And a different angel came and stood at*** (by) ***the altar*** (a place of sacrifice), ***having a golden censer; and there was given unto him*** (the angel) ***much incense, that*** (*Gr:hina-purpose, intent, result*) ***he*** (the angel) ***should offer it*** (incense) ***with the prayers of all saints*** (all believers, presumably of all dispensations, but certainly from the Trib) ***upon the golden altar, which is before the throne*** (God-the-Father's. <u>Q1: What was given to this different angel? -A1: Much incense</u> (interesting it doesn't say prayers were given to the angel, prayers are only to God, thru the name of Jesus). **8:4**-"***And the smoke of the incense, which came*** ("which came" are supplied words, are not in manuscripts, as noted by italics in KJV, and aren't really needed, but make it clearer) ***with the prayers of the saints, ascended up*** (God is above all) ***before God out of the angel's hand*** " (we see this picture of an angel jointly worshiping by holding up his hand with a censor in it pouring out/up the incense and men's prayers to God). **8:5**-"***And the angel took the censer, filled*** (*Gr:gemizo-filled entirely*) ***it with fire from the altar*** (<u>Q2: What</u>

does fire always do on the altar?-A2: Burns, consumes, punishes, or judges the quality of material on the altar), **and threw it into the earth** (now not a picture of prayerful petitions, but of judging justice; no sweet smells or heavenly prayers now, just earthly singeing fire): **and there came to be thunder, and voices, and lightnings, and an earthquake"** (interesting thunder, voices, and lightning are plural, but only 1 earthquake. Q3: Any guess as to what the voices may have been uttering while judging the earth? -A3: Truth about sins/crimes or maybe worship or thanks for coming holy justice).}

   C. **8:6**— {Title: The 7 Angels with 7 Trumpets Prepared to Sound}
      1. What do you think the angels' preparation to trump looked like? {**8:6**-"**and the 7 angels, which had the 7 trumpets, prepared themselves to sound**" (Q1: What do you think their preparation looked like?-A1: Bowing, licking lips, raising trumpets).}

   D. **8:7**— {Title: 1st Angel—Hail and Fire with Blood Burning 1/3 Trees and Grass}
      1. What judgment was the 1st Trumpet and its results? {**8:7**- "**The 1st angel sounded** (Gr:salpizo-trumpeted, blasted, sounded), **and there followed** (came to be) **hail and fire mingled** (mixed) **with blood, and they were cast upon** (thrown onto) **the earth: and the 3rd part of trees was burnt up, and all green grass was burnt up**" (Q1: What judgment was the 1st Trumpet and its results?-A1: Hail and Fire with blood burning 1/3 trees and grass).}

   E. **8:8-9**— {Title: 2nd Angel—Burning Mountain, Sea became Blood and Killed 1/3 and 1/3 Ships}
      1. What judgment was the 2nd Trumpet and its results? {**8:8**-"**And the 2nd angel sounded, and as it were a great mountain burning with fire was cast into the sea: and the 1/3 part of the sea became blood;**" **8:9**-"**And 1/3 part of the creatures which were in the sea, and had life, died; and the 1/3 part of the ships were destroyed**" (Q1: What judgment was the 2nd Trumpet and its results?-A1: A burning mountain on earth, the sea became blood and killed 1/3 and 1/3 of the ships were also destroyed).}

   F. **8:10-11**— {Title: 3rd Angel—Burning Meteor-"Wormwood" Fell on 1/3 Water, Killing Many}
      1. Was the star a real star/meteor or an angel/demon?
      2. What judgment was the 3rd Trumpet and its results? {**8:10**-"**And the 3rd angel sounded, and there fell a great star** (Q1: Was this star a real star or an angel/demon?-A1: "Star" is found 15 times in Bible, 2 in OT, one referring to Jesus (**Num. 24:17**) and the other to an

idol (**Amo. 5:26**); 13 in NT, 5 in **Revelation**, 6 or 8 a literal star (**Mat. 2:2, 7, 9-10; 1Co. 15:41**), 1 an idol (**Acts. 7:43**), 1 or 3 for an angel or demon (**9:1, 11**), and 3 for Jesus (**2Pe. 1:19; Rev. 2:28; 22:16**) as the "Day" or "Morning" Star). So the 2 in question are found here in **8:10-11,** where some believe the star is Satan, as Lucifer (cf. **Isa. 14:12-15**) means "Day Star" and Satan tries to be or counterfeit God/Jesus. Satan gets cast down to earth clearly seen later in **12:4, 7-13**, and seems if it were someone as important as Satan he would be identified clearly here if God intended this star to be him, for this reason some suggest a demon (e.g. C. S. Lewis in The Screwtape Letters)[11], but could be a demon or Satan. I currently lean to the star in **8:10-11** being a literal star/meteor as: 1) the majority verses re: a "star" in Scripture are not for angels, demons, or Satan, 2) demons are never shown that destructive and usually are following Satan's directive, not God's, 3) the star is named "Wormwood" not Satan, and 4) Satan is pictured as a 7-headed dragon that is cast down to earth 4 chapters later in **Rev. 12.** FYI "stars"-51 times, 35 in OT, 16 in NT, 9 in Revelation is similar in usage to star, yet highlights some men as also "stars" cf. **Gen. 37:9**; so there fell a great star) **from heaven, burning as it were a lamp** (like a torch)**, and it fell upon the 3rd part of the rivers, and upon the fountains of waters;" 8:11-"And the name of the star was called Wormwood: and the 3rd part of the waters became wormwood; and many men died of the waters, because they were made bitter."** (Q2: What judgment was the 3rd Trumpet and its results? -A2: Burning Meteor-"Wormwood" fell on 1/3rd of the fresh water, killing many by bad/bitter water).}

   G. **8:12**— {Title: 4th Angel—3rd of Sun, Moon, and Stars Smitten Shortening Day and Night by 1/3rd}

   1.   What judgment was the 4th Trumpet and its results? {**8:12-"And the 4th angel sounded, and the 3rd part of the sun, the 3rd part of the moon, and the 3rd part of the stars were smitten; so as** (Gr:hina-purpose, so that, the result was) **the 3rd part of them was darkened** (Gr:skotizo-obscured, darkened)**, and the day shown not for a 3rd of it, and the night likewise."** (Q1: What judgment was the 4th Trumpet and its results? -A1: 3rd of sun, moon, and stars smitten shortening day and night by 1/3rd or 8 hours). It's not clear whether our solar system went from 24 to 16-hour solar days or whether day and nights had less light from the sun and moon/stars. FYI-Venus day is < 6 hrs., while earth's is 24, Mars about 25 hrs., so if the distance or rotation of the earth changed, so could time on earth. **Mat. 24:22** and **Mar.**

13:20 say that God graciously shortened these days to save people, for the sake of the saved).}

   H. ***8:13***— {Title: An Angel Flew Crying "Woe, Woe, Woe" for the 3 Trumpets yet to Sound}

     1. How many "woes," "angels," and "trumpets" yet to sound? {***8:13***-"***And I*** (John) ***beheld, and heard another angel flying in mid sky/heaven, saying with a loud voice*** (Gr:megas phone), ***'Woe, woe, woe*** (an exclamation of grief) ***to the inhabitants of the earth because of the other trumpet voices of the 3 angels, yet to sound!'*** (Q1: How many "woes," "angels," and "trumpets" yet to sound? -A1: 3, the # of completion; to complete the 3 woes).}

Application (Activity/Questions)

A. Will Christians (the Church) be able to do anything to help the wicked during the Tribulation period? {No, nothing; the Church will be in heaven. Only Jewish believers after the Rapture (during the Trib) will be able to witness, while running from the Antichrist and plagues.}

B. What should we do now in light of God's patience and these 4 terrible trumpet judgments to the unsaved during the Trib? {Pray for them, warn them, and beg them to be reconciled so they can miss the Trib (the terrible wrath to come).}

Figure 11 – 14.1 The Four Angels of Death[12]

7th Seal and 5th Trumpet (1st Woe)-Locusts with 5-Month
Scorpion Stings; No Repentance.

5th Trumpet and 1st Woe Judgment.
{The Bottomless Pit, Its Angel, & Scorpion King.}

Introduction
A. Anyone ever been stung by a scorpion, bee, or wasp? {Yes, all of the
above, and the scorpion was the worst, and some even kill.}
B. Not comparing it to anything discovered after 100 AD., describe a
weapon firing from a helicopter. {Skip this question if concerned for
time. We will see some 1st century descriptions of what some say could
be an Apache helicopter or other 21st century weapons.}
C. What were the 3 responses of Pharaoh to the 8th Plague (locusts) on
Egypt (**_Exo. 10:7-11, 16-17, 20_**; **_8:15_**)? {Partial repentance, questions,
resisted God/Moses' request (**_Exo. 10:7-11_**); Repented (**_Exo. 10:16-17_**);
Hardened his heart to God again and God hardened his heart also by
the progression of plagues (**_Exo. 10:20_**; **_8:15_**). We'll see in **_Rev. 9_** the
wicked didn't repent either.}

Scripture (Observations/Interpretation/Commentary)
{"and" starts 10/11 verses, showing continued action}

A. **9:1-6**— {Title: 5th Trumpet/1st Woe—Bottomless Pit Opened
Sending Stinging Locusts. **_1_**-"**_And the 5th angel sounded, and I_** (John)
saw a star (figurative, shown is an angel or some believe a demon
using a key leading locusts further discussed in **_9:11_**) **_fall from_** (out of)
heaven unto the earth: and to him (an angel), **_was given the key of
the bottomless_** (Gr:abussos-depthless, abyss, deep, bottomless) **_pit_**"
(Gr:phrear-hole, abyss, well, pit; for holding something, as a prison). **_2_**-
"**_And he_** (the angel) **_opened the bottomless pit; and there arose_**
(ascended) **_smoke out of the pit, as_** (like) **_the smoke of a great
furnace; and the sun and the air were darkened by reason of_** (from)
the smoke of the pit" (a picture of judgment with smoke and
darkness). **_3_**-"**_And there came out of the smoke locusts upon the
earth: and unto them was given power_** (capability)**_, as the scorpions
of the earth have power_**" (capability. Locusts came with scorpion
stings. 3 main locust views: 1) Literal locusts led by an angel or demon,
maybe even gene spliced with scorpion stings, 2) figurative locusts

that were actually demons, and 3) figurative locusts that may be Apache helicopters, or Locust-like drones, or other modern war-machines with bio/poison; weaponry almost impossible for John to describe in the 1st Century prior to the invention of any gun, missile, bomb, car, or plane). *4-"And it was commanded them* (locusts) *that* (*Gr:hina-purpose*) *they* (locusts) *should not hurt the grass* (*Gr:chortos-court, garden, pasture, vegetation, grass, hay*) *of the earth* (what was left or grew back from the 1st Trumpet's hail judgment in *8:7*), *neither any green thing, neither any tree; but only those men which have not the seal of God in their foreheads"* (cf. *7:3-8*, God's seal of protection on His 144,000 Jewish witnesses). *5-"And to them* (locusts with scorpion stingers) *it was given that* (*Gr:hina-purpose*) *they should not kill them* (unsealed men. FYI, scorpion stings currently account for about 3,250 deaths/year (10 times that of poisonous snakes)[13], even without these increased plague like numbers), *but that* (*Gr:hina-purpose*) *they* (unsealed, wicked, unsaved men) *should be tormented 5 months: and their torment was as* (like) *the torment of a scorpion, when it strikes* (stings) *a man." 6-"And in those days shall men seek death, and shall not find it; and shall desire to die, and death shall flee away from them"* (Kind of a summary of this locust stinging judgment and repeats twice the pain will be so bad they want to die, but won't).

B. *9:7-11*— {Title: 5th Trumpet—Stinging Locust Description and Their Bottomless Pit King. (cf. *8:7*; *7:3-8*; *11:7*; *17:8*; *20:1, 3, 7, 10*; *Luke 16:19-31*; *2Pe. 2:4*; *Jude 1:6*) (Greek text starts a new paragraph here, but not all do as it starts with "and" and continues the 5th Trumpet). *7-"And* (now John sees 8 descriptions of these locusts; 3 in *9:7*) *the shape* (*Gr:homoioma-form, resemblance, likeness, shape, similitude*) *of the locusts were like unto horses prepared unto battle; and on their heads were as it were crowns like gold, and their faces were as the faces of men." 8-"And they* (locusts) *had hair as the hair of women, and their teeth were as the teeth of lions"* (2 more locust descriptions). *9-"And they* (locusts) *had breastplates* (*Gr:thorax-chest, thorax, breastplate*) *as it were breastplates of iron; and the sound of their wings was as the sound of chariots of many horses running to battle* (2 more locust descriptions). *10-"And they* (locusts) *had tails like unto scorpions, and there were stings* (*Gr:kentron-prick, sting, poison*) *in their tails: and their power* (capability) *was to hurt men 5 months"* (the 8th and final locust description was a tail that stings and hurts 5 months, repeated again from *9:5*). *11-"And they* (locusts) *had a king over them* (he is "the Locust/Scorpion King"), **which** (who) **is the angel of the bottomless pit, whose name in the Hebrew tongue is Abaddon** (means destroying angel), **and in the Greek tongue has his name Apollyon"** (means destroyer. Some believe this is Satan as he is certainly a destroyer, and some equate **11:7** and **17:8** as references to Satan ascending out of the "bottomless pit"-found 7 times in Bible. Others (including me), think this is another powerful angel, and not Satan or another demon as: 1) it names him Abaddon/Apollyon, 2) it doesn't specifically identify him as Satan here **9:11** or **9:1-2**, 3) he seems to obey God, and 4) clearly another powerful angel has the key to the bottomless pit, grabs Satan, chains him up, and locks him in the bottomless pit in **20:1, 3**. As a bonus, some see the "great gulf" in **Luke 16:19-31** as the chasm that looks across the "bottomless pit" and separates "hades," a place of torment, from Abraham's "bosom" or paradise, a place of comfort. Also, I believe the bottomless pit leads to "tartaroo," the place where some demons were cast into "chains of darkness, to be reserved unto judgment," cf. **2Pe. 2:4**; **Jude 1:6**; as Satan also gets chained there prior to also being cast into hell, cf. **20:1, 3, 7, 10**).}

C. **9:12**— {Title: 1 Woe is Past, 2 Woes to Come. **12**-(**9:6, 12, 20-21** are really summary statements about men and the woes); "**1 woe** (exclamation of grief) **is past; and behold, there come 2 woes more hereafter"** (a little summary that the 5th Trumpet and 1st Woe is past; the 6th Trumpet and 2nd Woe, plus the 7th Trumpet and 3rd Woe are still to come).}

Figure 12 – 15.1 The Opening of the Seventh Seal and the Eagle Crying 'Woe'[14]

<u>Application</u> (Activity/Questions)

A. What do you believe the locusts are (1-Literal Locusts, 2-Demons, or 3-Modern Warfare)? Does it matter that much since the results are the same anyway? {1-Literal locusts since 8 specific descriptions of them, they are called locusts, they are led by a demon, and locusts were part of the OT plagues. My 2nd choice would be modern warfare by flying bio-weaponry drones-with poisonous hypodermic needles to keep from killing but disabling an enemy for months; which are currently rapidly proliferating the battlefield and even civilian law-enforcement. But it really doesn't matter that much as God judges the wicked with 5 months pain either way.}

B. Do you believe the star, "the Locust/Scorpion King," the angel of the bottomless pit, Abaddon and Apollyon is Satan, a Demon, or another powerful good angel, why? {Another powerful good angel as he is named Abaddon/Apollyon, not called Satan, he obeys God, and Satan is actually chained up and thrown into the bottomless pit by this angel later in **_Rev. 20:1-6_**. So, I would not think a demon either, since he obeys God, and it doesn't make since for him to get to throw his boss into the bottomless pit.}

C. How does God show mercy to the wicked by not permitting these "locusts" to kill them? {He provides a witness of Himself, motivation to believe Him, and more time to repent.}

D. How does God's judging only the wicked, justify, comfort, and show mercy to His people? {Demonstrates God's laws are true, those who follow Him and His laws are wisest, it weakens the wicked's ability to persecute the righteous, and it withholds judgment from the righteous who also deserve judgment for their sin; and God is just to do so since Jesus took that judgment for us.}

7ᵗʰ Seal and 6ᵗʰ Trumpet (2ⁿᵈ Woe)-
200M Army Kill 1/3ʳᵈ Men; No Repentance.

200M Army Kill 1/3ʳᵈ Men; 2/3ʳᵈ Still Don't Repent.
{Drugs, Demon Worship, and Idols.}

Introduction
A. How many do you think fought in World War 2 (1939-1945)?
{About 100M; the world population was 2.3B then. Now is the 1ˢᵗ time in world history where there could be an army of 200M.}
B. Not comparing it to anything discovered after 100 AD, describe an attacking tank. {Or 50 caliber or flame thrower military vehicle—An iron chariot that shoots fire, smoke, and brimstone from its head and tail killing many.}
C. Do you think God allows hurricanes, tornadoes, earthquakes or other disasters as a witness or punishment today, why/why not? {Yes, sometimes and allows Christians to be a witness in how they help most and minister to those impacted.}

Scripture (Observations/Interpretation/Commentary)
A. _9:13-19_— {Title: 6ᵗʰ Trumpet/2ⁿᵈ Woe Judgment-200M Army Kill 1/3ʳᵈ Men. _13_-"**And the 6ᵗʰ angel** (2ⁿᵈ Woe) **sounded** (his trumpet)**, and I** (John) **heard a voice from** (out of) **the 4 horns** (a symbol of strength, honor, and power/dominion) **of the golden altar** (a place of worship and sacrifice), **which is before God," _14_-"Saying to the 6ᵗʰ angel** (2ⁿᵈ Woe), **which had the trumpet, 'Loose** (release) **the 4 angels, which are bound in the great river Euphrates'** (longest river in SW Asia, over 1,700 miles long, many boats, separates the middle east from Asia, e.g. China, originates in the mountains of Turkey=22% of their fresh water, Syria=11%, Iraq=46%, and Iran=19%, emptying into the Persian Gulf; the Tigris is the other large river and water supply in the area. FYI-not just water, but 8/13 of the world's largest oil reserve countries are in the Middle East). _15_-"**And the 4 angels were loosed, which were prepared for an hour, and a day, and a month, and year** (God's sovereign perfect timing. Wonder why He says the time backward? I think to emphasize the specific hour), **for to** (Gr:hina-purpose) **kill the third part** (1/3) **of men." _16_-"and the number of the army of the horsemen** (Gr:hippikon-cavalvry force, horsemen; the idea of men transporters) **were 200,000,000** (Gr: duo murias murias-two

10,000/myriad/indefinite number [*] 10,000/myriad/indefinite number): **and I** (John) **heard the number of them** (not only saw this 200M in John's vision, but also heard it stated. Who are these 200M army? -2 main views of who the 200M army that kills 1/3 (2.5B of the world's >7.5B as of June 2017.[15] 1) Demonic hoard. Could fit the description and tie to the 4 angels or demons leading. In the OT you see angelic horsemen with Elijah-**2Ki. 2:11** and Elisha-**2Ki. 6:17**). 2) Human army. China Chairman Mao boasted in the 1960s an army of 200M, 14% of their about 1.4B population as of 2019.[16] In 2000, China surpassed that number in their fighting age men and has steadily grown that by about 5% a year. Others see Arabs/Islamic fielding an Army of 200M or 12.5% of their about 1.6B,[17] those just around the Euphrates are Iran, Turkey, Syria, Iraq, Kuwait, and Saudi Arabia. Others, the European Union [EU] nations and those led by Antichrist or those battling against the Antichrist. Some believe a non-literal or large human army. I lean towards a coalition of nations including China, Russia, with some EU and Islamic nations fighting. **Dan. 11:44** says, "But tidings out of the east and out of the north shall trouble him: therefore, he shall go forth with great fury to destroy, and utterly to take away many." Notice the "east" [China and maybe India, 37% of worlds pop],[18] and the "north" [Russia]. **Rev. 16:12** says, "And the sixth angel poured out his vial upon the great river Euphrates; and the water thereof was dried up, that the way of the kings of the east might be prepared." Again, kings of the "east" [China]. I believe a literal 200M human army crossing the dried-up Euphrates certainly makes way for China and others in Asia in automated vehicles including tanks to go to the Middle East, probably motivated to get oil). **17-"and thus** (in this way) **I** (John) **saw the horses in the vision, and them that sat on them** (the horses), **having breastplates of fire, and of jacinth** (Gr:huakinthinos-hyacinthine, jacinthine, deep blue, jacinth-golden, red-brown, purple), **and brimstone** (Gr:theiodes-sulpher like, sulfurous, brimstone): **and the heads of the horses were as the heads of lions; and out of their mouths issued fire and smoke and brimstone"** (Gr:theion-flashing, sulfur, brimstone). **18-"By these 3 was the third** (1/3) **part of men killed, by the fire, and by the smoke, and by the brimstone, which issued** (projected) **out of their mouths." 19-"For their power** (force/ capability) **is in their mouth, and in their tails: for their tails were like unto serpents** (Gr:ophis-snake-sly cunning, sharpness of vision, artful malicious person), **and had heads** (more than 1), **and with them they do hurt."** (Most consider this to be describing armored vehicles like Tanks, Rocket Launchers...Summarizing—so the voice out of the heavenly altar tells the 6th Trumpeting Angel to release the 4 angels bound to the Euphrates, that were sovereignly prepared and awaiting this very hour, an army of 200M in horse power with cunning fierce like-lion and serpent-like heads and tails that projected fire, smoke, and flashes of sulfur like yellowish explosions kill 1/3 of men crossing the dried up Euphrates.}

B. **9:20-21**— {Title: 2/3rds Still Living Don't Repent of their Demonology/Idolatry/Wickedness. **20**-"*And the rest of the men, which were not killed* (2/3rds) *by these plagues yet repented not of the works of their hands, that* (Gr:hina-purpose) *they should not worship devils* (or the probably possessed Antichrist, who was also a false idol that couldn't bring peace), *and idols of gold, and silver, and brass, and stone, and of wood: which neither can see, nor hear, nor walk* (but the true God surely can):" **21**-"*Neither repented they of their murders, nor of their sorceries* (Gr: pharmakeia-medication, pharmacy, magic, sorcery, witchcraft), *nor of their fornication, nor of their thefts.*" (Summary—The 2/3rds wicked men still alive didn't repent/change their mind about the works of their hands to stop worshiping devils, or blind, dumb lame idols, nor stop murdering, drugs, sexual perversion, or stealing. How sad, still breaking the 1st 3rd, and 6th, 7th, and 8th [60%] of the 10 Commandments, another silent witness to the nation of Israel to whom God gave the 10 Commandments to make them a blessed people over all the nations of the world).}

Application (Activity/Questions)

A. What purpose does God use earthly judgments to accomplish? {To lead men to repentance, to turn to worship God from their wicked works and idolatry, before His final eternal judgment.}

B. How does Pharaoh's response to God's plagues on Egypt mimic those here in **Rev. 9**? {Both hardened their hearts and didn't repent from the progressively worst plagues.}

C. What normally does persecution, war, and death cause men's heart to ponder? {God, an afterlife, an eternity, prayerfully having them turn to God for help for eternal salvation.}

D. Why do you think many will worship devils and are getting caught up in witchcraft or other occult practices today? {Don't want to be responsible to God; like a belief that allows them to indulge their flesh like occult fornication practices; enjoy lawlessness; are deceived; want to have God-like power; want to belong; want to be out there, spiritual, but not Godly.}

A Mighty Angel, a Secret Message, and Eating a Little Book.

A Mighty Angel Cries, 7 Thunders Speak a Secret.
{A Message Not to Write, But John Must Prophesy Again.}

Introduction

A. Do you think there are any really amazing angels that get to be daily in God's presence? {Yes, and I can't wait to experience the same someday...}

B. What impact do you think daily being in God's presence might have on an angel or anyone? {Greatly increase knowledge, understanding, and wisdom; face might shine, reflecting His glory; gain eternal perspective; learn a lot; want to go do something for Him.}

C. Do you have a daily opportunity to be in God's presence (**_Heb. 4:16_**; **_Isa. 58:2_**)? {Yes, though I may feel distant, we are made close through Jesus by God's Spirit and can draw closer daily.}

Scripture (Observations/Interpretation/Commentary)
{10/11 verses begin with "and;" showing continued action; only **_10:7_** starts with "But;" have learners Read and Title Paragraphs.}

A. _10:1-7_— {Title: A Mighty Angel with a Little Book Thunders and Says Don't Write This. **_1_**-"**And I** (John) **saw another** (different) **mighty angel** (mentioned 3 times in Bible; **_5:2_**; **_10:1_**; **_18:21_**) **come down** (descend) **out of heaven, clothed with a cloud: and a rainbow** (a sign of God's promised everlasting covenant to not destroy every living creature upon the earth by a flood; **_Gen. 9:16_**) **upon his head, and his face was as it were** (like) **the sun, and his feet as pillars of fire:**" **_2_**-"**And he had in his hand a little book** (1st time a "little book" is referenced in Bible and only found in **_10:2, 8, 9, 10_**) **open: and he set his right foot upon the sea, and his left foot on the earth,**" **_3_**-"**And he cried with a loud voice, as when** (just like) **a lion roars: and when he had cried, 7 thunders** ("7 thunders"-only 3 times in Bible, all here in **_10:3-4_**; is not defined for us. They could be 7 other angelic voices, could be 7 important glorified believer's voices, could be actually 7 thunders, or some see this from a Jewish Idiom meaning the "voice of God," which sounds like thundering (cf. **_John 12:28-30_**; **_Job 40:9_**). I believe this is 7 other angels thundering a message when this mighty angel speaks as in **_10:4_**, John is told not to write what they thundered, and I don't believe an angel would kick off God's speaking, normally God tells angels to speak or thunder) *uttered their voices."* (Gr: phone-noise, sound, or voice; by indication an address or disclosure. Who is this mighty angel? -3 main views, some believe: 1) Jesus-as so many corollary heavenly and high priest descriptions, cf. *1:14-16*; *4:3*; *5:7*; but he is not identified as Jesus and is actually called a mighty angel. 2) *"Another mighty angel"*-as that is what Scripture says in *5:3*; *10:1*, and there are some differences in the descriptions of Christ and this mighty angel, e.g. *"book"* vs *"little book,"* eyes like fire instead of feet... 3) Michael the Archangel-clearly a part of view 2. Archangel means chief angel, angel with authority over others. He is Israel's Chief Angel/Prince/Protector in *Jude 1:9*; *Dan. 10:13, 21*, he is clearly one of the mightiest angels who will defeat Satan, cf. *12:7-10*, his voice is heard at the Rapture, cf. *1Th. 4:16*; *Jud. 1:9*. Michael means *"who is like God?"* *Dan. 12:1*-*"And at that time shall Michael stand up, the great prince which standeth for the children of thy people* [Israel/Jews]: *and there shall be a time of trouble, such as never was since there was a nation even to that same time* [The Great Tribulation]: *and at that time thy people* [Jews] *shall be delivered, every one that shall be found written in the book."*) *4*-*"And when the 7 thunders had uttered their voices, I was about to write: and I heard a voice out of heaven* (the unknown voice from heaven like several other voices, cf. *4:1*; *6:6-7*; *9:13*...) *saying to me* (John), *'Seal up* (a command) *what the 7 thunders uttered, and don't write them'"* (cf. *Pro. 25:2*a- *"It is the glory of God to conceal a thing:"* keeping some mystery. We need to trust Him. God shows John who is probably overwhelmed by much of this, to probably comfort and encourage him, make him know he is special, but doesn't allow him to share some words with the rest of the church. The Apostle Paul was also given heavenly words, which were also not allowed to be uttered, cf. *2Co. 12:4*). *5*-*"And the angel* (the mighty one) *which* (who) *I* (John) *saw stand upon the sea and upon the earth lifted up his hand to heaven"* (a picture of worship/prayer), *6*-*"and sware by Him* (God) *that lives forever and ever* (Jesus, cf. *1:18*), *who created heaven, and the things that therein are* (in heaven)*, and the earth, and the things that therein are* (in earth)*, and the sea, and the things that therein are* (in the sea. So, 7 descriptions of the eternally living creator God and Jesus, cf. *Joh. 1:3*; *Col. 1:16*; *Heb. 1:2*. They start with Life and He created all, 6 aspects, 3 environments-heaven, earth, and sea, and 3 things contained in each environment. Now the mighty angel swore by God-the living creator of all), *that there should be time* (Gr:chronos-interval, delay, time; seems to be summing up "time" as in the universe-created for mortal man on earth and further delay) *no longer"* (more): **7**-*"But in the days of the voice of the 7ᵗʰ angel* (mentioned only in **10:7**; **11:15**; **16:17**), *when he shall begin to sound* (his trumpet)*, the mystery* (Gr:musterion-secret or mystery) *of God* (what a mouthful! if any of God's creation could ever fully know the mystery that is God, but at least His plan for His creation in time) *should be finished* (Gr:teleo-ended, completed, executed, concluded, discharged, accomplished, expired, finished, paid, performed), *as He* (God) *has declared* (Gr:euaggelizo-announce good news, evangelize, declare, bring glad tidings, preach the gospel) *to His* (God's) *servants the prophets"* (Gr:prophetes-fortellers, prophets, inspired speakers. So, when the 7ᵗʰ Angel begins to trumpet, God's mystery of this time-bound universe will be "completed," "paid" by Christ's blood as God evangelized/ preached the good news thru His servants, the inspired prophets in God's precious Holy Bible).}

B. **10:8-11**— {Title: John Told To and Eats the Book, But He Will Prophesy Again to Many. **8**-*"And the voice, which I* (John) *heard from heaven spake unto me again, and said, 'Go and take* (depart and receive; 2 commands) *the little book, which is open in the hand of the angel* (the mighty one), *which stands upon* (or over) *the sea and upon* (or over) *the earth'"* (So many angels are involved now and John wants to make sure we know which one). **9**-*"And I* (John) *went unto the angel* (the mighty one), *and said to him, 'Give me the little book.' And he said to me, 'Take it and eat it up* (2 commands); *and it shall make your belly bitter, but it shall be in your mouth sweet* (Gr:glukus-sweet, fresh; believe where we get the word glucose) *as honey.'"* (**Psa. 119:103**-God's Word is sweeter than honey. Here provides a metaphoric picture of devouring a good book. **Eze. 3:3**-sweet in mouth to Ezekiel and here to John, but bitter in belly or coming out to hearers, as both Ezekiel and John and all proclaimers of God's Word will find a bitter experience in their own gut and frequently the reception by wicked). **10**-*"And I* (John) *took the little book out of the angel's* (the mighty one's) *hand, and ate it up; and it was in my mouth sweet as honey: and as soon as I had eaten it, my belly was bitter."* **11**-*"And he said to me, 'You must prophesy again to many peoples, and nations, and tongues, and kings.'"* (Even though John was forbidden to reveal some of what was uttered in heaven, he is still commissioned to continue prophesying to many more; to all of us in the millennia to follow. John returns to receiving more Revelation of Trib events).}

Application (Activity/Questions)

A. Who is the mighty angel (another mighty angel or Jesus as an unnamed messenger)? {Another mighty angel that clearly was in the presence of Christ in heaven, so reflected some of God's glory like Moses did (e.g. *Exo. 34:29-35*). I believe Michael the Archangel as specifically Israel's protector and called out as key in Christ's end time plans.}

B. Have you ever had to share a tough message from God's Word (e.g. on divorce, family roles, homosexuality) that almost made your stomach sick, though you knew it was sweet and needed? {Yes, on all those topics, plus following Church discipline on almost any sin...}

C. Has God ever revealed something impressive to you that He didn't want you to communicate to others (please don't share it if He did, but can you share the reason or circumstances)? {Yes, on mature gray areas that a weaker brother wasn't ready to receive yet, and on personal sin that would make someone else stumble who heard it...}

D. How much of an appetite do you have for God's Word, and is it sweet to you? {Yes, amazing how my appetite grows when I'm in the Word or I need answers and taste and see He is good; and I find my appetite wains for His Word when I sin or stay away from It...}

Figure 13 – 17.1 St. John Eating the Book[19]

A Tale of 2 Witnesses and the 7th Trumpet—
Christ's Judgment Reigning.

A Tale of 2 Witnesses and the Response.
{Rebuilt Jewish Temple Measured, Courts Stay Gentile Controlled.
A Tale of 2 witnesses for 1,260 Days of Miracles; Rejected,
Killed, Resurrected, and Translated to Heaven.}

Introduction

A. Have you ever had to meticulously measure something, but not report the measurements? {Yes, and that was frustrating when it took a lot of time. But sometimes that is for our own good.}

B. Do you consider our world to be gentile or Jewish run, why? {Gentile now, since Jews have only recently even become a nation again in 1948, and recently gotten Jerusalem back in 1967, most still don't believe Israel's temple site is back from the Muslims yet, and we are in "the times of the gentiles" (cf. ***Luk. 21:24***).}

Scripture (Observations/Interpretation/Commentary)
{Read ***11:1-14***; Divide into groups and have them answer questions}

A. ***11:1-13***— {Title: A Tale of 2 Witnesses and the Response}
1. Is this Temple, earthly or heavenly (***11:1-2***), why?
2. Where is *"the holy city"* (***11:2***), *"the great city"* (***11:8***), *"the city"* (***11:13***), why and why is it called so?
3. Do you believe this *"42 months,"* *"1,260 days"* (***11:2-3***), the 3 ½ years is in the 1st or final part of the Tribulation, why?
4. Who do you think these 2 witnesses (***11:6***) are, why?
5. Who is *"the beast"* (***11:7***), why?

{**1**-"***And there was given me a reed like a rod*** (like a ruler or yard stick): ***and the angel*** (the last angel mentioned was the mighty angel) ***stood saying, 'Rise, and measure*** (Gr:metreo-measure by a fixed standard; where we get metrics) ***the temple of God*** (This is not the church, the true Church is in heaven. <u>Q1: Is this Temple, earthly or heavenly? -A1: This is the Jewish earthly temple that will be rebuilt but hasn't been in existence since AD 70 when the Roman Emperor Titus destroyed it, and with it the Jewish sacrificial system. So, this is the earthly temple, not heavenly.</u> cf. ***11:2***), ***and the altar, and them*** (those) ***that worship therein*** (in it. Measuring the temple and altar is clear and would show it is to specifications, and those worshiping would just be a count of their number. Interesting, he doesn't tell us the measurements). *2-"But the court, which is without* (outside) *the temple (earthly) leave out, and measure it not* (So exclude the court outside the temple itself, which was the, Court of the Gentiles. The Temple areas from West to East: 1-Holy of Holies, 2-Holy Place [90' Long x 30' Wide x 45' High], 3-Court of the Priests, 4-Court of Israel/Court of Men of Israel, 5-Court of the Women, 6-Court of the Gentiles. So it was this 6th outside court, or Court of the Gentiles that is left out of the measurements); *for* (because) *it is given unto the Gentiles* (everyone not Jewish): *and the holy city* (Q2: Where is "the holy city" [*11:2*], "the great city" [*11:8*], "the city" [*11:13*]?-A2: Jerusalem. All 10 times "holy city" is found in the Bible [*Neh. 11:1, 18*; *Isa. 48:2*; *52:1*; *Dan. 9:24*; *Mat. 4:5*; *27:53*; *Rev. 11:2*; *21:2*; *22:19*] it refers to Jerusalem. Why called "holy," because God was in Temple); *shall they tread under foot 42 months."* (3 ½ yrs. Jesus says in *Luk. 21:24*, "*And they shall fall by the edge of the sword, and shall be led away captive into all nations: and Jerusalem shall be trodden down of the Gentiles, until the times of the Gentiles be fulfilled.*" (Q3: Do you believe this is the 1st or last 3 ½ years?-A3: Due to the signed peace pact with Israel in the 1st 3 ½ years, I think it will be in the last 3 ½ years after the peace pact was broken by "*the abomination of desolation,*" cf. *Dan. 8:13*; *12:11*; *Mat. 24:15*; *Mar. 13:14*; when the Antichrist and gentile nations will be attacking Israel/Jerusalem). *3-"And I* (seems to be the mighty angel that was talking to John which may have been the same angel that gave power/strength to Daniel working with the mighty Archangel, Michael in *Dan. 10*; of course, this empowering came from God) *will give power* ("power" is not in the Greek, but is implied, and thus supplied by KJV translators) *unto my 2 witnesses* (Gr:martus-witness, record, martyr; not only witnesses, but we'll see are martyrs later; more to come on them), *and they* (2 witnesses) *shall prophesy 1,260 days* (Jewish calendar is a 360-day year, so 3 ½ years), *clothed in sackcloth"* (a sign of mourning; mourning because most reject the witness and witnesses). *4-"These* (2 witnesses) *are the 2 olive trees, and the 2 candlesticks* (lampstands) *standing before the God of the earth"* (cf. *Zec. 4*, prophesying of Zerubbabel rebuilding the temple, seen in Ezra, "*Not by might, nor by power, but by my Spirit says the Lord of hosts. Who art thou, O great mountain? before Zerubbabel thou shalt become a plain: and he shall bring forth the headstone thereof with shoutings, crying, Grace, grace unto it*"-*Zec. 4:6-7*. So, these 2 witnesses are filled by God's Spirit and power, not man's.

God's Spirit, pictured as olive oil, is poured out by these 2 witnesses, called *"the 2 anointed ones, that stand by the Lord of the whole earth"*-***Zec. 4:14***, that bring God's grace to Israel, light and witness, and powerful witness of the cornerstone/headstone-a witness for the righteous and against the wicked that are killed, reject the Word of the 2 witnesses' testimony, and receive immediate judgment). ***5***-***"And if any man will hurt them*** (2 witnesses), ***fire proceeds out of their*** (2 witnesses) ***mouths and devours their*** (2 witnesses') ***enemies*** (haters/adversaries)***: and if any man will hurt them*** (2 witnesses; repeats again; double trouble)***, he must in this manner*** (fire out of the witnesses mouths) ***be killed."*** ***6***-***"These*** (2 witnesses) ***have power*** (capability/ authority) ***to shut heaven, that*** (Gr:hina-purpose) ***it rain not in the days of their prophecy: and have power over waters to turn*** (convert) ***them to blood, and to smite the earth with all plagues, as often as they will."*** (Q4: Who do you think these 2 witnesses (***11:6***) are, why? -A4: 3 main views: 1) **Moses and Elijah**-as Elijah calls fire from heaven and no rain and Moses brought all plagues including water into blood. You also see in the last Book of the OT, God references Moses and promises Elijah to come before the 2nd Coming in ***Mal. 4:4-5***- "*Remember ye the law of Moses my servant, which I commanded unto him in Horeb for all Israel, with the statutes and judgments. Behold, I will send you Elijah the prophet before the coming of the great and dreadful day of the LORD:*"-a euphemism for the Tribulation period. And they even cite ***Mar. 9:2-13*** where Moses and Elijah did come as witnesses of Jesus during His 1st Advent and Jesus even says that Elijah *"verily cometh 1st...but I say unto you, that Elijah is indeed come"* (2nd perfect active indicative; *"has come"* with continued results). 2) **Elijah and Enoch**-"*as it is appointed unto men once to die,*" cf. ***Heb. 9:27***, and they were the only 2 recorded in the Bible who didn't die *"once,"* so many make the argument that Moses couldn't die twice, although Lazarus died once, then was resurrected, and apparently died a 2nd time, cf. ***John 11:14. 43-44***, as well as all the others that had been raised from the dead. 3) **2 Witnesses in the spirit and power of Elijah and Moses** (but not them)-these 2 witnesses definitely have the spirit and power of Elijah, cf. ***Luk. 1:17***, and seemingly Moses. All these views seem to be consistent with prior prophecies, so this doesn't seem to matter that greatly. Clearly these are 2 OT-like prophets who are Spirit filled witnesses for this special powerful witness to the unsaved during the Trib). ***7***-***"And when they*** (2 witnesses with God's Spirit and great power) ***shall have finished their testimony, the beast that*** (who) ***ascends out of the bottomless pit***

(Q5: Who is this beast [**11:7**], why?-A5: ***Rev. 17:8*** is the only other place a "beast" ascends out of the bottomless pit. We have seen angels/demons, but no beasts. In **13:7**, this beast, who we'll learn is the Antichrist, is said to have been given power *"to overcome"* the saints as he does with the 2 witnesses here. More re: this beast later) ***shall make war against them*** (2 witnesses)***, and shall overcome them*** (2 witnesses)***, and kill them*** (once God's mission for the 2 witnesses and miraculous judging of the wicked is complete, the "beast"/Antichrist will be allowed to kill them). **8**-"***And their*** (2 witnesses) ***dead bodies*** (corpses) ***shall lie in the street of the great city*** (Jerusalem, where the earthly temple will be, and is the main focus of the world governments, Antichrist, Satan, and God), ***which is spiritually called Sodom and Egypt*** (only found here in the Bible. Not Sodom and Gomorrah-sin/sin or twin sin cities, but Sodom-licentious/lawlessness/sexual perversion and Egypt-law/legalism/idolatry. 2 extremes people have always used not to trust God), ***where also our Lord*** (Jesus) ***was crucified"*** (So, 2 witnesses are martyred in the same place where Jesus was accursed on the cross to save both the perverted and proud, Jesus died for both, for all, cf. ***2Co. 5:14-15***). **9**-"***And they of the people and kindreds, and tongues, and nations shall see their*** (2 witnesses) ***dead bodies 3 ½ days, and shall not permit their*** (2 witnesses) ***bodies*** (corpses) ***to be put in graves."*** **10**-"***And they*** (the wicked) ***that dwell*** (Gr:katoikeo-dwell, *house permanently*; not just their actions, but further showing this is the wicked who believe this world is all there is, so they settle permanently, but "our citizenship is in heaven"-***Php. 3:20***. So this is the wicked) ***upon the earth shall rejoice*** (cheer) ***over them*** (2 godly faithful dead witnesses), ***and make merry*** (rejoice the 2nd time; double the rejoicing at misfortunes of saved witnesses), ***and shall send gifts one to another*** (partying when should sober at a funeral); ***because these 2*** (Gr:duo-two; dynamic duo; find someone to be dynamic with for God, maybe your spouse, a close friend, someone you're mentoring; 2) ***prophets tormented them*** (wicked, persecutors of saved) ***that*** (who) ***dwell upon the earth."*** **11**-"***And after 3 ½ days*** (maybe uses such precision of 3 ½ days to parallel the 3 ½ years of the Great Tribulation or just to show they were dead and it was "high noon" so clearly visible and not a hoax) ***the [Ss]pirit of life*** (God's or their spirit[s]?-surprisingly only 1 other time phrase used in Bible is ***Rom. 8:2***-"For the law of the Spirit of life in Christ Jesus has made me free from the law of sin and death."-***Romans 8***'s context is the Holy Spirit, but there is true life when in the Spirit, and our spirit is quickened or given life from God's Spirit. So unsure, but think both Holy Spirit and 2 witnesses' spirits, as believers are indwelt by the Spirit of God-*Joh. 14:16-17*; *Rom. 8:9-11*; *1Co. 3:16*; *6:19-20*; *2Ti. 1:14*; and have their own spirit) *from God* (All life is from God. God's Spirit is with God and their spirit was with God-*2Co. 5:8*-"*absent from the body, and to be present with the Lord*") *entered into them* (2 dead witnesses, now alive. God never leaves His own), *and they* (2 witnesses) *stood upon their feet; and great fear* (Gr:megas phobos-mighty terror; wondering how, and maybe if they would get tormented again) *fell upon them* (wicked, as this encourages the righteous, which have "*no fear in love...perfect love casts out fear*," cf. *1Jn. 4:18*) *which* (who) *saw* (Gr:theoreo-saw, spectator, considered; not normal word for saw, but experienced and theorized how/why) *them*" (The resurrected witnesses. This resurrection is prior to the great resurrection of all, and these witnesses going to heaven in the next verse is pointed to by both Mid and Partial Rapture proponents as support for their view, but it is not. This is special, just like Enoch and Elijah's translation to be with God in heaven in the OT, cf. *Gen. 5:24*; *2Ki. 2:11*, which was prior to the Church even existing). *12*-"*And they* (doesn't say whether unsaved wicked or saved witnesses, but probably both, but clearly witnesses) *heard a great voice from heaven saying unto them* (clearly 2 resurrected witnesses), *'Come up hither'* (here, heaven. A command that all will love to obey). *and they* (2 resurrected witnesses) *ascended up to heaven in a cloud; and their enemies* (wicked persecutors and rejectors of God, them, and their message) *beheld* (again Gr:theoreo; probably coming up with wild theories how to explain this miracle, but not repenting or believing the obvious truth of the gospel message from these 2 witnesses) *them*" (2 dead witnesses, now alive, and ascended into heaven). *13*-"*And the same hour* (as wicked contemplated this miracle, but didn't repent yet) *there was a great earthquake* (Gr:seismos-gale, earthquake, tempest; big on Richter scale/seismograph, used to measure earthquakes), *and the tenth part* (1/10th) *of the city* (Jerusalem, we know this because this is where the temple is and it is called "*the holy city*" and "*the great city*" now under Gentile control; *11:1-2, 8*) *fell* (after abominable desolation it wasn't able to be used by God's people anyway), *and in the earthquake were slain* (killed) *of men 7,000* (plus unmentioned # of animals): *and the remnant* (Gr:loipoi-remaining ones, remnant, rest; some have suggested this refers to the saved remnant and KJV translates it as remnant as we'll see they give God glory, but in context it seems to be referring to the remaining 9/10th maybe saved and unsaved) *were affrighted* (terrified), ***and gave glory*** (*Gr:doxa-dignity, glory, honor, praise, worship*) ***to the God of heaven***" (Not just the God of earth, cf. __**11:4**__. So, saved continue to give God glory and I believe earlier the wicked didn't respond to the miraculous resurrection. But here, the additional earthquake made them realize that they could easily be judged to death and so have some repentance. Some may have been eternally saved, and some are not sorry for their sin, but at least give God glory out of fear).}

B. __**11:14**__— {Title: The 2nd Woe is Past, the 3rd is Coming. __**14**__-"***The 2nd Woe*** (exclamation of grief) ***is past*** (behind); ***and behold, the 3rd Woe*** (associated with the 7th Trumpet) ***comes quickly.***"}

Application (Activity/Questions)

A. What does giving glory mean? {Giving praise, honor, worship, glory, showing dignity. Most like to take, but not give glory...}

B. How do you give God glory? {Talking good about Him to Him, to others, and to myself, singing songs to Him by yourself and with others; praying to Him; obeying Him; seeking Him.}

C. What does it take to motivate you to give God the most glory? {Usually, God allows valleys to force me beyond myself to be on my back so I will look up to Him. Mountain top experiences usually make me want to rejoice and praise Him more, but sometimes I'll try to take credit for those. Also, others encouraging me to do so.}

D. How can you give more glory to God this week, will you, and if so when? {Consciously plan more time, Yes. 1st thing in morning. During devotions, before each meal, before bed, to co-workers...}

Christ's Judgment Reigning Over the Kingdoms of this World.

Christ's Judgment Reigning.
{When the 7th or Final Trumpet Sounds, Christ's Judgment is
Complete and He Will Reign Over All the World's Kingdoms.}

Introduction
A. What do you think it will be like when Christ reigns over all the world? {Wonderful for just who are saved and rewarded, painful for the wicked who are unsaved and judged.}
B. How do you think the Seals, Trumpets, and Vials are sequenced and relate to each other? {Below you will see each of of the 3 types of judgments and the specific judgments. Some are similar. Let's look at the 2 main views of how they relate and are sequenced.}

Figure 14 – 19.1 Seals, Trumpets, and Vials Overview

#	Seals (6:1-17; 8:1)	Trumpets (8:7-12; 9:1-21; 11:15-19)	Vials (16:2-21)
1	White Horse-Conquering (6:1-2)	Hail Fire:1/3 Land/Plants (8:7)	Boils (16:2)
2	Red Horse-Killing (6:3-4)	Fiery Mountain:1/3 Sea/Fish/Ships (8:8-9)	Sea as Blood/Death (16:3)
3	Black Horse-Famine (6:5-6)	Meteor=Wormwood:1/3 Rivers/Lakes (8:10-11)	Rivers/Lakes as Blood (16:4-7)
4	Pale Horse-Death (6:7-8)	Darkness:1/3 (8:12)	Scorching Sun (16:8-9)
5	Martyrdom (6:9-11)	Demonically Led Locusts:5mos Sting (9:1-12)	Darkness (16:10-11)
6	Earthquakes/Meteors (6:12-17)	200M Army:1/3 Men Killed (9:13-21)	Dried Euphrates (16:12-16)
7	Heavenly Silence:1/2 hr (8:1)	Heavenly Voices-Christ's Wrath & Reign (11:15-19)	Worst Earthquake & Hail (16:17-21)

{View 1: Traditional/7th Starts Next 7 (Show as seen below)
Seals: 1 2 3 4 5 6 7   -->|
Trumpets: 1 2 3 4 5 6 7   -->|
Vials: 1 2 3 4 5 6 7 -->|

View 2: Repetitive/Parallel/Simultaneous (Show as seen below:)
Seals: 1 2 3 4 5 6 7 -->|
Trumpets: 1 2 3 4 5 6 7 -->|
Vials: 1 2 3 4 5 6 7 -->|

As can be seen, the Traditional view ends all judgments with the 7th of each ending at the same time, the end of the Tribulation Period. It really doesn't matter that much, besides the order. Although View 2 combines or synchronizes 21 Tribulation plagues making it either 7 snap shots or different camera angles of the same plagues or at least the plagues occur simultaneously. So, let's look at the 7th or final Trumpet judgment that once complete begins Christ earthly reign, although we haven't yet come to the Vial judgments.}

Scripture (Observations/Interpretation/Commentary)

A. **11:15-19**— {Read and have learners come up with Title; The 7th Trumpet-Christ's Judgment and Reign Over the Kingdoms of this World. Have learners answer questions Q1-Q3, as you step through verse-by-verse exposition/commentary.}

1. What is the 2-fold response to Christ's Return and Kingdom reign (**11:16-18**)?
2. What are the 3 groups of saved listed in **11:18**?
3. Is this Temple, earthly or heavenly in **11:19**, why?

{**15**-"*And the 7th angel sounded* (trumpeted)*; and there were great voices in heaven, saying, 'The kingdoms of this world are become the kingdoms of our Lord* (God-the-Father and/or God-the-Son. The Kingdom here is a technical word for the Millennium, which we will learn more about in **20:1-6**)*, and* (Gr:kai-and, even, also) *of His Christ* (Gr:Christos-anointed, Messiah, Christ; Kings are anointed to rule as is Christ. That is why God intentionally uses Christ instead of Jesus, which means "Savior")*; and He shall reign forever and ever.'"* (Christ's reign will not end. Glad I'm with Him. Can you see and hear the earthly ovation and sounds of "The Hallelujah Chorus"?) **16**-"*And the 24 Elders* (found 12 times in **Revelation**; referring to the Church leaders)*, which* (who) *sat before God on their seats* (Gr:thronos-thrones, seats; shows the exalted position of the Church, on thrones)*, fell upon their faces, and worshiped God*" (A normal response to the announcement that all rulers of the world are now under God's/Christ's reign is to leave their seats and fall prostrate before Him), **17**-"*Saying, 'We give thanks* (to You)*, O Lord God Almighty, Which art* (Who is)*, and wast* (was)*, and art* (is) *to come* (the only Eternal 1)*; because Thou* (You) *have taken to Thee* (You) *Thy* (Your) *great power, and have reigned.'"* (God is ruling over all kingdoms-**11:15**, will reign forever-**11:15**, and has reigned-past tense, even when we are unaware of His reigning) **18**-"*And the nations were angry* (some reject and don't like Christ's rule; Q1: What is the 2-fold response to Christ's Return and Kingdom reign?-A1: Thankful worship or rejecting anger)*, and Your* (Lord God Almighty's) *wrath* (Gr:orge-justifiable wrath, violent passion, vengeance, anger, indignation) *is come* (He is no longer going to be patient, the prayers for justice will be answered)*, and the time of the dead* (righteous and wicked) *that they should be judged* (sentenced)*, and that You shouldest give reward unto*

(Q2: What are the 3 groups of God's saved servants listed in **11:18**?-A2:
1) Prophets, 2) Saints, and 3) Those who fear God's name) *Thy* (Your)
servants the prophets, and to the saints, and them (those) *that* (who)
fear Thy (Your) *name, small and great* (all); *and shouldest destroy them
which* (who) *destroy the earth"* (God is an environmentalist. Not in
valuing things or animals over people, but He is concerned with our
stewardship of the earth, both physically and spiritually. Spiritually the
wicked were also destroying the earth and all those on it, so God will
destroy those unrepentant ones). *19-"And the temple of God was
opened in heaven* (Q3: Is this an earthly or the heavenly temple?-A3:
Not the earthly temple like in **11:1-2**, but the 1 true heavenly temple
that the earthly one is patterned after, cf. *Heb. 8:1-5*; *9:11, 23*f) *and
there was seen* (formerly unable to see into this Holy of Holies and
especially the Ark without dying, but believers have been made near by
the blood of Jesus Christ-*Eph. 2:12-22*) *in His temple* (the real heavenly
1) *the ark of His Testament* (Covenant/Promise): *and there were
lightnings, and voices, and thunderings, and an earthquake, and great
hail."* (No mention of the Mercy Seat here protecting from judgment of
the Holy presence of God Almighty reigning over all).}

Application (Activity/Questions)
A. We will humbly worship and give thanks for Christ's Millennial
Reign, so what should our response be to His patient sovereign reign
now? {Humble, trusting, patient, and thankful worship.}
B. What should be our response to the angry rejecters of God's rule
now? {Prayer and pleading with them about the reality that is to come
and reasoning with them of how much better His rule is than their own
fleshly enslavement or this world's politically correct, but Biblically
incorrect system.}

The Dragon and his demons battle Christ, are cast out
by Michael and his angels, and persecute Israel.

God Sustains Israel from Satan's Attacks.
{An Interlude of Famous Personages in History of an Earthly War
Between a Wondrous Woman and Son vs a Dragon and Demons.
A Heavenly War Shows Michael and Angels Casting the Dragon
and Demons to Earth, so Dragon Persecutes God's
Protected Israel 3 ½ years.}

Introduction
{Expect this to be long or take 2 lessons.}
A. What is the purpose or spirit of prophecy? {"the testimony of Jesus
is the spirit of prophecy" (**_19:10_**). We've seen John the Apostle
imprisoned for His witness/testimony of Jesus on the Isle of Patmos
but protected from death (**_Rev. 1_**). We've seen Jesus, the eternal
witness Himself, crucified, risen, and ascended in heaven (starting in
Rev. 1 and continuing). We've seen 7 Churches overcoming Satan by
the Word of His testimony (**_Rev. 2-3_**), and then get Raptured into
heaven, and all heaven and earth searching for someone holy and
worthy enough to judge, and all conclude and testify that Jesus alone
is "worthy" (**_Rev. 4-5_**). We've seen Angelic Beasts in heaven, telling
John to come see Jesus ("the Lamb") opening the 7 seals bringing
judgment on the wicked; and we see the Trib saints that were
martyred for their witness of Jesus testifying again of the holy and true
Jesus (**_Rev. 6_**). We've seen 144K witnesses, 12K from each tribe of
Israel, sealed in their foreheads, so as not to receive the Tribulation
judgments (**_Rev. 7_** and **_14_**). We've seen Trib martyrs and saints again
who gave their lives for the testimony of Jesus glorified in heaven with
the Church and Angels testifying blessing, glory, wisdom, thanksgiving,
honor, power, and might be to God forever and ever (**_Rev. 7_**). We've
seen a silent witness, almost a holy hush for a sobering ½ hour and
then saw the witness of all the prayers of all the saints being offered
saying that Jesus is just as He begins opening the 7 Trumpet judgments
on the wicked that refuse to believe the testimony of Jesus Christ (**_Rev._
_8_**). We've heard a voice from the horns of the golden altar before God
releasing the 6th Trumpet judgment and the wicked still do not repent
of their wickedness and listen to the testimony of Jesus (**_Rev. 9_**).
We've seen a Mighty Angel and 7 thundering voices swearing by God

at the time of the 7th Trumpet Angel that God's mystery testified by His servants the prophets will be completed (**Rev. 10**). We've seen the 2 witnesses, given miraculous power to protect themselves as witnesses of the risen ascended Savior, who after their witness is complete, are martyred, resurrected, and translated to heaven; and we've seen great voices and the 24 Church elders in heaven at the 7th Trumpet worshiping and thanking God for the testimony of Christ's eternal reign (**Rev. 11**). That brings us to **Rev. 12**.}

B. What Title might you give Rev. 12, just based on a 60 second review, why? {Short-The Beauty, the Son, and the Beast. Longer-The Dragon and his demons battle the ascended Son, is cast out by Michael and his angels, so persecutes the woman and her seed. You will see the rule of the Woman and Her Son, 1st attacked by the Dragon as the fierce Beast who can't get the Son, so goes after the Woman. You'll later see that this Dragon empowers the Beast who is the Antichrist who leads the beast of the 1-World Government and Dragon empowers the Beast who is the False Prophet who leads the 1-World Religion supporting the Antichrist. All of these Satanically empowered Beasts, Kings, and Kingdoms try to usurp the true reign and testimony of the 1 and only King of Kings and Lord of Lords, Who the Book of Revelation reveals reigns over all now and we will perfectly praise God forever with 20/20 sight, and so clearly see that Jesus Christ is reigning over all, for all eternity.}

Scripture (Observations/Interpretation/Commentary)
{16/17 verses begin with *"and,"* showing continued action; only **12:12** doesn't have *"and,"* but begins with *"Therefore."* Divide into groups, read and give paragraph titles for the 3 paragraphs; some will be used in the 2nd lesson. Could have 2 Groups for question 1-3; may want to save questions 4 and 5 for the 2nd lesson.}

A. **12:1-6**— {Title: The Woman and the Son vs the Red 7-Headed, 7-Crowned, and 10-Horned Dragon.}

1. Defend who is this special woman (**12:1-2, 5-6, 14-17**; cf. **Gen. 37:9-10**); 3 main views: Church, Mary, or Israel (including Jewish moms, including Mary)? {Israel, detail follows.}

Figure 15 – 20.1 The Woman of the Apocalypse
and the Seven-Headed Dragon[20]

2. Who is the special Child born, to rule the nations, and ascend to heaven (**_12:2-5_**)? {Christ, detail follows.}
3. Defend who is the 7-headed dragon/serpent (**_12:3-4, 7-9, 12-17_**; cf. **_20:2_**)? {Satan, detail follows.}
4. Defend who are the 3ʳᵈ part of the stars of heaven (**_12:4, 7-9_**)? {Fallen Angels/Demons, detail follows.}
5. Defend when was Satan banished from heaven (**_12:7-12_**)? {Middle of the Tribulation, detail follows.}

{After introducing the 7ᵗʰ Trumpet of Christ's judgment and eternal reign at the end of **_Rev. 11_**, John takes an interlude to picture famous persons battling in heaven and on earth for and against God's people throughout history culminating in the last 3 ½ years of the 7-year Tribulation. **_1-_** **_"And there appeared_** (Gr:optanomai-to gaze, as with wide open eyes at something remarkable, with continued inspection) **_a great wonder_** (Gr:semeion-miracle, sign, token, wonder; a frequent word John used in his Gospel to show Jesus was God) **_in heaven; a woman_** (described as very special, more to come) **_clothed with the sun_** (a bearer of divine/bright testimony, to whom comes the Law and the prophets of God's Word, cf. **_Exo. 20_**; **_Deu. 5_**; **_Gen.-Mal._**, "a light to the gentiles," cf. Isa. **_49:3-6_**), **_and the moon under her feet_** (to reflect the light of sun/Son and walk in the light of the gospel with beautiful feet, cf. **_Isa. 52:7_**; **_Rom. 10:15_**), **_and upon her head a crown of 12 stars"_** (14 verses with sun, moon, and stars, and only this 1 and **_Gen. 37:9-10_** mention them in a non-literal, metaphorical sense, where the Sun is Israel, the Moon Rebekah, and the Stars the 12 sons/tribes of Israel, although some see the 12 stars as angels protecting these tribes and reference **_21:12_**): **_2-_** **_"And she_** (this special woman) **_being with Child_** (pregnant; Q1: Who is the special Child to be born, rule the nations, and ascend to heaven in **_12:2-5_**?-A1: We'll see later He is clearly Christ) **_cried, travailing in birth, and pained to be delivered_** (Give birth. Q2: So, who is this special woman?-A2: 3 main views: 1) Church-who is clearly related to Christ, but not as mother, but as Bride, cf. **_21:9_**; **_22:17_**. Also, the Church is already Raptured and in heaven in **_Rev. 4-19_** so can't be persecuted on earth by Satan during the Trib. And Christ wasn't born through the Church, the Church was born through Christ. 2) Mary-Mostly Catholics, and she surely was special as the Angel Gabriel said to her, "You who are highly favored, the Lord is with thee: blessed are you among women," cf. **_Luk. 1:28_**, but doesn't seem to fully fit the woman of **_12:6, 13-17_**, whom Satan is persecuting in the last 3 ½ years of the Trib, as Mary is already in heaven. 3) Israel-including all her Jewish moms down to including the virgin Mary-this view seems to fit the context of the Trib purpose-"*a time of Jacob's* [Israel's] *trouble,*" cf. ***Jer. 30:7***, is consistent with ***Gen. 37:9-10*** language of Israel being the Sun, his wife the moon, and his sons the 12 tribes, fits the lineage of Christ prophesied and He came through Israel, cf. ***Mat. 1***, permits Israel/Mary to birth our Savior, cf. ***Luk. 2:5-11***, Israel as this woman is also historically validated as Satan has persecuted the Jews: Nazi exterminations, antisemitism, and Islamic hatred and attacks, and best fits context of how Satan will also ferociously attack Israel during the last 3 ½ years of the Great Trib. For more detailed coverage and references, see Wikipedia's "Woman of the Apocalypse," summarizing views including extreme liberal positions and even cult perspectives; besides the 3 main views included: "astrological symbolism," "astrological alignment," "generic man," "Eve," and amalgamated views combining more polyvalent symbolic interpretations.[21]). **3**-"***And there appeared another wonder in heaven; and behold,*** (Q3: Who is the 7-headed dragon/serpent-***12:3-4, 7-9, 12-17***; cf. ***20:2***?-A3:) ***a great red*** (A3 continues; fire-like/ flame-colored; red like blood as Satan "*was a murderer from the beginning,*" cf. ***Joh. 8:44***; "*a flaming fire*" like all angels, cf. ***Psa. 104:4***; and fire-like as Satan's "*fiery darts*" we are to quench by the shield of faith, cf. ***Eph. 6:16***) ***dragon*** (A3 continues; *Gr:drakon-fabulous kind of serpent, dragon*; we'll see even clearer that he this red dragon is Satan later. A familiar icon, but no pitch fork; pictured as a crafty serpent in the Garden cursed with hatred between the Woman and her Seed, Jesus, cf. ***Gen. 3:1-15***; ***Gal. 3:16***), ***having 7 heads, and 10 horns*** (A3 continues; "*7 heads, and 10 horns*" found 4 times in Bible. Personified as Satan here in ***12:3***, and Satan possessing the blasphemous Antichrist in ***13:1***, and Satan leading the evil 10 kings that give their power to the Antichrist "Babylon" in ***17:3, 7*** against Christ and His people), ***and 7 crowns upon his heads*** (A3 continues; these 7-heads with 7-crowns and 10-horns picture Satan as this dragon/serpent that has perfect or complete agreement between these locations and rulers who receive power from Satan to lead the gentile nations against God and His people Israel). **4**-"***And his*** (Satan's) ***tail drew*** (drug) ***the third part*** (1/3rd) ***of the stars of heaven*** (Q4: Who are these stars of heaven?-A4: Figuratively angels where 1/3rd are said here to be demons; cf. ***Job 38:7***; ***Isa. 14:13***; ***Dan. 8:10***; ***Jud. 1:13***; ***Rev. 1:16, 20***; ***2:1***; ***3:1***; ***12:4, 7-9***), ***and*** (he, Satan) ***did cast*** (throw) ***them to the earth: and the dragon*** (Satan) ***stood before the woman*** (Israel), ***which*** (who) ***was ready to be delivered*** (give birth), ***for to*** (*Gr:hina-*

purpose, intent) *devour her Child* (Gr:teknon-Child, Son; Christ) *as soon as It* (He, Christ) *was born"* (Satan through Herod tried to kill the Child and coming King Jesus, but instead killed many Israelite children, cf. *Mat. 2:12-18*). *5-"And she* (Israel/Mary) *brought forth* (birthed) *a Man (male, emphasizing Christ's humanity; A1 continues) Child* (Gr:uihos-Son; emphasizing Christ's kinship with humanity), *Who was to rule* (Gr:poimaino-tend as a shepherd, feed, rule; emphasizing His role as King and Shepherd over sheep) *all nations with a rod* (scepter/staff) *of iron* (powerful rule): *and her* (Israel's) *Child* (Gr:teknon-Child, Son; probably emphasizing that was not yet time for His earthly rule as Messiah) *was caught up* (Ascension, cf. *Acts 1:9-11*) *unto God, and to His throne"* (Jesus has always had an eternal reign over all, and today rules in Heaven. FYI-In between *12:5-6* is *Acts 1*-Christ's Ascension in *12:5*, and *Acts 2*-starts the Church Age, where individual Jews can join the Church but are nationally set aside, cf. *Rom. 11*, the Church is then Raptured, and national Israel resumes their final 7-years in the Trib, discussed in *12:6*). *6-"And the woman* (Israel), *fled* (escaped) *into the wilderness, where she* (Israel) *has a place prepared* (provided) *of* (by) *God, that* (Gr:hina-purpose) *they* (unstated as to who, maybe the U.N., U.S., or group of Trib believers) *should feed her* (Israel) *there 1,260 days."* (3 ½ years. Summarizing, Israel's greatest light and witness pictures a pregnant woman, Israel/Mary, with Satan, pictured as a red serpent-like 7-headed and 7-crowned dragon with 10-horns casting 1/3rd of the angels or demons following Satan as he was cast to earth, who are ready to kill her Son Jesus at His birth, Who was to rule the world with a strong scepter, but He ascends up to God's throne, and Israel flees Satan into the desert for 3 ½ years into a place prepared and fed by God).}

B. *12:7-12*— {Title: A Heavenly War: Michael and Elect Angels Cast Out Satan and his Demons. *7-"And there was war in heaven* (normally a place of peace and holiness): *Michael* (the Archangel, chief of angels) *and his angels* (all good/elect angels) *fought against the dragon; and the dragon fought and his angels"* (who by their sinful act of rebellion against God, here have become demons/non-elect angels), *8-"And prevailed not* (Satan and his demons didn't have the strength); *neither was their place* (room) *found any more* (no longer) *in heaven. 9-"And the great dragon was cast out* (of heaven), *that old* (Gr:archaios-original, primeval, old; conjures memory of the Garden of Eden, the 1st temptation of man, cf. *Gen. 3:1-6, 14-15*) *serpent* (Gr:ophis-snake, artful malicious person, Satan, serpent), *called the Devil* (Gr:diabolos-

Satan, false accuser, Devil, slanderer), *and Satan* (in case you really were unsure this is Satan), *which* (who) *deceiveth* (is deceiving) *the whole world: he was cast out into the earth, and his angels* (now demons) *were cast out with him* (Satan). *10-"And I* (John) *heard a loud* (great) *voice saying in heaven, 'Now is come salvation, and strength* (power), *and the Kingdom* (Millennium) *of our God, and the power* (authority) *of His Christ* (Messiah): *for* (because) *the accuser* (complainant at law, Satan) *of our brethren* (believers) *is cast down, which* (who) *accused* (Gr:kategoreo-plaintiff, charged with offense, accused, objected. Why? -Satan doesn't believe God is just to save us, since we've sinned, so wants to destroy us, cf. *Job 1:6-12*; *2:1-10*) *them* (elect/believers) *before* (in the face of) *our God day and night."* *11-* *"And they* (saved/elect/ believers) *overcame him* (Satan) *by the blood of the Lamb* (Jesus' blood, the only eternal victory over Satan and the charges against us by Satan's temptations and accusations when we sin) *and by the Word of their testimony* (the only thing we can point to when accused is we have God's eternal assurance by His promises in His Word. And Jesus is also called the Word in *John 1:1, 14*. Is this your testimony now? If not, it can be...); *and they loved not their lives* (Gr:psuche-life, heart, mind, soul) *unto the* (until) *death"* (Because of God's love to them, to us, we should want to die to our flesh now to be rewarded and truly live in our glorified bodies later, cf. *Php. 1:21*- *"For to me to live is Christ, and to die is gain."* Unfortunately, we usually live the opposite of that verse: to live is gain, and to die is Christ. Forgive us Father). *12-"Therefore* (whenever you see a therefore, you must look to see what it is there for. So, in light of God's plan throughout the ages for Israel, His Son, Satan, and us (believers) to overcome Satan through His Son's blood and the witness of the Word) *rejoice, you heavens, and you that* (who) *dwell in them* (in heaven. Church and those Trib martyrs). *Woe to the inhabiters* (inhabitants) *of the earth and of the sea! For the Devil* (Satan) *has come down* (descended) *unto you, having great wrath* (Gr:thumos-passion-as if breathing hard, fierceness, indignation, wrath; you can also picture Satan as a dragon painting and snorting from the heavenly battle), *because he* (Satan) *knows he* (Satan) *has but a short* (brief) *time."* (He has already been defeated in Heaven and knows he will be on earth. So has a short hunting season on those God loves. At least as much as God allows, to refine and bring saints to God. Q5: When is Satan banished to earth? -A5: 6 main views: 1) Before creation-cf. *Isa. 14*; *Eze. 38*, as how could God let evil be in heaven and some see part of a

Gap theory in creation. But I don't believe Gap theory and God did let Satan in heaven after this in *Job 1-2* and casts him out of heaven in *Rev. 12:9*. 2) After Creation, but before man's sin- e.g. *Gen. 3*-it is clear Satan was on earth, but doesn't say he was confined there, and again not consistent with Satan in heaven in *Job 1-2*. 3) Right before Jesus' Birth-cf. *12:3-4* pictures Satan in heaven and coming to earth ready to attack Jesus at His birth-but seems to say that Satan cast the demons to earth, not that God or Michael did. Also *12:5-6* shows a time lapse with Christ's birth and Ascension, and the first half of the Tribulation, prior to the war in heaven where Satan is thrown out in *12:7-14*, where he angrily persecutes Israel (as a result), the last 3 ½ years of the Trib. 4) During Jesus' earthly ministry-after return of 12 commissioned Apostles and 70 disciples, in *Luk. 9:1*; *10:1*; In *10:18*, Jesus *"said unto them, I beheld Satan as lightning fall from heaven."*- clearly Jesus empowered these Apostles/Disciples to cast out demons out of people and overcome them with His power and that hurt Satan's rule enough for him to probably quickly come down to earth, but doesn't say God or Michael cast him to earth, doesn't explain the reasons in view 3, nor explain how prior to the cross, believers could have *"overcame him [Satan] by the blood of the Lamb"* (*12:11*), prior to Christ's blood being shed as the sacrificial Lamb on the cross. 5) At the Cross or Resurrection-cf. *Heb. 2:14*-says that through Christ's *"death He might destroy"* Satan who had power of death-clearly Christ defeated Satan on the cross or bruised Satan's head, cf. *Gen. 3:13-15*. Also, Jesus talking about His death says in *Joh. 12:31*, *"Now is the judgment of this world: now shall the prince of this world [Satan] be cast out."* A clear reference to Christ defeating sin and Satan on the cross, judging the world, its system and ruler, and even refers to him being cast out. If that is not a summary statement of what the cross would accomplish, but is Satan being finally cast out "of heaven?" It could have been Satan temporarily cast out, but later allowed back in, and that wouldn't be the correct view, as *12:8* says, *"neither was there place found [for Satan] any more in heaven."* It doesn't specifically say Satan was cast out of heaven at that time and we (church believers) still do experience Satan's attacks and accusations today, as *Rev. 12:10* says *"the accuser [Satan] of the brethren is cast down, which accused them before God [who is in heaven], day and night."* This is probably the most popular Amillennial view but could be held by all views. 6) During the Trib-most maintain the middle of Trib, as it twice mentions the 3 ½ years that Israel is fleeing and is protected by God and then

Satan is cast to earth in **12:6-9, 12-17**. This is clearly in the *"things which shall be hereafter"* (**1:19**) future section of the outline, so after all the prior views hold it occurred. **Rev. 12:12** mentions the 3rd "Woe" of the 7th Trumpet, which is during the future Trib, and we'll see **12:13-17** talks about Satan making war with Israel and trying to flood Israel during the last half of the Trib period. This timeframe, context, also coupled with **12:5** saying that Christ had ascended to heaven (which obviously was later than the cross and resurrection), before **12:7-10** events where Satan is finally cast out of heaven with all the demons that still remained with him causes me to hold this 6th, during the Trib view. Also, Satan has been permitted to be in heaven and earth deceiving and accusing throughout history as cited above, has been *"the prince of the power of the air,"* **Eph. 2:2**, and permitted to be *"the god of this world,"* **2Co. 4:4**, is why Church believers are now commanded to *"put on the whole armor of God, that you may be able to stand against the wiles of the devil,"* **Eph. 6:11**, and we are now commanded to *"resist the devil,"* cf. **Jam. 4:7** on earth now. Also believe the whole point of this passage is Satan, during the Trib, knows his time is short so persecutes Israel fiercely during the Great Trib. This is probably the most popular Pre-Trib and Pre-Millennial view. The most important thing is the fact that Satan does fight with God and His angels and gets defeated and then tries to hurt believers, and believers are protected by God and able to overcome him by Jesus' blood and the testimony of His Word.)}

C. **12:13-17**— {Title: A Woman Flees the Dragon, God Nourishes Her for 3 ½ Years.} **13**-"**And when the dragon** (Satan) **saw** (understood) **that he was cast** (thrown) **unto the earth, he** (Satan) **persecuted the woman** (Israel) **which** (who) **brought forth the man** (male) **Child** (Child is not in the Greek text, but implied, as shown by italics in the KJV, that she had a male child, Jesus). **14**-"**And to the woman** (Israel) **were given 2 wings of a great eagle** (Some view this eagle like safety transport as coming from the US, as an eagle is our national emblem/symbol and we've been Israel's strongest ally, but probably most see this as how God swiftly carried Israel and provided for them in the wilderness, like He did when he brought Israel out of Egypt, cf. **Exo. 19:4**; **Isa. 40:31**. Clearly God will carry and provide for Israel in the Trib), **that** (Gr:hina-purpose) **she** (Israel) **might fly into the wilderness, into her place** (unstated as to where this is, but does tell us), **where she is nourished** (fed there) **for a time, and times, and half a times** (3 ½ times or years; seen as 1,260 days in **12:6**. Those that hold a non-literal interpretation of Scripture change the *"time, times, and half a time," "middle of the week"* [of years], 3 ½ years, *"42 months,"* and *"1,260 days"* quoted to only mean a figurative period of time in Israel's, the Church's, or the World's history, not the last 3 ½ years of the 7-year Trib period. Clearly these many specific literal time frames of the last 3 ½ years indicate this has to be a literal 3 ½ years and not figurative), *from the face* (presence/person) *of the serpent* (Satan). *15-"And the serpent* (Satan) *cast* (threw) *out of his mouth water as a flood* (or river; cf. *Dan. 9:26*; a flash flood or maybe diverting of a river like the Euphrates to where Israel goes in the desert. Some see this as symbolic like floods of wicked men or demons, cf. *Isa. 59:19*; *Psa. 18:4, 16*; *124:2-6*) *after* (towards the back of) *the woman* (Israel), *that* (*Gr:hina-purpose*) *he* (Satan) *might cause her* (Israel) *to be carried away* (overwhelmed) *by the flood"* (or river). *16-"And the earth helped the woman* (Israel), *and the earth opened her* (its) *mouth* (again a figurative picture where John is seeing God's providential hand in the desert and had just referred to God as *"the God of the earth"* in *11:4*, only found 1 other time in Bible, cf. *Gen. 24:3*; but *"God of heaven"* is found 24 times, and 27 times for *"heaven and earth"*), *and swallowed up the flood* (or river) *which the dragon* (Satan) *cast* (sent) *out of his mouth."* *17-"And the dragon* (Satan) *was wroth* (*Gr:orgizo-provoked, enraged, exasperated, angry; summons the image of Satan as* a fire breathing, smoke snorting dragon), *with the woman* (Israel), *and went* (departed) *to make war with the remnant of her seed* (specifically Jews, but could include other believers during the Trib as would be of her *"seed"* in Christ as seen in the next phrases), *which keep* (are keeping) *the commandments* (the Law) *of God, and have the testimony of Jesus* (Savior) *Christ."* (Messiah; *"Jesus Christ,"* both as savior from sin and Jewish Messiah for Trib saints; out of 198 times *"Jesus Christ"* is found in Bible, only 7 in *Revelation*, 983 times *"Jesus,"* with 14 in *Rev*, 571 times *"Christ,"* with 11 in *Rev*, and 40 times *"the Lamb,"* with 26 in **Rev**. So summarizing, once Satan is thrown down to earth, he persecutes Israel who bore the Son of God-Jesus, and during the 3 ½ year Great Trib, God provides Israel a swift escape, maybe the American Air Force or another way, to escape from Satan and the Antichrist in the desert, so Satan causes a *"flood"* towards Israel, which the earth swallows up, so angry Satan makes war with the remaining Jews and faithful obedient believers in God and Jesus Christ).}

<u>Application</u> (Activity/Questions)

A. Who is the most important person ever born and what is His nationality? {Jesus Christ/Jewish.}

B. Are Satan and his demons stronger than God's elect angels, why? {No, there are twice as many elect/good angels as bad/non-elect/ evil angels/demons (2/3rd to 1/3rd). Also, Michael and good angels defeat Satan and his demons, and even kicks them out of heaven. Also, 1 angel beats Satan as we'll see in **_20:1-3_**.}

C. Why does Satan try to attack Israel and why do we see him attacking the Church today? {He is angry, he can't hurt God, so hurts those God loves.}

D. Can Satan hurt or go even 1 inch beyond God's walls/hedges of protection (cf. **_Job 1:10_**)? {No, although sometimes God allows Satan to do some things that accomplish a higher more eternal purpose than even our temporary pleasure.}

E. How does the church overcome Satan today and how will Israel in the Tribulation (cf. **_12:11_**)? {"*By the Blood of the Lamb*" and "*the Word of their Testimony;*" "*By faith through grace*" (**_Eph. 2:8-9_**), and not loving their own life unto death, but loving it for all eternity, "*For to live is Christ, and to die is gain.*" (**_Php. 1:21_**).}

F. When Satan is cast down to earth, why is there such rejoicing in heaven even before the Millennial Kingdom (cf. **_12:10-12_**)? {Heaven cleansed from bad. No more continuous accusations from Satan in heaven. Yes, we were saved by Christ's blood and testimony, but don't like to hear him accusing believers on earth either. Maybe also knowing that the gun lap was sounding for the Millennium...}

G. What are 3 of the greatest historical events/almost paragraph titles for Israel and all believers? {Christ's Birth; Satan Cast Out of Heaven; Israel/Believers Protected from angry Satan...}

Figure 16 – 20.2 Saint Michael Fighting the Dragon[22]

The Anti-Christ, the Mark of the Beast (666), and the False Prophet.

Antichrist, His Mark, and the False Prophet.

Introduction
A. Are you Pro-Christ? How? Why? {Yes. Support through obedience, words, sharing the Gospel. He saved me, loves me, advocates for me, is coming back for me, is preparing a place for me...}
B. What is the last thing we saw happen to Satan and what did he set out to do (**_Rev. 12_**)? {Satan and demons kicked out of heaven and so fiercely setting out to attack Israel, since he can't hurt God.}
C. Who will greatly deceive the earth after the Church is Raptured? {Satan, thru Antichrist and False Church.}
D. What have you heard might be the Mark of the Beast? {Biochip, tattoo, bar-code...}
E. Who do you think is the most significant global religious leader today? {Think it was Billy Graham, now probably the Pope.}

Scripture (Observations/Interpretation/Commentary)
A. _13:1-4_— {Title: Blasphemous 1st Beast Empowered to Conquer Saints 3 ½ Years. **_1_**-"**And I** (John) **stood upon the sand of the sea, and saw** (sea saw :)) **a beast** (more to come about who or what later) **rise up** (ascending) **out of the sea** (when figurative, the "sea" often refers to gentiles, nations, or many people, cf. **_17:15_**, or could be a literal sea since John is standing on the sand by the sea as he sees this beast, like a monster beast/dragon coming out of the sea), **having 7-heads** (the beast described in **_17:9_** says, "_The seven heads are seven mountains_" and some believe **_17:10_** also associates them to be "_seven kings._" Rome is called the city on 7 hills or mountains, where the Vatican is, 7 mountains=Quirinal, Viminal, Capitoline, Esqualine, Palatine, Caelian, and Aventine; and Rome was the gentile world power when this was written) **and 10-horns** (Scripture often envisions symbolic beasts with symbolic horns that symbolize rulers or kingdoms, as they are here; in **_17:12_** it says, "_And the ten horns which thou sawest are ten kings;_" believe these horns on the beast represent a 10-nation confederacy), **and upon his horns 10 crowns** (Gr: diadema-diadem, crown, a symbol of royalty; they rule), **and upon his heads, the name of blasphemy**" (Some believe this is the Mark of the Beast that we'll see later in this chapter and all see it as each speaking evil against God, His ways, and

people. So after Satan attacks Israel and Jesus in **Rev. 12** and he and his demons are cast to earth by Michael and the good angels, a beast from the sea with 10 crowned blasphemous kings on 7 mountains arises to also war against Israel). **2-"And the beast which I** (John) **saw was like** (similar in appearance or character; cf. **Dan. 7:3-8, 17-27**) **unto a leopard** (swiftness), **and his feet as the feet a bear** (strength), **and his mouth as the mouth of a lion** (ferociousness): **and the dragon** (Satan), **gave him** (this beast) **his power, and his seat** (Gr:thronos-seat, throne)**, and great authority"** (So this quick moving leopard-like and strong bear-like and ferocious lion-like composite beast was given a powerful rule with great authority by the *"god of this world,"* Satan-**2Co. 4:4**. Daniel in his vision also saw these prophetic gentile world powers in the idolatrous image of a man, cf. **Dan. 2**. Daniel's image of a man was later ground to powder by a stone made without hands-by God that *"became a great mountain, and filled the whole earth."* Then Daniel also saw these 4 beasts, then future, now historical gentile world powers. The 1st like a Lion-Babylonian [Gold Head] under King Nebuchadnezzar [~600-539 BC], the 2nd like a Bear-Medo-Persian [Silver Chest and Arms] empire [~539-331 BC], the 3rd like a Leopard-Grecian [Brass Belly and Thighs] empire [~331-48 BC] under Alexander the Great and his 4 generals, and a 4th dreadful powerful Roman [Iron Legs] empire [~48 BC-364 AD], that would continue to loosely exist and ultimately lead to the final revival of this future *"dreadful and terrible"* beast [Iron and Clay Feet] different from the others with 10-horns [10-kings/kingdoms/nation confederacy]. So who or what is this Beast out of the sea?-3 main views. 1) The Antichrist-as this powerful beast is empowered by Satan and counterfeits the Messiah and leads the pagan gentile world against Israel, *"Antichrist(s)"* is not used in **Revelation**, is only found 5 times in Bible, all by John in **1Jo. 2:18, 22**; **4:3**; **2Jo. 1:7**, although is doctrinally taught elsewhere. There have always been people against Christ or Christ's Spirit, but this man embodies and impersonates Christ, while being against Jesus and blaspheming Him. 2) Gentile/Pagan World Government/Military/Political Rule-consistent with Daniel, embodies all world empires since Daniel's time, ending in the revived Roman Empire. 3) The Antichrist leading this final future revived Roman Empire (combination beast of both leader and empire), seems most complete view. **3-"And I** (John) **saw 1 of his heads** (a mountain or a king; consistent with both 7 mountains of Rome and its leader), **as it were wounded to death; and his deadly wound was healed: and all the world wondered** (who and how could this be?) *after the beast."* (What is the deadly wound that was healed? -If the Antichrist, sounds physical to this king/ruler. If a world empire, sounds like its mountain of power/ influence/standing in the world. Scofield notes say that it was the imperial form of Roman government that died and will be revived. Scofield also sees this beast as the king and kingdom, maintaining *13:1-3* is the 10-nation/kingdom power and *13:4-10* is its ruler, clearly the beast, the Antichrist, who leads these gentile world rulers[23]). *4-"And they* (unsaved Tribulation folks) *worshiped the dragon* (Satan), *which* (who) *gave power* (authority) *unto the beast* (Antichrist leading gentile nations): *and they* (unsaved) *worshiped the beast* (Antichrist), *saying, 'Who is like unto the beast* (Antichrist)*? Who is able to make war with him?'"* (The Antichrist; A blasphemous worship as truly only God is unique and has that said of Him in truth, cf. *Exo. 15:11*; *Psa. 35:10*; *71:19*; *113:5*).}

B. *13:5-8*— {Title: Blaspheming Beast Waring with Saints, Worshiped by Wicked. There is a paragraph division in Greek here, but some keep *13:1-8* together. *5-"And there was given unto him* (the beast/Antichrist) *a mouth speaking great things and* (even) *blasphemies; and power* (authority) *was given unto him* (Antichrist) *to continue 42 months."* (3 ½ years) *6-"And he* (1st Beast/Antichrist) *opened his mouth in blasphemy* (Gr:blasphemia- vilification, blasphemy, evil speaking, railing) *against God, to blaspheme His* (God's) *name, and His* (God's) *tabernacle* (temple, habitation), *and them that dwell* (those residing) *in heaven."* *7-"and it was given* (granted) *unto him* (1st beast, the Antichrist, truly Satan thru him) *to make war with the saints* (those saved-believers), *and to overcome them: and power* (authority) *was given him* (Antichrist) *over all kindreds, and tongues, and nations."* *8-"and all that dwell* (house permanently; the wicked, not saved, as our *"citizenship is in heaven,"* cf. *Php. 3:20*) *upon the earth shall worship him* (Antichrist), *whose names are not written in the Book of Life of the Lamb* (the Lamb's-Jesus' Book of Life-where all believers names are written and are never blotted out, nor can be *"plucked from Jesus' hand,"* *John 10:28-29*) *slain from the foundation of the world."* (Even though killed at the cross, God, in order to be holy and just, counted Christ's death even before creating the universe, so He could be merciful, gracious, and forgiving throughout all time).}

C. *13:9-10*— {Title: Listen Up and Be Patient. *9-"If any man* (one) *have an ear* (even 1), *let him hear"* (understand). *10-"He that leadeth* (goes) *into captivity shall go into captivity: he that kills with the* *sword* (war) **must be killed with the sword** (war). ***Here is the patience*** *(Gr:hupomone-cheerful endurance, patience)* ***and the faith of the saints."*** (Saved. In other words, listen and understand, some will get imprisoned, others will kill or be killed, but believers need to patiently believe in God-He will judge the wicked).}

D. ***13:11-18***— {Title: False Prophet Deceives Wicked to Worship Beast by Mark and Miracles. ***11***-"***And I*** (John) ***beheld another*** *(Gr:allos-different, another, an other)* ***beast*** *(Gr:therion-dangerous animal, wild or venomous beast.* Some consider this beast the same as the 1st beast, but this is a *"different,"* 2nd beast, more to come) ***coming up out of the earth*** (not *"out of the sea,"* like the 1st Beast. Some see this earth meaning a Jew who was concerned with every inch of the promised land, others see this as he is earthy/worldly, and some see this beast as not mysteriously emanating from the water, but who has been around in plain sight on the land/earth); ***and he*** (2nd Beast) ***had 2 horns*** (rulers or kingdoms) ***like a lamb*** *(Gr:anion-small young lamb;* mild like Jesus, instead of wild poisonous beast like he really is), ***and he*** (2nd Beast) ***spoke as*** (like) ***a dragon"*** (or serpent. He is nothing like a humble little lamb like Jesus but is Satanically proudly roaring like a dragon and lying like the forked tongue of a serpent). ***12***-"***And he*** (2nd Beast) ***exercises all the power*** (authority) ***of the 1st Beast*** (Antichrist) ***before*** (in the presence of) ***him*** (Antichrist), ***and causes the earth and them which dwell*** *(Gr:katoikeo-house or reside permanently, dwell;* so these are unsaved wicked) ***therein to*** *(Gr:hina-purpose, intent, result, that, to)* ***worship the 1st Beast*** (Antichrist), ***whose deadly wound was healed."*** (So this powerful 2nd Beast's purpose was to get all to worship the Antichrist). ***13***-"***And he*** (2nd Beast) ***does great wonders*** (signs, miracles), ***so that*** *(Gr:hina-purpose)* ***he*** (2nd Beast) ***makes fire come down from*** (out of) ***heaven on the earth in the sight of men"*** (his purpose is to deceive men by these miracles; mimicking a true witness, like the prophet Elijah in ***Rev. 11***), ***14***-"***and*** (2nd Beast) ***deceives them that dwell*** (permanently house; unsaved wicked) ***on the earth by the means of*** (*"the means of"* are not in Greek, but supplied to explicitly show how he deceives, as italicized in KJV) ***those miracles, which he*** (2nd Beast) ***had power to do in the sight of the beast*** (1st beast, Antichrist. Interesting, doesn't say in man's sight this time, but sight of the beast, who is accepting the miraculous witness from the 2nd Beast. So, who is this 2nd Beast? -4 Main Views. 1) USA-Only government powerful enough to exercise control over the nations, they view *"out of the earth"* as not from the *"sea"* or nations, so separated by water, and view *"like a lamb,"* as having attributes of Christ, but *"spoke like a dragon,"* as relinquishing those attributes for those of Satan. But this ignores the spiritual nature and miracles-proponents describe that as the battle between Roman Catholicism and American Protestantism and seem to reach for another symbolic political power/state. 2) Artificial Intelligent Supercomputer-an integrated very "aware," almost demonically possessed, powerful computer, that can speak, spy, track earnings and expenditures, and control or affect any connected device. Interesting, there is a supercomputer called the beast that boasts these capabilities in Europe already. I'm confident these types of tools will be used by this 2nd beast but doesn't seem to have the religious and personal capacity described. 3) Antichrist-point to ***13:11*** where he like a lamb and cite he is a religious leader that leads in worship like a high priest, also cite ***13:1-10*** is a world-wide government and ***13:11-18*** is a world leader [contradictory as doesn't receive worship, but 2nd Beast causes all to worship 1st Beast, also contradicts some info pointing to the Antichrist as the 1st Beast, and this beast is *"different"* from the 1st Beast]. 4) The False Prophet-a title ***19:20*** and ***20:10*** use specifically of this beast, who looks like a lamb and can deceive with miracles. This individual leads the 1-World Religion/Ecumenical movement/ the False Church in idolatry of the Antichrist/political power. Seems most literal view, consistent with ***16:13***; ***19:20***; ***20:10*** title, and explains why not a normal government out of the sea of Gentile nations, but an earthly religious authority, that is *"out of the earth,"* maybe Jewish and worldly. Some see this as the final Catholic Pope, a prominent Protestant Pastor, or an Islamic Prophetic Caliphate; will discuss more in ***Rev. 17***); ***saying to them that dwell*** (house permanently, unsaved wicked) ***on the earth, that they*** (wicked) ***should make an image*** (*Gr:eikon-likeness, statue, profile, representation, resemblance, image*; where we get "Icon;" notice John uses *"image"* 4 times in 2 verses) ***to the beast*** (Antichrist), ***which*** (who) ***had the wound by a sword, and did live." 15-"And he*** (2nd Beast; the False Prophet) ***had power*** (was given to him) ***to give life*** (*Gr:pneuma-breath, spirit, life, soul, mind; could even be a demonic spirit*) ***unto the image of the beast*** (Antichrist), ***that*** (*Gr:hina-purpose*) ***the image of the beast*** (Antichrist) ***should both speak, and cause that*** (make) ***as many as would not worship the image of the beast*** (Antichrist; *"the image of the beast"* is repeated 3 times for emphasis) ***should*** (*Gr:hina-purpose, result*) ***be killed."*** (So, the False Prophet heals, resurrects, or some believe removes a deadly wound possibly by a demon or possibly even the False Prophet using a TV/phone/computer image and voice of the Antichrist, compelling all to worship the image of the Antichrist). *16-*"*And he* (False Prophet) *causes* (makes) *all, both small and great,* (even) *rich and poor, free and bond* (slave)*, to receive a mark* (Gr:charagma-scratch, etching, stamp, graven, mark; cf. *13:16-18*; *14:11*; *16:2*; *19:20*; more to come) *in* (or on) *their right hand, or in* (or on) *their forehead:*" *17-*"*And that* (Gr:hina-purpose) *no man* (one) *might* (was able to) *buy or sell, save* (unless, except) *he that had the mark, or the name of the beast* (the Antichrist, but doesn't tell us his name)*, or the number* (next verse shows is 666) *of his* (Antichrist's) *name.*" *18-*"*Here is wisdom* (listen up to know better this riddle). *Let him that has understanding count* (innumerate, compute) *the number of the beast* (Antichrist)*: for it is the number of a man* (man's generic number is said to be 6)*; even his* (Antichrist's) *number is six hundred threescore and six.*" (4 main views of "*666.*" 1) World Political and Religious Greed-666 only found 4 times, here, *1Ki. 10:13; 2Ch. 9:13*, re: Solomon's annual taxing gold talent amount, and *Ezra 2:13* re: Adonikam's descendants returning from Babylonian captivity to rebuild the temple. So, this conjecture ties together the Antichrist and False Prophet's worldly economy/ greed. But this has happened throughout man's history and doesn't help identify the Antichrist. 2) Mankind's material makeup-is carbon based, and carbon is made from 6 electrons, 6 neutrons, and 6 protons, so man materially is 666. But this really wouldn't help identify the Antichrist either as a specific man. 3) Numeric counting of the letters in the Antichrist's name=666 [each letter equals a number and added together=666]-this practice is called Gematria in Hebrew/Greek and Isopsephy in Latin, e.g. "Nero Caesar," if Greek letters: "Neron Kaisar" are transliterated into Hebrew "nrwn qsr," the letter numbers add up to 666=50+200+6 +50+100+60+200. This is a compelling view as persecution by Nero or another specific emperor might put someone to death if their name was identified, so this provided plausible deniability. But many names equal 666 and the Antichrist hasn't come yet, though proponents say they believe in the law of double reference [prophecies could refer to 2 or more events separated by time] where it could have meant something historically to John's 1st century readers re: Nero's persecution [as John would say, "*even now are there many Antichrists,*" *1Jo. 2:18*] but will still have ultimate fulfillment with the actual Antichrist. But it is easy to get many names or things to equal 666, but almost impossible to get 1 name from the number. Also, Nero was dead when **Revelation** was written, though they would probably point to another name that equals 666. A subset of this view is 666 equals the Antichrist's or False Prophet's title. 7th-Day Adventist, Uriah Smith writes: *"The pope wears upon his pontifical crown in jeweled letters, this title: "Vicarius Filii Dei," "Viceregent of the Son of God;" the numerical value of which title is just six hundred and sixty-six...It is the number of the beast, the papacy; it is the number of his name, for he adopts it as his distinctive title; it is the number of a man, for he who bears it is the "man of sin."*[24] Catholics believe they are the true universal, not the false church, they deny existing popes are the Antichrist, but agree he represents Christ on earth, and they rightly state that many names can be shown to equal 666 discussed above. Catholics acknowledge some improper government union and historical tyranny during the Crusades and Medieval tortures and executions during numerous Inquisitions, though this Antichrist was not historical, he could be now, or is soon to come. 4) 666 is a technical mark or device the Antichrist requires that identifies him. Many have cited the three 6's currently found on every bar code on almost everything bought and sold. Some prefer the more recent bio-chip popular to place in between the bones of child's hand or animal with GPS location services. Some envision DNA scanning /identification of a man...I hold a combination of views 3 and 4, where the Antichrist's name will equal 666 and require a technology in the right hand or forehead to buy or sell to fits his worship, control, and arrogance. FYI-666 here, from 3 Greek letters spelled out: *chi xi stigma* [used as numbers are 600, 60, and 6]. What many say, 3 is completion-beginning, middle, and end, and 6 is for man, so three 6's is the completion of man, and man's final attempt to become and bring down God and all God loves. I believe that believers living at the time of the Antichrist will be clearly able to figure out or count the number of the Antichrist to equal his 666 name, see its tie to the economic system, his worship, and identify the Antichrist. Interesting that the true Christ gives believers a new personalized meaningful name [**Rev. 2:17**], where the Antichrist seems to require all to display a mark with his name/ number and make his worshipers only a number).}

Figure 17 – 21.1 The Beast with the Lamb's Horns and the Beast with Seven Heads[25]

<u>Application</u> (Activity/Questions)

A. Who is the 1st Beast from the sea (***13:1-8***)? {The Antichrist leading the final future 1-World Gentile Government/Revived Roman Empire /Political/The State.}

B. Who is the 2nd Beast from the earth (***13:11-17***)? {The False Prophet leading the false church/1-World Religion/The ecumenical church.}

C. What is the relationship between the 2 Beasts (***13:12***)? {Like the Church and State today; the False Prophet/1-World Religious leader pushes all to worship the Antichrist (Man's Government); like the false church seems to support the secular political leaders today and will during the Trib.}

D. What were Jews commanded to do with False Prophets (***Deu. 13:1-5***)? {Kill them.}

E. How can you help keep yourself from being deceived by False Prophets today? {Read and run everything through God's Word and watch out for governmental political correctness.}

F. What is *"the Mark of the Beast"* (***13:16-18***; ***14:11***; ***16:2***; ***19:20***)? {*"666," "the name of the beast," "the number of his name," "a mark in their right hand, or in their foreheads," "no man might buy or sell,"* without the mark of the beast; and is coupled with worship of the Antichrist; so God will judge all who take it with earthly sores and eternal judgment in hell.}

G. Can a person who takes the Mark of the Beast be eternally saved (***14:11***; ***16:11***; ***19:20***)? {No; only the unsaved can take it. So please, don't take it, no matter what.}

H. What does John tell us to do in ***13:10***? {Patiently endure in faith.}

I. What does John imply we should be in ***13:18***? {Be wise and understanding.}

The Lamb, 144K Choir, 3 Angel Messages, and God's Judgment.

Heavenly Singing, Angel Messages, and Coming Judgment.
{Virgin Witnesses With Harps Sing a New Song.}

Introduction

A. What do you think would clearly convince the unsaved today of God and his gospel? {An angel flying and proclaiming it in the sky?- probably not.}

B. What do you think you might be doing in heaven while God is judging the earth? {Praising and being thankful to God for His grace and mercy to me and all; and His justice to oppressors.}

C. How did Israel receive the testimony of Jesus during His 1st Advent? {Rejected; stumbled, only a small remnant believed; at His 2nd Coming they will receive Him joyfully.}

{So after an overview of Israel, her Son (Jesus and His ascension), during the Trib, Michael, and his angels cast Satan and demons out of heaven; Satan fiercely steps up his attacks on Israel (**_Rev. 12_**), and Satan establishes the Antichrist to lead the 1-world global Gov't and the False Prophet to lead the 1-world global religion, supporting the Antichrist (**_Rev. 13_**); it brings us to **_Rev. 14_**, where John overviews the righteous in heaven with Jesus, and the angelic judgment from God to the wicked on the earth.}

Scripture (Observations/Interpretation/Commentary)
{Major Paragraphs: **_14:1-5_** (The Lamb and 144K Choir); **_14:6-13_** (3 Angel Messages); **_14:14-20_** (God's Wrath Judging the Earth); 16/20 verses begin with "and;" Have groups: provide paragraph titles.}

A. _14:1-5_— {Title: 144,000 witnesses with the Lamb sing their special song accompanied by Heaven. **_1_**-"**And I** (John) **looked, and lo** (behold)**, a Lamb** (Jesus) **stood on the mount Sion** (Zion, a holy hill/stronghold in Jerusalem; Sion-9 times in Bible and Zion-153 times; prophesied as the place of the coming King, who initially was a Rock of offense or stumbling Stone-1st Advent, but will come to Israel as the Deliverer-2nd Advent; cf. **_Mat. 21:5_**; **_Joh. 12:15_**; **_Rom. 9:33_**; **_11:26_**; **_Heb. 12:22_**; **_1Pe. 2:6_**)**, and with Him** (Jesus) **144,000, having His** (Jesus') **Father's name written in their foreheads." _2_**-"**And I** (John) **heard a voice** (sound)

132

from heaven, as the voice (sound) of many waters, and as the voice (sound) of a great thunder: and I heard the voice (sound) of harpers (harpists) harping on their harps:" 3-"And they sung as it were a new song ("new song," 9 times in Bible, 6 in Psalms, 1 in Isaiah, all encouraging praise to God; 2 in Rev. 5:9 and 14:3; 5:9 is a different song, as here in 14:3, we'll see that only the 144K could learn it) before the throne, and before the 4 beasts (angelic creatures), and the elders (Church leaders): and no man could (was able) to learn (Gr:manthano-learn, understand) that song, but the 144,000, which (who) were redeemed from the earth." 4-"These are they which (who) were not defiled with women; for they are virgins (a picture of their most intimate relationship is not physically with a woman, but spiritually with God). These are they which (who) follow the Lamb (a picture of Jesus as the perfect, without spot or blemish lamb/sacrifice) whithersoever (where-ever) He goes. These were redeemed from among men, being the first-fruits (the Jewish beginning sacrifice, 1st given to God, recognizing 1st received from God; so seem to be the 1st saved Jewish Christians in the Trib) unto God and to the Lamb" (Jesus). 5-"And in their (144,000 witnesses') mouth was found no guile (deceit; the Truth of the Gospel, the Truth-Jesus was on their lips): for they are without fault (unblemished; a picture of their righteous sacrifice, because of the Lamb) before the throne of God." (So the Lamb is followed by these singing, sealed, redeemed, pure, virgin, and Jewish witnesses, singing a song that none could learn, while being accompanied by heavenly harpists, angels, and the Church, before God's throne and Jesus).}

B. 14:6-7— {Title: Another angel flies and preaches the everlasting gospel to worship (trust) the God of all creation cause it's judgment time. 6-"And I (John) saw another (a different) angel fly in the midst of heaven (mid-sky), having the everlasting (eternal) gospel (good news) to preach (to evangelize, to announce good news) unto them that dwell (housing permanently, unsaved, wicked) on the earth, and to every nation, and kindred (race, tribe), and tongue, and people," 7-"Saying with (in) a loud voice, 'Fear (Gr:phobeo-fear exceedingly, be in awe of, revere, reverence) God, and give glory (Gr:doxa-glory, dignity, praise, honor, worship) to Him (God); for the hour (Gr:hora-hour, day, instant, season, time) of His judgment is come: and worship (like a dog kissing/licking his masters hand) Him that made heaven, and earth, and the sea, and the fountains (original spring) of waters.'"}

C. 14:8— {Title: Another angel says Babylon is fallen because it enticed nations into idolatry. *8-"And there followed another* (a different) *angel, saying, 'Babylon is fallen, is fallen,* (repeated to show certainty and sometimes surprise) *that great city, because she made all nations* (non-Jewish) *drink out of the wine of the wrath of her fornication'"* (or idolatry).}

D. 14:9-12— {Title: A 3rd angel says those who worship or receive the Mark of the Beast will be forever tormented in Hell and obedient faithful will cheerfully endure. *9-"And the third angel followed them* (1st 2 angels), *saying in a loud voice, 'If any man* (one) *worship the beast* (1st Beast, the Antichrist) *and his image, and receive his* (Antichrist's) *mark* (Gr:charagma-scratch, etching, stamp, graven, mark) *in* (or on) *his forehead, or in* (or on) *his hand,'"* *10-"The same shall drink of the wine of the wrath of God, which is poured out without mixture* (undiluted) *into the cup of His* (God's) *indignation* (passionate punishment); *and he* (wicked rejecting Jesus and taking the Mark of the Beast) *shall be tormented with* (in) *fire and brimstone in the presence of the holy angels, and in the presence of the Lamb"* (Jesus, Who died for their sin): *11-"And the smoke of their* (Antichrist worshipers/Mark of the Beast receivers) *torment ascends up forever and ever* (not annihilation, but forever torment): *and they have no rest day nor night* (continuous), *who worship the beast* (Antichrist) *and his image, and whosoever receives the mark of his* (Antichrist's) *name;"* *12-"Here is the patience* (cheerful endurance; because of their belief of what Jesus has endured and accomplished for them and what God has promised for their future) *of the saints* (saved): *here are they that keep the commandments of God, and the faith of Jesus"* (obedient and faithful; trust and obey).}

E. 14:13— {Title: Happy are the saved that die in Trib so they can rest from works. *13-"And I* (John) *heard a voice* (last voice referenced was the 3rd angel in *14:9*) *from heaven saying unto me, 'Write, Blessed* (happy, well off) *are the dead which* (who) *die in the Lord* (in Christ; saved) *from henceforth'* (from this point on; now it should be, *"For to me to live is Christ, and to die is gain."*-**Php. 1:21**; but then due to severe persecution it will be even more true): *'Yea'* (Yes/truly), *says the Spirit* (the Holy Spirit), *that* (Gr: hina-purpose) *they* (saved) *may rest from their labors* (God's promised rest to His people, cf. **Heb. 3:11-4:11**); *and their works do follow after them."* (Faithful works are the only thing you can take with you).}

F. **14:14-16**— {Title: An angel tells a crowned one on a cloud to judge the earth and he does. **14**-"**And I** (John) **looked, behold a white cloud, and upon the cloud one sat like** (similar) **unto the son of man** (Christ or an angel-discussion to follow), **having on his head a golden crown** (Gr:stephanos-wreathe, chaplet [badge of royalty, prize in public games, symbol of honor], crown), **and in his hand a sharp** (Gr:oxus-keen, rapid, sharp, swift) **sickle."** (A symbol of reaping a harvest (what has been sown, cf. **Gal. 6:7-9**) in judgment. Is this crowned one Christ or an angel?-some see this one in a cloud ready to judge-and in **14:15** told by an angel to judge the earth, like **Rev. 10:1**, "another mighty angel" that had been close to and reflecting the glory of Christ, maybe Michael-Israel's protecting angel, crowned after casting out Satan and his demons, since it was "like" or "similar to" one who looked like the "son of man"-197 times in Bible, a title for men, also a title used of Christ, 85 times in the Gospels alone, for Christ's humanity, John uses it 14 times, 12 in **John** and 2 in **Rev.**; **John** also uses "Son of God" more when talking about Jesus, 19 of the 48 total times, in **John, 1Jo.,** and **Rev.**; but most see this as Christ as His 2nd Coming is in judgment and He is crowned and coming in the clouds [cf. **Psa. 18:11**; **97:2**; **Dan. 7:13**; **Mat. 24:30**; **26:64**; **Mar. 13:26**; **14:62**; **Rev. 1:7**], but a little strange if so, to be told by an angel to judge the world-**14:15**. I lean towards a mighty angel, like the Archangel Michael, that looks like a man, reflecting God's glory, protecting Israel from Satan, also the context is of angelic judgment, and I think John of all Apostles [beloved], would have recognized and called out Jesus instead of saying this one looked "like" the "son of man," a phrase commonly used of men; but probably doesn't greatly matter). **15**-"**And another** (a different) **angel came out of the temple, crying with a loud voice to him that sat on the cloud** (either a mighty angel or Christ), '**Thrust in your sickle, and reap; for the time is come for you to reap; for the harvest of the earth is ripe'**" (or dried up/withered. So 2 reasons for judgment on the earth: 1) the time has come-God's patience has limits and there is a time and place for everything, and, 2) the harvest or crop is ripe/ready, or worthless, so remove it). **16**-"**And he that sat** (was sitting) **on the cloud** (a mighty angel or Christ) **thrust in his sickle on the earth; and the earth was reaped**" (judgment came upon the earth).}

G. **14:17-20**— {Title: Another angel from the heavenly altar tells an angel from the heavenly temple to judge the ripe earth and he does causing the bloodiest battle ever. **17**-"**And another** (a different) **angel**

135

came out of the temple, which is in heaven (not the defiled earthly one, but the holy one near God), *he also having a sharp* (rapid) *sickle."* **18**-*"And another* (a different) *angel came out from the altar* (a place of sacrifice within the holy heavenly temple), *which had power* (authority) *over fire; and cried with a loud cry to him that had the sharp* (rapid) *sickle* (an angel)*, saying, 'Thrust in your sharp* (rapid) *sickle, and gather the clusters of the vine of the earth; for her grapes are fully ripe."* (So an angel told another angel to rapidly reap/judge the earth as it is fully ready). **19**-*"And the angel thrust in his sickle into the earth, and gathered the vine of the earth, and cast it into the great wine-press of the wrath* (indignation) *of God."* (So the angel obeyed the other angel, and gathered presumably the wicked from the earth together into a place to be crushed by God's wrathful judgment). **20**-*"And the wine-press was trodden* (trampled) *without* (outside) *the city* (presumed Jerusalem), *and blood* (not wine, but real blood; avg person has 6 quarts or 1.5 gallons) *came out of the wine-press, even unto the horses bridles* (avg is 4' 10" high), *by the space of 1,600 furlongs."* (950,400' or 180 miles; this is describing the gathering of the armies of the world to a bloody battle believed by most as the battle of Armageddon that we'll discuss more in **16:16**, as part of the 6th vial/bowl judgment).}

Application (Activity/Questions)

A. Will there be incredible special songs sung by pure lips in heaven (**14:3**)? {Yes.}

B. Is the NT gospel different from the OT gospel (**14:6-7, 12**)? {No, it is universal in time and its applicability (to every nation, kindred, tongue, and people) of all who will believe. It has always been by grace through faith in God's promise of Jesus' death, burial, and resurrection. Fear/reverentially trust and give God glory and worship the Creator, who is starting judgment.}

C. Will the gospel be preached everywhere to every nation and language in the Trib (**14:6**)? {Yes, praise God.}

D. Will people who reject the gospel spend eternity in a fiery Hell? {Sadly, yes.}

E. Why will it be hard for folks to trust God during the Trib and be saved (**13:13-14;** cf. **2Th. 2:9-12**)? {Great deception and lying signs.}

F. What should that motivate us to do more today? {Loudly proclaim the truth of the everlasting glorious gospel of Jesus Christ, the Savior.}

G. Will those rejecting God in the Trib be judged on earth and for all eternity? {Sadly, yes.}

The Final Plagues (7 Vials) Culminate God's Earthly Judgment—Heavenly Saints Praise God with Moses' and the Lamb's Song.

Finally, God's Just Judgment.
{Earthly Judgment and Heavenly Singing}

Introduction

A. Should we rejoice or be sober when our enemy is judged (cf. **_Pro. 24:17-18_**), why? {Be sober, for if not for the grace of God, that would be us; we don't want to be judged for disobeying; we should plan to testify of God's grace, while there is still time for the wicked to believe.}

B. Can we rejoice, worship, and even sing when God is judging (**_15:2-4_**), why? {Yes; that often delivers us from evil, we know God is holy, just, and even loving, and we sing for His greatness, mercy, and grace.}

C. Anyone ever been stressed watching a recording of a close sporting event, and then reminded yourself to relax, remembering your team wins? {I have and we definitely win with Christ in God at the end; so we can have confidence, celebrate early, and even have peace, knowing He will and we will be victorious.}

Scripture (Observations/Interpretation/Commentary)

{This is the shortest chapter in **_Rev._** It doesn't provide much new info, it is an overview or prelude to prepare us for the final 7 judgments coming.
Have class Read verses and Title paragraphs.}

A. _15:1_— {Title: The Last 7 Plagues Completing God's Earthly Judgment; **_1_**-"**And I** (John) beheld **_another sign_** (miracle, **_Rev. 12_**-Overviewed signs/wonders of war between Israel, Christ, Michael, and 2/3rd good angels against Satan and His 1/3rd demons) **in heaven, great and marvelous** (wonderful), **7 angels having the 7 last** (*Gr:eschatos-final, farthest, end, last; the root where we get eschatology or last/final events*) **plagues; for in them is filled up** (*Gr:teleo-end, completed, concluded, accomplished*) **the wrath** (indignation) **of God.**" (The good news is these judgments are on the Antichrist, the wicked, and they are the final ones-Yea, the end is in sight...Those who won't positively respond to God's gospel and loving rebukes, will receive God's judgment and final wrath).}

B. 15:2-4— {Title: Trib Saints Sing Songs Praising God's Just Judgment; **2**-"And I** (John) **saw** (beheld) **as it were a sea of glass** (transparent) **mingled with fire** (cf. **4:6**; **Exo. 24:10**; **Eze. 1:22**; mirroring God's glory and picturing His holy pure, separating refining judgment fire): **and them** (those saved in Trib now in heaven, possibly martyrs) **that** (who) **had gotten the victory over the Beast** (1st, the Antichrist), **and over his** (Antichrist's) **image, and over his mark** (the mark of the beast/Antichrist), **and over the number of his name** (got victory over 1 person and 3 things), **stand on the sea of glass** (could even be streets or areas of pure transparent gold, cf. **21:21**), **having the harps of God** (interesting shown standing with God's harps, probably peacefully praising Him as the rightful ruler of a great eternal economy). **3**-"And they** (Trib saved in heaven) **sing the song of Moses** (Law; singing to God for His strong judgment/deliverance of Israel, based on His righteous standard, from their enemy miraculously crossing the sea into the promised land of rest; only place in Bible *"the Song of Moses"* and also the only place in Bible *"the Song of the Lamb"* directly quoted, but Moses' song is referred to in **Exo. 15:1**; **Deu. 31:22, 30**; **32:44**) **the servant of God, and the song of the Lamb** (Grace; Jesus, as savior, loving sacrificial substitute to allow eternal deliverance; both songs come from grateful hearts celebrating God's merciful deliverance to those trusting Him), **saying, 'Great and marvelous** (wonderful) **are your works** (God did the works for Israel and us through His Son Jesus and also His might judging works of the wicked; so some see Moses' Song from Israel's point of view and the Lamb's Song from the Church's as He is the Church's Bride-groom and soon Husband; showing the unity of all believers, OT-Israel and NT-Church), **Lord God Almighty** (Gr:pantokrator-all ruling, universal sovereign, omnipotent; the most powerful ruler and judge); **just** (holy/right) **and true are your ways** (God's judgment is always just), **King of Saints'"** (set apart, holy, saved; You'll notice God's works, person, and ways were highlighted as great worship entails). **4**-"Who will not fear Thee** (God), **O Lord** (supreme ruler), **and glorify your name?** (Good question for us today as this is reasonable). **For You only** (alone) **are holy** (Gr: hosios-right, intrinsic divine character, pure, holy): **for all nations** (heathen) **shall come and worship** (bow; cf. **Php. 2:9-11**; even unsaved will bow in worship; interesting *"all nations"* is the same phrase used in the Great Commission of our evangelizing and edification scope, cf. **Mat. 28:19**) **before You** (God; this is being sung by saints); **for Your** (God's) **judgments** (equitable works) **are made manifest** (known, rendered apparent; no more deception, the truth of God's righteous ways/judgments will be clear and He will be worshiped by all unsaved and saved).}

C. **15:5-8**— {Title: God's Empty Temple Awaiting Completion of the Final 7 Vial Judgments; **5**-"**And after that** (What?-worshipful singing in the midst of impending world judgment) **I** (John) **looked** (considered), **and, behold, the temple** (dwelling) **of the tabernacle** (tent) **of the testimony** (Gr:marturion-testimony, witness; the Law/Decalogue/ evidence housed in the sacred temple; "*the testimony of Jesus*" is the only reason why saints can be standing and singing during judgment; "*tabernacle [or tent] of [or the] testimony*" repeated 5 times in OT, cf. **Exo. 38:21**; **Num. 1:50, 53**; **9:15**; **10:11**) **in heaven** (the real temple, not the copy on earth, that now is defiled) **was opened:**" **6**-"**And the 7 angels came out of the temple, having the 7 plagues** (of final earthly judgment), **clothed** (arrayed) **in pure and white** (radiant) **linen, and having their breasts** (chests) **girded with golden girdles** (or belts; 7 angels clothed as Christ has also given saints and He also appears). **7**-"**And 1 of the 4 beasts** (10th of the 11 times "*four beasts*" quoted in Bible, all in **Revelation** referring to 4 living, 6-winged, 4-faced, many eyed Seraphim holy creatures; **4:6, 8**; **5:6, 8, 14**; **6:1, 6**; **7:11**; **14:3**; **15:7**; **19:4**; although referred to as Seraphim in other places, cf. **Isa. 6:2-7**) **gave unto the 7 angels 7 golden vials** ("*golden vials*" quoted only 1 other time in Bible, **5:8**, full of the saints prayers for justice) **full** (overflowing) **of the wrath** (indignation) **of God** (the Father, giving justice; where the plagues of the wicked is God's response to the prayers of the righteous), **Who lives forever and ever**" (the only eternal one and eternal life). **8**-"**and the temple was filled** (entirely) **with smoke from the glory of God, and from His power** (Gr:dunamis-miraculous power, ability, might, strength; where we get dynamite); **and no man** (no one/nothing) **was abl**e (had the power; Gr:dunamai-ability, power, might...) **to enter into the temple, until the 7 plagues of the 7 angels were fulfilled**" (completed/finished; evokes imagery of **Exo. 40:35**: "*And Moses was not able to enter into the tent of the congregation, because the cloud abode thereon, and the glory of the LORD filled the tabernacle.*" Moses, under Israel's economy was the only one able to enter and his face glowed previously, but not even he was worthy to enter when God's holy glory was there. None can stand in God's presence when He is judging, but Christ, Who enters by Himself, with His own blood, to take upon Himself "*once for all*" (cf. **Heb. 10:10**), the judgment we all deserve.}

Application (Activity/Questions)

A. How can you celebrate now (even in tough times), knowing we ultimately win with God? {Think about eternal rewards, sing, praise, and tell others...}

B. The temple is a place of judgment and worship, why? {Sin required death and when God paid death by His own Son, we worship and praise Him for His love and holiness.}

C. Will the unsaved ultimately bow and worship God, even for His judgment (**15:4**; **Php. 2:9-11**)? {Yes; the truth of God, His worth, and just judgments/equitable works will be made so clear that bowing in worship with our bodies and lips will be the only reasonable response.}

D. Does God ever give you a song of praise to Him (like David or Trib Saints)? Want to share any words or ideas? {Yes. Thanksgiving, praise, worship, love, gratitude, acknowledging Who He is now...}

E. Who do you think praises more, blessed Christians or persecuted ones? {Persecuted; pray we increase our praise without increased persecution; but sometimes it takes that to appreciate the eternal things God is accomplishing for, in, and thru us...}

The 7 Last Vial Plagues on the Wicked and Jesus is Coming Soon.

The 7 Vial (Bowl) Judgments.
{(1-Ulcers, 2-Sea like Blood, 3-Rivers like Blood, 4-Sun Scorching Men, 5-Darkness, 6-Euphrates Dried & 3 Demons Gather for the Battle of Armageddon, and 7-Earthquake/Hail) and Jesus' Soon Coming. Includes a Timeline Overview Chart of 40+ Prophesied Events.}

Introduction
A. Looking at the world today (with the Church), what type of hopelessness, evil, and deception will exist (without the Church) in the Great Trib? {Unbelievable bloody wickedness/despair.}
B. What have you heard of the Battle of Armageddon? {A Battle to end all battles; bloody; wicked world against Christ with His Church...}

{As way of reminder and overview, the 7th Seal, seemed to start the 7 Trumpets and continue, and the 7th Trumpet seemed to start the 7 Vials. These 7 vials are the last plagues (_15:1_) and they reenact some of the early OT plagues on Egypt. John's 1st starts with Moses 6th plague of boils, moving to Moses' 1st where the seas and rivers turn to blood for John's 2nd and 3rd vials/plagues, John's 4th has the sun scorching fire, Darkness is Moses' 9th and John's 5th Plague, and John's 6th and 7th has the Euphrates dry up and the worst earthquake/hail ever, where hail was Moses' 7th plague, and part of John's 6th plague has 3 demons like frogs, where frogs was Moses' 2nd plague. These last plagues/vials of John's were not sent to free God's people from slavery (the redeemed are already free, though it might have distracted the wicked from persecuting Israel/Saints some), but as a last effort to bring the earth's inhabitants to faith and repentance to God, which unfortunately mostly will not repent, just like Pharaoh and his response to God, Moses, and the Israelites.}

Scripture (Observations/Interpretation/Commentary)
{18/21 verses begin with *"and"* for continued action; May want to divide into Groups that Read a paragraph; come up with a Title; and draw pictures of plagues and/or their results on board.}
A. _16:1_— {Title: 7 Angels Commanded to Pour Out God's Judgment Vials or Bowls. _1_-"**And I** (John) **heard a great** ("great"-72 times in _Rev._, 11 in _16:1-21_, showing the intensity/immensity of these final

judgments) *voice out of the temple saying to the 7 angels, 'Go your ways* (Depart), *and pour* (gush) *out the vials* (or bowls or cups) *of the wrath* (indignation) *of God upon the earth.'"* (Summary Thesis command; followed by vial number sequenced obedience by the 7 angels).}

B. 16:2— {Title: 1st Angel—Harmful Grievous Ulcers Upon Wicked. **2-**
"And the 1st (Angel) *went, and poured out his vial upon the earth* (immediate and direct obedience to God); *and there fell* (came) *a noisome* (bad/harmful) *and grievous* (hurtful/diseased/vicious; doubly bad) *sore* (ulcer) *upon the men* (human beings; unsaved/ wicked) *which* (who) *had the mark of the beast* (1st, Antichrist), *and upon them which* (who) *worshiped his* (Antichrist's) *image."* (Satan attacking Israel and saints through the Antichrist's followers/Christ Rejectors and God begins 7 vial judgments on wicked).}

C. 16:3— Title: 2nd Angel—Sea like Blood So Creatures Died. **3-**"*And the 2nd angel poured out his vial* (of judgment) *upon* (into) *the sea; and it became as the blood of a dead man* (coagulated; dead)*: and every living soul* (vitality) *died in the sea."*

D. 16:4-7— {Title: 3rd Angel—Rivers like Blood, Wicked Shed Blood, so Sovereign God is Just Judging. **4-**"*And the 3rd angel poured out his vial upon* (into) *the rivers and fountains* (source) *of waters; and they became* (or seemed) *blood. **5-**"And I heard the angel of the waters* (3rd angel) *say, 'You are righteous* (just/equitable/ innocent), *Oh Lord* (Master/Supreme), *Who are, and was, and shall be* (ever present, eternal), *because You have judged thus"* (this way). **6-**"*For they have shed* (*Gr:excheo*-poured, shed, spilled; same word as angels pouring out vials) *the blood of saints* (saved) *and prophets* (inspired speakers of God's Word by which wicked could be saved, but will be judged), *and You* (God) *have given them* (the wicked) *blood to drink* ("*an eye for an eye,*" blood for blood, cf. **Gen. 9:6**; **Mat. 5:38**; equitable/just); *for they* (Antichrist followers) *are worthy* (deserving/due; You're giving them the judgment they deserve). **7-**"*and I* (John) *heard another* (different angel) *out of the altar* (place of holy sacrifice) *say, 'Even so* (Yes/Truth), *Lord God Almighty* (Universal Sovereign/All ruling), *true and righteous* (equitable/just) *are Thy judgments* (justice).'" (Another angel couldn't control himself but had to say Amen and talk about God's rightful position—Sovereign Lord/Judge and rightful works/actions—bringing true and righteous justice).}

E. 16:8-9— {Title: 4th Angel—Sun Scorching Men Who blasphemed God More. **8-**"*And the 4th angel poured out his vial upon the sun; and* power was given to him (4th angel) to scorch (burn) men (human beings) with fire." 9-"And men (human beings) were scorched (burnt) with great heat, and blasphemed (spoke evil of) the name of God (the 1 they should be praising and trusting), Which (Who-God) has power (authority) over these plagues (the 1 Who could stop the plagues): and they (wicked) repented not to give Him (God) glory." (Praise/worship; men pridefully continue to reject God's rule rather than repent and be saved and avoid the heat).}

F. 16:10-11— {Title: 5th Angel—Darkness on Antichrist and Followers Who Still Blaspheme. 10-"And the 5th angel poured out his vial upon the seat (throne) of the beast (1st, Antichrist); and his (Antichrist's) kingdom (realm) was (became) full of darkness (Gr:skotoo-obscurity, blindness, full of darkness); and they (Antichrist's wicked followers) gnawed (chewed) their tongues for (out of) pain," 11-"and they (Antichrist and his wicked followers) blasphemed the God of heaven (and earth, but pictures Him in heaven above them) because of their pains and their sores (ulcers), and repented not of their (wicked/unsaved) deeds." (Acts/works/ doings. Ironic that the Antichrist's throne/realm and followers are in darkness, wanting light, while Christ is the creator of light, and the "light of the world," cf. Joh. 1:1-11; 8:12; 9:5; Christ has "delivered us from the power of darkness," cf. Col. 1:13; and "the light of the glorious gospel of Christ" brings light, while Satan blinds in unbelief, cf. 2Co. 4:4; 11:13-15; and rejected light always blinds, brings darkness, hardening, unbelief, and ultimately leads away from Christ "into outer darkness," cf. Mat. 8:12; 22:13; 25:30).}

G. 16:12-16— {Title: 6th Angel—Euphrates Dried and 3 Demons Gather Wicked Armies for Battle of Armageddon. 12-"And the 6th angel poured out his vial upon the great river Euphrates (important river in Asia supplying water to many countries; it was a natural divider between the East and the West-including ancient Rome. It was the eastern boundary for Israel's promised land (Gen. 15:18; Deu. 1:7; 11:24; Jos. 1:4); 21 times in Bible, twice in Rev., here in 16:12, and also 9:14, by the 6th angel of the Trumpet judgments opening the way for the 200M army); and the water thereof (of it-Euphrates) was dried up (cf. Isa. 11:15-16), that (Gr:hina-purpose, result) the way of the kings of the east (rising of the sun. Since kings is plural, seems a reference to both Japan and China, who probably will be coming to the middle east for oil and China, India, Iraq, and Afghanistan could cross directly by land with the Euphrates dried up) might be prepared." 13-"And I

(John) *saw 3 unclean* (ceremonially, morally, often demonic) *spirits like frogs come out of the mouth of the dragon* ("*dragon*"-19 times in Bible; the 13 times in **Rev.** all refer to Satan), *and out of the mouth of the beast* (1st/Antichrist), *and out of the mouth of the false prophet.*" (2nd Beast. Kind of a Tribulation Trinity of Evil-Satan, Antichrist, and False Prophet). **14**-"*For they* (unclean spirits) *are the spirits of devils* (demons)*, working miracles* (signs/wonders)*, which* (who) *go forth unto the kings of the earth* (countries/land) *and of the whole world* (globe; implies global Roman empire of leaders and followers), to gather (assemble) *them* (wicked leaders and followers) *to the battle* (*Gr:polemos-battle, fight, war*; can be a single war or series of battles that occur in the last 3 ½ years of the Trib period; battle(s) of Armageddon, cf. **16:16**) *of that great day of God Almighty"* (a technical term for "*the Day of the Lord*" a period of judgment where patience ends and justice prevails, emphasizing God is powerfully judging; calls this, God's battle; we'll see in **Rev. 19** that Christ (as God-man) finishes this battle at His Return with us the Church). **15**-"*Behold, I* (Jesus; so this verse should be in red for the red letter editions as they are words of Jesus) *come* (2nd Coming; 1st Coming Jesus came in peace as a Man-child, His 2nd Coming will be in Judgment as the God-man) *as a thief.* (Not stealing, but Paul, Peter, and Jesus use the imagery of a thief to encourage us to watch and be ready as Jesus will come quickly in a day/time of judgment when the world won't expect him; cf. **3:3**; **1Th. 5:2, 4**; **2Pe. 3:10**; By the way, **1Th. 5:7-11** tells us "*God has not appointed us*" [Christians/Church Age believers] "*to wrath, but to obtain salvation,*" so we should be faithful, loving, hopeful, and comforted that we will be "*together with Him*" at His 2nd Coming). *Blessed* (Happy) *is he* (the one) *that watches* (*Gr: gregoreuo-keeping awake, watching, being vigilant*; "*is watching*")*, and keeps* (*Gr:tereo-watch, guard, keep [a military fortress]*; "*is keeping*") *his garments, lest* (*Gr:hina-purpose; me-not*; "*that not*") *he walk naked, and they* (wicked) *see his shame* (indecency)." (So Jesus interjects a reminder to believers now and in the Trib to live in the Spirit, confessed up, and a sanctified life for an example/ witness to all the wicked/unbelievers because after only 1 more vial judgment He is coming for the remaining wicked and their eternal judgment; wicked cannot see Christ's imputed righteousness in us, but they can see our righteousness actions that Christ lives out through us and understand by our works and words the testimony of Jesus). **16**-"*And he* (6th angel, Satan, Antichrist, False Prophet, Demonic spirits, or Jesus?-It is

144

he [singular], not they [plural], which rules out the demonic spirits here, but truly God/Jesus is sovereignly leading them together, and God tasked the 6th angel, and Satan, the Antichrist, and even the False Prophet are gathering armies; so seems all, except demons, which we are told explicitly in **16:14** gather them, so all of the above) **gathered** (assembled) **them** (the kings and by implication their armies of the whole world) **together into a place being called in the Hebrew tongue** (Israel's native tongue) **Armageddon.**" (Name only found 1 time in the Bible; generally interpreted as the "*mountain of Megiddo.*" Megiddo is found 11 times in the Bible regarding it's kings, towns, countries, inhabitants, wars, waters, hills, or valleys; all in the OT, a place in northern Israel, south of Bethlehem and Galilee, west of the Jordan river and Jezreel; a large excellent place for a great epic battle. This will be a world war, the last earthly battle of good and evil. We'll see more in **19:11-19** that Christ Returns with His Church and defeats all the armies of the Antichrist and world and saves His promised people in their promised land to commence His glorious earthly Kingdom; cf. **Dan. 11:41-45**; **Joel 3:1-3, 9-16**; **Zec. 12:1-14**; **14:1-16**; **Mat. 24:21-31**; folks are "*Armed and Gettin*" trouble at Armageddon-sorry I know that was horrible humor but may have made you smile re: this sober somber battle).}

H. **16:17-21**— {Title: 7th Angel—Worst Earthquake/Hail Dividing Babylon and Wicked Blaspheme God. **17**-"**And the 7th angel poured out his vial into the air** (strange as we'll see earthquakes effect the earth, hail is from the air, but also aimed at Satan who is now "*the prince of the power of the air,*" cf. **Eph. 2:2**); **and there came out a great voice out of the temple of heaven** (the true heavenly temple), **from the throne** (God's throne is in the temple, as it is a place of holy/just judgment, and it is holy because He/His throne is there. In fact, no men [even saved] were holy enough to enter until these plagues were complete, cf. **15:8**), **saying, 'It is done.'**" (Fulfilled/Finished; Summary statement of 7th Vial Judgment). **18**-"**And there were** (4 powerful things) **voices, and thunders, and lightnings; and there was a great earthquake, such as was not since men** (human beings) **were upon the earth, so mighty an earthquake, and so great.**" (Such a huge earthquake, bigger than all before. In Shaanxi, China under emperor Jiajing, there was recorded an earthquake that killed about 830,000 in 1556 AD, that leveled mountains, cities, started floods, fires...There was an even bigger one that was a 9.5 on the Richter scale in 1960, in Chile, that spawned a Tsunami that itself was larger than the Jiajing Great Earthquake. This one is the biggest one ever, even bigger than those killing millions). _19_-"**And the great city** ("*great city*," 10 times in _Rev._; 17 times in Bible: 1 for Resen-_Gen. 10:12_, 1 for Gibeon-_Jos. 10:2_, 4 for Nineveh-_Jon. 1:2_; _3:2-3_; _4:11_; 2 clearly for the earthly Jerusalem-_Jer. 22:8_; _Rev. 11:8_; and 1 for the heavenly new Jerusalem-_21:10_; 7 where it is clearly Babylon-_14:8_; _17:18_; _18:10, 16, 18, 19, 21_; and here in _16:19_, where it may be Jerusalem if it is contrasted with the gentile nations, or Babylon or Rome if included with the 1-world gentile government run by the Antichrist. I believe its Babylon as _**Revelation**_ uses "*great city*" most for Babylon, Babylon is the great city of _Rev. 16-18_, and this 7th Vial judgment is on the wicked gentiles, not Israel or it would be Jerusalem) **was divided into 3 parts, and the cities of the nations fell: and** (or even) **great Babylon** (that literal 1st wicked world empire that Daniel mentions, which is also symbolic of many world empires, like Rome, and other capitols of evil that we'll see more of in _Rev. 17-18_ that corrupts the people of God, and the world, and must be judged) **came into remembrance before God** (like a docket comes up or due before a judge; not that God forgot, but that He is mindful of all their evil deeds and answers the righteous demands of His holiness and the prayers of His saints at this fullness of time), **to give unto her** (Babylon, believed to be the modern day revived Roman empire) **the cup of the wine** (a frequent metaphor of judgment that is about to be drunk) **of the fierceness** (wrath/ indignation) **of His** (God's) **wrath** (vengeance/ justifiable anger)." _20_-"**And every island fled away, and the mountains were not found** (a massive earthquake could cover islands and level many mountains; or could be a metaphorical picture of remote places hiding or trying to escape and high places brought low before God). _21_-"**And there fell upon men** (human beings) **a great hail out of heaven** (heavenly hail; probably seemed hellish), **every stone about the weight of a talent** (about 75 pounds each): **and men** (wicked mankind) **blasphemed God** (instead of repenting, they spoke evil against God Who could have stopped it, and demonstrating why it was just and needed) **because of the plague of the hail; for the plague thereof** (of it) **was exceeding** (vehemently) **great**." (Interesting, the greatness of this plague is emphasized twice. John's, truly God's final 7th plague is much worse than Moses' final 10th plague of the death of the 1st born that let Israel go from Egypt, this is the deaths of many wicked around the world, destroying Satan's warring governments of the Antichrist and where Christ returns and saves all Israel, cf. _**Rom.**_

11:26. How sad: the worst earthquake with enormous hail leveling nature, man's structures, man's hopes and dreams apart from Christ, and man's stony heart remains hardened, unrepentant, and rejecting the gracious love of a God Who died for their every sin. Not only does ***Revelation*** reveal the testimony of Jesus, but it also reveals a testimony, a witness of the wickedness of man).}

Application (Activity/Questions)
A. What effect did the plagues have on righteous and wicked in Egypt and during the Trib? {Greater trust and faith by righteous; greater heart hardening, anger, and rejection of God by wicked.}
B. How can you help keep your heart from growing hard or callous towards God (cf. ***Heb. 3***; ***1Co. 10:10***)? {Daily trusting, confessing, not complaining, hoping, forgiving, praising, exhorting, letting circumstances bring us to Him and not away from Him.}
C. Why do you think the wicked still will not trust and will even blaspheme God (when not atheistic or agnostic as they know these 7 last plagues are from God, cf. ***16:9, 11, 21***)? {Pride; rebellion; trusting man-made government, false idols/religions. They know God exists, but still persist in rejecting and blaspheming, not trusting God; so they are blinded by sin/pride.}
D. Is God just judging on earth and eternally (***16:5-7***), why? {Yes, He is eternal and the standard; men break His standard and His laws and are deserving; He has given all a way out; His is almighty and righteous.}
E. For the believers on earth during the Trib, what should be their response (***16:15***)? {Same as ours now; watching and worthy confessed up clean living, positively anticipating Christ's Return.}
F. Before we see the 1-World Government and the 1-World Church, can you draw a timeline chart showing what chapters some of the great prophetic events fit in? {See Figure 18 below, to remember and prepare you for some to prophetic events to come.}

147

Figure 18 – 24.1 Revelation Timeline Overview of 40+ Events

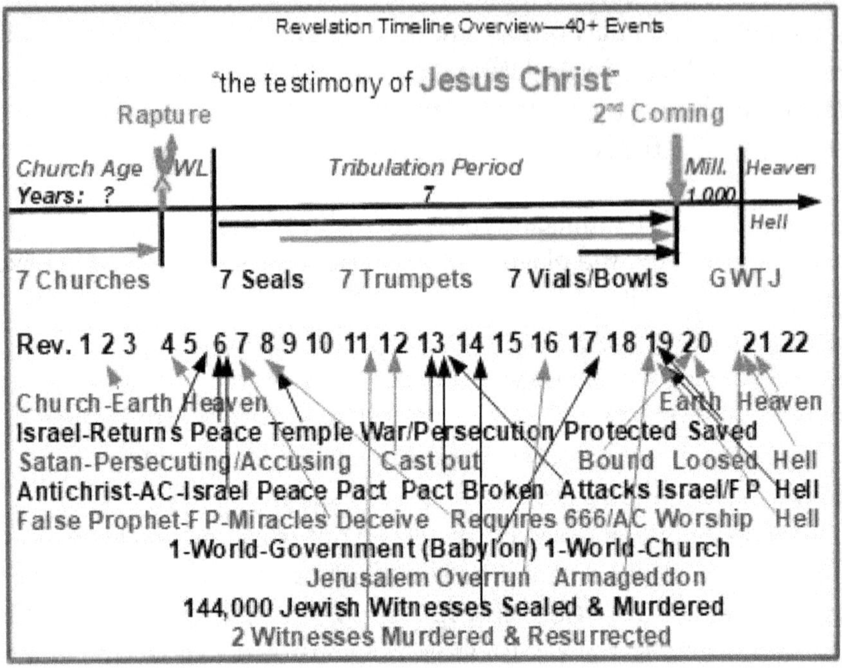

Revelation Timeline Overview—40+ Events

"the testimony of Jesus Christ"

Rapture   2nd Coming

Church Age WL   Tribulation Period   Mill.   Heaven
Years: ?   7   1,000

                                                         Hell

7 Churches   7 Seals   7 Trumpets   7 Vials/Bowls   GWTJ

Rev. 1 2 3   4 5 6 7 8 9 10 11 12 13 14 15 16 17 18 19 20   21 22

Church-Earth Heaven   Earth Heaven
Israel-Returns Peace Temple War/Persecution Protected Saved
Satan-Persecuting/Accusing Cast out   Bound Loosed Hell
Antichrist-AC-Israel Peace Pact Pact Broken Attacks Israel/FP Hell
False Prophet-FP-Miracles Deceive Requires 666/AC Worship Hell
1-World-Government (Babylon) 1-World-Church
Jerusalem Overrun Armageddon
144,000 Jewish Witnesses Sealed & Murdered
2 Witnesses Murdered & Resurrected

Murderous Idolatrous Harlot Destroyed by Blasphemous "Babylonian" Beast, Conquered by Christ.

Ugly and the Beast.
{Or Church and state Beasts Beaten by the Lamb. The Harlot, Babylonian Beast, 7 Kings, and 10 Horn Views Listed with Rationale and Rebuttal for Each, and Significance Explained.}

Introduction

A. Provide a short overview or title for ***Rev. 17***? {The False Church gives power to the Antichrist, who is given power by government to lead the final revived Roman Empire. Short Title1: Ugly and the Beast. Both main similes/metaphors: Woman=False Prophet leading Ecclesiastical Rome and Beast=Antichrist leading Political/ Economical/Secular City/State Rome. Short Title2: Church and State Beasts Beaten by the Lamb. At the 1st Advent Satan showed Jesus "*all the kingdoms of the world*" in a moment of time, and said, "*all these things will I give you*" for it was given to me and to whoever I will give it... Jesus said to worship and serve God alone (cf. ***Mat. 4:8-10***; ***Luk. 4:5-8***). ***Rev. 13*** pictures 2 arrogant Beasts-1 political power and the other with religious power, both against the Lamb. ***Rev. 17*** pictures 1 powerful woman (who failed as a wife and as a mother) riding a powerful beast.}

B. Do you know of any governments today where it is politically correct to follow Jesus? {No.}

C. If the government outlawed Christianity, would your life change, if so how? {Yes; teaching, speech, writing...}

D. Do you see or feel any idolatry and persecution in our government or church today? {Yes, both.}

E. https://www.youtube.com/watch?v=Olahc83Kvp4 {4:30; play great video song by Andrew Peterson, "*Is He Worthy?*"[26]}

Scripture (Observations/Interpretation/Commentary)

{2/3rd verses begin with "and" showing continued action; this Harlot and Beast are tied closely with ***Rev. 13***'s 2 Beasts; have the Learner read paragraph and come up with Titles; cross references are up front, so learners have them up front; expect 2 lessons.}

A. 17:1-6— (cf. *17:18*; *17:15*; *Jer. 3:8, 14*; *Isa. 50:1*; *54:5*; *Rev. 17*; *17:9, 12*; *Dan. 2:41-44*; *Rev. 17:10, 18*; *Isa. 13:19-22*; *Jer. 51:24-26, 62-64*; *Rev. 14:8*; *16:19*; *17:5*; *18:2, 10, 21*). {Title: Mystery: Great Babylon and Mother of Harlots, Drunk with Martyr's Blood. *1-"And there came* (appeared) *1 of the 7 angels, which* (who) *had the 7 vials* (of God's judgment), *and talked with me* (John), *saying to me (John), 'Come here; I will show unto you the judgment of the great whore* (harlot. *17:18* explains this woman as the great city Babylon, which reigns over the earthly kings) *that sits* (is sitting) *upon* (a picture of dwelling or resting on or with the support of) *many waters'"* (*17:15* explains waters are a metaphor for lots of people with different tongues from different nations): *2-"With whom* (the Great Harlot) *the kings of the earth have committed fornication* (harlotry/adultery/idolatry), *and the inhabitants* (house permanently, wicked, unsaved) *of the earth* (a reference to their location and worldliness) *have been made drunk* (intoxicated; slowed and dulled imagery) *with the wine of her fornication."* (Idolatry; a picture of an unfaithful married woman [frequent comparison of Israel and God her husband, cf. *Jer. 3:8, 14*; *Isa. 50:1*; *54:5*], but here is starting to describe this False Church or congregation of believers that are "in bed" with the government, "*the kings of the earth.*" 1 of the big reasons America was founded was to get away from the sickness/idolatry/adultery of the church and government controlling, compromising, and corrupting each other). *3-"So* (*Gr:kai-and, even, also, so; really continued like an "and," but used to tie back to the angel of verse 1*) *he* (1 of the angels with 1 of the last 7 vial judgments) *carried me* (John) *away in the spirit* (seemingly John's spirit, not the Holy Spirit, like an Ebenezer Scrooge imagery) *into the wilderness: and I* (John) *saw a woman* (wife; the harlot) *sit* (sitting) *upon a scarlet* (crimson) *colored beast* ("*beast,*" 44 times in *Rev.*; the 1st 7 times were good angelic beasts or living creatures; the majority of times, 16 in *Rev. 13* alone, refer to the 1st Beast or Antichrist and the 2nd Beast or False Prophet; 9 times in *Rev. 17*, where many believe is a composite beast supporting Babylon of both the Antichrist's political/economical/secular Babylon and the ecclesiastical/ religious Babylon and carry or support the harlot, the great city, which many believe is Rome. Satan used Rome to attack Christ and authorize His death in His 1st Advent and most believe Satan will again use the revived Rome to attack Christ at His 2nd Advent. Explained further in the following verses) *full of names* (authority/ character) *of blasphemy* (speaking evil against God), *having "7 heads*

and ten horns." (**17:9** says, "*7 heads are 7 mountains.*" Rome is called the city on 7 hills or mountains, where the Vatican is, and Rome was the gentile world power when this was written. **17:12** says, "*10 horns...are 10 kings.*" These 10 kings seem also the 10 toes of the final revived 4th beast and image in **Dan. 2:41-44**. Most believe these horns represent a loose 10-nation confederacy [as iron and clay do not adhere in those feet and toes]. We will later see a double metaphorical meaning, where the 7 heads are also described as 7 kings in **17:10**). **4-"And the woman** (wife and harlot) **was arrayed in purple and scarlet** (crimson) **color** (the scarlet dressed harlot wife of God in stark contrast with the white dressed bride of Christ), **and decked** (gilded) **with gold and precious stones and pearls, having a golden cup in her hand full of abominations and filthiness** (moral impurity) **of her fornication:"** (Adultery/ idolatry. The woman, "*that great city*" [**17:18**], appears most like the 2nd Beast of in **Rev. 13**, the False Prophet who leads the False Church or Apostate Christendom, the Woman or Ecclesiastical Babylon, which most believe is Rome, where the Vatican is, though some believe it will actually be Babylon revived, but **Isa. 13:19-22** and **Jer. 51:24-26, 62-64** seem to preclude that. So Babylon seems a representative name for the Gentile world empire prophesied to be judged, while God preserves Israel in so many places throughout Scripture. God mentions Babylon=294 times, Babylonian=4 times, Chaldea=7 times, Chaldean=2 times, or the Chaldeans=66 times by name in 19 Books, 6 times in **Rev. 14:8**; **16:19**; **17:5**; **18:2, 10, 21**; 373 total times in the Bible. The Book of Habakkuk only includes the name once, but the entire Book is devoted to Habakkuk's complaint of how God can be just to use the wicked Babylonians to judge wicked Israel, but by faith he comes to rejoice and see God's holiness/justice. These 5 names for the city, area, or Gentile world empire of the historical and future metaphorically stated Babylon are found in these Biblical Books: **2 Kings, 1 and 2 Chronicles, Ezra, Nehemiah, Esther, Job, Psalms, Isaiah, Jeremiah, Ezekiel, Daniel, Micah, Habakkuk, Zechariah, Matthew, Acts, 1 Peter**, and **Revelation**), **full** (Gr:gemo-full, swell out; like a picture of an unwanted pregnancy. 3 main views for who is this ornately dressed morally filthy Harlot or 2nd Beast. 1) The Final Pope leading the Roman Catholic church, and some include leading other false churches, based on the attire, the golden cup, the affluence, the Roman location, and has been a world renown religious leader powerful and influential enough to lead the false 1-World Church. This view is held by many including an American Founding Father and President John Adams. He wrote that the government is represented as *"Babylon"* and the *"Whore"* is the Catholic Church, describing their unholy union and it was this tyrannical threat to liberty that *"accomplished the settlement of America."*[27] 2) A prominent Protestant Pastor of a united False Church that will be an affluent world leader maybe even uniting religions, where all views will be tolerated, except the only 1 true gospel and way to God, cf. **John 14:6**, which is by grace through faith in Jesus' death, burial, and resurrection to remove sin and reconcile 1 to God. See the World Council of Churches that currently includes 350 churches with ½ billion members, whether true or false, attempting unity and unification of leadership and doctrine now. 3) An Islamic Prophetic Caliphate, Imam, or state religion, which is 1 of the fastest growing religions, as they average 4 times the number of births than most other religions, Islamism is the required religion of numerous middle eastern governments encircling Israel and across Europe, they clearly have great influence and affluence through oil revenue, and obviously have martyred numerous true Christians by state executions and world-wide terrorism. Many discard this view by claiming no true fornication can exist with a Muslim leader or people who were never married to God as they reject Christ as Savior and God. But that could also be said of all views, since all are of the false church. Remember, during this tribulation period the true Church believers will be Raptured to heaven and so only a remnant will get saved and be fighting the Antichrist and this Harlot /False Prophet. I believe view 1 or 2 is most likely as difficult to believe that Islamic leaders could peacefully galvanize all world religions with their current strategy of killing all infidels/non-Muslims or at least are silent when Islamic extremists continue murder and terrorism on innocent men, women, and children. Clearly, this harlot seems to represent the False Church in an adulterous affair with the government and not God): **5**-"***And upon her*** (the adulterous harlot's) ***forehead was a name written, 'Mystery, Babylon the Great, the Mother of Harlots and Abominations of the Earth.'***" (The Greek text doesn't have it capitalized, but KJV puts this writing in all capital letters. *"Mystery Babylon,"* not the literal old revived Babylon, but a new representative one. *"Mother of Harlots,"* as spawning false man-made and led religions and ecumenical cult groups not following Scripture or the true gospel, but man's work-centered writings. This type of church union with the government is 1 of the reasons why the United States

1st Amendment prohibits any law establishing or restricting the free exercise of religion, which many refer to as a Separation of Church and State. Historically and today you can readily observe many governments forcing registrations and adherence to a state religion or creed, such as North Korea, China, and numerous Islamic states). *6-"And I* (John) *saw the woman* (wife; this harlot) *drunken* (being drunk) *with the blood of the saints* (pictured drinking up their blood, like a vampire bat, draining their life), *and with the blood of the martyrs* (witnesses; 2nd time mentions the blood of saints in this verse and here shows they bled to death for the testimony of our Savior) *of Jesus* (since knowing of the true Savior Jesus and dying for Him, e.g. "martyrs of Jesus," indicates these are NT saints)*: and when I saw her* (the bloodthirsty whore), *I* (John) *wondered* (Gr:thaumazo-wonder, admire, marvel) *with great admiration* (Gr:thauma-from form of thaumazo, wonder or admiration; probably best translated "wonder" again here. John didn't know who this wealthy well-dressed whore was. If you maintain she is the Catholic Church, she really wasn't around yet for John to know about, although Catholics often state they started with Jesus, or Peter as the 1st Pope. John wondered as he didn't know who this was, and probably wondered how God was so patient and the Harlot was so cruel).}

B. *17:7-14—* (cf. *17:1, 3*; *12:3*; *13:1*; *17:3, 7*; *Dan. 7:7, 23-24*); *John 3:31*; *8:23*; *Rev. 1:8, 17-18*; *3:5*; *17:8*; *20:12, 15*; *22:19*; *Php. 4:3*; *Rev. 13:8*; *21:27*; *Jer. 51:24-25*; *Dan. 2:35, 44-45*; *Rev. 13:3, 12, 14*; *Dan. 2 and 7*; *Rev. 13*; *17-18*; *17:14*; *19:16*; *Deu. 10:17*; *Psa. 136:3*; *1Ti. 6:15*). {Title: The Angel Explains the Mystery of the Harlot Carried by the Beast. *7-"And the angel* (1 of the 7, the same 1 that carried John to see the harlot, cf. *17:1, 3*) *said unto me* (John), *'Wherefore* (why) *did you marvel* (or wonder)? *I will tell you the mystery of the woman* (wife; harlot), *and of the Beast* (political and religious Babylon) *that carries her* (the Harlot), *which has the 7 heads and 10 horns.'"* ("7 heads and 10 horns;" again, 4 times quoted in Bible, all in *Rev.*; refers to Satan in *12:3*, the Antichrist empowered by Satan in *13:1*, and in *17:3, 7* is this blasphemous, adulterous prostitute empowered by Satan, riding this beast). *8-"The Beast* (see *Rev. 13* commentary; the Beast carrying the Harlot; most believe this is Political Babylon, secular, the City/State, the 10-nation confederacy, the revived Roman empire, the last Gentile world government. Beast=Kingdom and Horns=Kings, cf. *Dan. 7:7, 23-24*) *that you saw was, and is not; and shall ascend out of the bottomless pit* (from below, this demonically possessed, clearly empowered beast from the depthless pit, is counterfeiting Jesus *"from above,"* **John 3:31**; **8:23**, Jesus, *"which is, and which was, and which is to come, the Almighty,"* Jesus, *"the first and the last,"* and Jesus, *"that liveth, and was dead; and, behold, I am alive for evermore,"* cf. **1:8, 17-18**), **and go into perdition** (ruin/ destruction; again the opposite of where Jesus is): **and they that dwell** (are dwelling/housing permanently; unsaved wicked) **on the earth shall wonder, whose names were not written in the Book of Life** (*"The Book of Life,"* **3:5**; **17:8**; **20:12, 15**; **22:19**; **Php. 4:3**, had everyone's name written in it before *"the foundations of the world"* of all who would be conceived. A person's name gets blotted out of it if they blaspheme the Holy Spirit/reject Jesus as their Savior. *"The Lamb's Book of Life,"* cf. **13:8**; **21:27**, never get anyone's name blotted out of it;) **from the foundation** (conception/founding) **of the world** (*Gr:kosmos-world, orderly arrangement including people*), **when they beheld the beast** (political and religious Babylon) **that was, and is not, and yet is."** (Repetition of his deceptive counterfeit; more to come on him). **9-"And here is the mind which has wisdom.** (So the angel is going to somewhat explain the harlot riding a beast; and this is 1 of those places that really takes some discernment and wisdom to even understand the angel's explanation of this beast). **The 7 heads are 7 mountains** (or hills), **on which the woman** (wife; harlot) **sits."** (Dwells/resides. So this unfaithful woman resides on 7 hills. Most see this an obvious picture of Rome, who was the gentile world ruler at the time John wrote Revelation, and Rome had 2 ½ decades prior, destroyed the temple in Jerusalem in 70 AD. Biblically, metaphorical mountains are often symbolling of world kingdoms, e.g. **Jer. 51:24-25**; **Dan. 2:35, 44-45**). **10-"And there are 7 kings: 5 are fallen, and 1 is, and the other is** (has) **not yet come; and when he comes, he must continue** (remain) **a short space."** (*Gr:oligos-puny, brief, short, season, time; "brief time;"* some say the 7 heads or 7 mountains are also the 7 kings; more on these kings to follow). **11-"and the beast that was, and is not,** (seems the same political/religious beast. The 3rd time this phrase is repeated, twice in **17:8**,) **even he is the 8th** (king/ ruler)**, and is of the 7** (kings/rulers)**, "and goes into perdition."** (Destruction or damnation. Uses the same descriptive phrase and end result for the beast in **17:8**. So, who are these 7 kings (5 fallen, 1 current, 1 to come)? 4 main views: 1) Roman Emperors-there were 10 before Domitian who was the current emperor at the time of John's writing, and many after, so difficult to have only *"5 fallen,"* 1 that *"is,"* and 1 *"yet to come,"* when there were 71 unified Roman emperors and 16 more if you consider only the western empire, though those that hold this view discuss the end-times start the 5 fallen.[28] 2)-Roman Catholic Popes-again this is greatly disputed as to the real names, numbers, beginning, succession, and all lists have lots of caveats of what most Catholics believe is currently 266 Popes, which doesn't reconcile to the 7 kings, and the kings seem more politically or militarily focused than religious, and the Pope(s) would more logically align with the end time Harlot or 2nd Beast/ False Prophet fighting with and then finally destroyed by the 10 kings, but some write interesting timings relating to 1798 pope removal and the 1929 Lateran Treaty establishing the papal state in Rome, Italy. 3) Roman Forms of Government- the *"5 fallen"* are Kings, Consuls, Dictators, Decemvirs, and Military Tribunals, and the 1 that *"is,"* or the 6th king or rule during the time John was in prison, was the Imperial form of government that had replaced the other forms, and they believe that the 7th king *"yet to come,"* is the rise of this fallen empire after several hundred years, and the beast is the 8th, or deadly wounded and then healed head of ***Rev. 13:3, 12, 14***-interesting, Walter Scott and Dr. C.I. Scofield,[29] hold this view, though the fallen government forms seem so similar as to not make as much sense to me. 4) World Empires-7 evil gentile global/world empires persecuting Israel, culminating with the 8th king, the beast, *"that was"*-several lists of these exist, but I like: Egypt, Assyria, Babylon, Medo-Persia, Greece (1st 5), held by *Dr. Roy L. Aldrich*[30] *and Dr. John MacArthur in his Study Bible.*[31] *T*hese Gentile global empires persecuting Israel had already fallen in John's time. All are familiar with Egypt in Exodus, and Assyria battled and finally took Israel captive in 722 BC; and Babylon, Medo-Persia, and Greece were clearly prophesied in ***Daniel 2*** and *7*], *"is"*- Rome [during John's time and also prophesied by Daniel, the 6th], *"yet is to come," "not yet is"*-Rome Revived [7th and the beast that is 8th and of the 7, that is wounded and revived; what most describe as the Roman empire loosely enduring, but the imperial aspect of the Roman empire is what is to be restored that had died, although many describe the beast as the individual Antichrist dying and being miraculously healed by the False Prophet. The next most popular list starts with Babylon and ends with Rome, that gets repeated to get the 7/8 kings, but not as clear as 1st list]-I lean towards View 4 [Roman Empires] as it seems most consistent historically, consistent with the context of ***Revelation***, with ***Rev. 13*** and ***17-18*** beast descriptions, and with the OT, including Daniel's descriptions of the 5 gentile beasts/kingdoms/

empires going forward from John with the final revived 1 being destroyed by Christ. See *Dr. J. Dwight Pentecost, "Things To Come," for detail and* discussion of main views.[32] It seems evident that this evil empire ending in the Beast, truly embodies the final push of the gentile world rulers/governments against the King of Kings, as we'll see in *17:14*). *12*-"*And the 10 horns which you saw are 10 kings, which have received no kingdom yet; but receive power* (authority) *as kings 1 hour* (season) *with the beast."* (So horns/ kings later receive their rule for a short time with the beast in this final gentile world government/empire). *13*-"*These* (10 kings) *have 1 mind* (Gr:gnome-cognition, opinion, resolve, judgment, mind, purpose, will), *and shall give their power and strength (*authority and power) *unto the beast."* (The 10 kings are united voluntarily giving their strength to the beast, this leader of the final world government/empire). *14*-"*These* (the Beast's 10 kings) *shall make war with the Lamb* (Jesus, pictured as the substitute sacrificed Savior), *and the Lamb* (Jesus) *shall overcome* (conquer) *them* (10 kings, leading world governments): *for He* (Jesus) *is Lord* (Supreme authority) *of lords* (5 times in Bible, all of Jesus, *17:14*; *19:16*; *Deu. 10:17*; *Psa. 136:3*; *1Ti. 6:15*), *and King of kings* (the only time Lord of lords and King of kings is together in the Bible, applies only to Christ. He is the true sovereign king vs the beast and 10 earthly temporary subservient ones)*: and they* (the Church, Christians, believers, saved) *that are with Him* (Jesus. We'll then be ecstatic to say, "we're with Him") *are called* (invited), *and chosen* (elect/ selected), *and faithful."* (Believing/true/sure. We will be sure and faithful because Jesus has saved us and made us that way-here even bodily glorified. Praise to our conquering Lord and King).}

C. *17:15-18*— (cf. *17:7*; *Mat. 5:18*) {Title: The 10 Kings Unite to Burn the Harlot According to God's Will. *15*-"*And he* (the angel explaining the mystery, cf. *17:7*) *says to me* (John), '*The waters which you* (John) *saw, where the whore* (harlot) *sits, are peoples, and multitudes, and nations, and tongues.'"* (This harlot has a great world-wide influence). *16*-"*And the 10 horns which you saw upon the beast* (carrying the Harlot. Most believe this is Political Babylon, secular, the City/State, the 10-nation confederacy, the revived Roman Empire, the last Gentile world government), *these* (10 kings) *shall hate* (detest) *the whore* (harlot, seems the religious world leader), *and shall make her* (harlot) *desolate and naked, and shall eat her* (harlot) *flesh, and burn* (down/consume wholly) *her* (harlot) *with fire."* (So these 10 horns/kings will hate and destroy the Harlot-leading the 1-world religion, which people now seem to only worship the beast or they die). *17*-"*For* (Because) *God has put* (given) *in their* (10 kings') *hearts to do His* (God's) *will* (purpose)*, and to agree* (do 1 will/purpose/ judgment)*, and give their* (10 kings') *kingdom unto the beast* (political/economical/ military 1-world government)*, until the words of God shall be fulfilled."* (Completed. God's sovereign will and judgment is being accomplished on the harlot by the unified evil 10 kings. Not 1 jot or tittle will pass away until God's Word is fulfilled, cf. *Mat. 5:18*). *18*-"*And the woman* (wife; Harlot) *which you* (John) *saw, is that great city* (symbolic Babylon believed to be Rome)*, which reigns over the kings* (sounds like more than just the 10) *of the earth."* (Again, the natural, worldly government and system).}

Application (Activity/Questions)

A. The Harlot and the Beast are both Religious and Political Babylon. Which is more like the 1st Political Beast led by the Antichrist and which is more like the 2nd Religious Beast led by the False Prophet in *Rev. 13*, and why? {The Harlot-like Religious False Prophet 1-World Religious Leader-dress, communion cup, unfaithful to God; Beast-like Antichrist leading the 1-World Political/Economic/Military Government as has kings, empires, and ultimately destroys the harlot/1-World False Church once the Antichrist has the false church's power.}

B. What false church leader (now and historically) is strong enough to lead the 1-World church, and why? {A Pope is probably the only current world-wide religious leader capable and tied to past and some current governments, that has been responsible for many martyrs of believers and infidels in Crusades and Inquisitions, that has had many idols or expensive artifacts, and is on the 7 Hills of Rome, Italy.}

C. Who do you think are the 7 Kings: Emperors, Popes, Government Forms, or World Empires, and why? {I believe World Empires as most consistent historically, best fits context, aligns with OT and Daniel beasts/kingdoms/empire prophecies, numbers best agree, and the last seems to be the final gentile 1-World government.}

D. Who are the 10 Kings? {Leaders of the final 10-nation confederacy who voluntarily give their power to the Antichrist and his final Revived Roman/Evil Gentile Empire.}

E. What will happen to all who fight against Jesus and those faithful to Him (*17:14*)? {Those against Jesus will be overcome/judged and sadly ultimately be in Hell; and those with Him will win and rule with Him in heaven for all eternity.}

F. How does secular Political Babylon and man's works centered Religious Babylon's substitutes pull on your heart, mind, and time today? {I seem to chase money, fame, materialism, works/ tasks... instead of Jesus and eternal things...but want to stop now!}

Figure 19 – 25.1 The Whore of Babylon[33]

Wicked Wail but Righteous Rejoice at God's Final
Just Judgment on Babylon.

The Final Fall of Babylon

Introduction

A. What worldview, value system, or cravings does the unsaved world pursue? {Wealth-$, materialism-things, hedonism-pleasure, sex, comfort, temporary happiness, fame; control, self-our way vs God's way.}

B. How separate do you live from the unsaved, and can those around you tell a difference? {Not as much as I should, some, especially when mention Jesus, Bible, gospel, or politically incorrect... *FYI, just shortly after the flood (_**Gen. 11:1-10**_), wicked men tried to unite the earth to build a city and tower to heaven for man's rule, not God's, and God separated all their languages at the Tower of Babel, in Shinar which many believe became Babylon.}

Scripture (Observations/Interpretation/Commentary)
{13/24 verses begin with and showing action.}

A. **_18:1-3_**— {Title: Great Babylon is Fallen, Fornicating with Nations, Kings, and Merchants. **_1_**-"**_And after these things_** (overview of the Babylonian Harlot and Beast, conquered by Christ) **_I_** (John) **_saw another_** (a different) **_angel come down_** (descending) **_from heaven, having great power_** (privilege/authority); **_and the earth was lightened_** (_Gr:photizo-brightened up, enlightened, illuminated_) **_with his glory._**" (Every angel or person in God's presence reflects the light of God's glory). **_2_**-"**_And he_** (angel) **_cried mightily_** (forcefully) **_with a strong voice, saying, 'Babylon the great is fallen, is fallen_** (doubly emphasized and true, contrary to belief), **_and is become the habitation_** (dwelling place) **_of devils_** (demons), **_and the hold_** (_Gr:phulake-guarding, place, cage, hold_) **_of every foul_** (impure) **_spirit_** (demon), **_and a cage of every unclean_** (or foul; Jewish picture of unclean, like a vulture eating dead...) **_and hateful_** (detestable) **_bird_** (foul)." (Pictures an unseen spiritual battle of demons in man's Babylonian empire). **_3_**-**_For all nations_** (non-Jewish/pagans) **_have drunk of the wine of the wrath of her fornication_** (adultery/ idolatry; all pagans have been impaired by the Harlot's adultery/idolatry), **_and the_**

kings of the earth have committed (practiced) **fornication** (adultery/idolatry) **with her** (the married Harlot), **and the merchants** (wholesalers) **of the earth** (again worldly) **are waxed rich** (Gr:plouteo- to become wealthy, to be made or wax rich; Aorist Active Indicative, "have become wealthy") **through** (out of) **the abundance** (Gr:dunamis- force, power, strength) **of her** (Harlot's) **delicacies.'"** (Gr:strenos- straining, strenuousness, voluptuousness, luxuries. A picture of the world government and system straining to compel the hearts and attentions of mankind. So, a glorious angel announces that the Great Babylon, the Gentile 1-World Government (not just the literal original Babylon that took Judah captive in 586 BC, but the metaphorical global gentile governments throughout history) that culminate in the final Babylon (revived Roman empire) that men have looked to to save them truly has fallen, the 1 that every pagan nation, king, and businessman has been in bed with and worshiped at the idol of power, money, and sexual infidelity...Now they have a hangover, the Harlot's wrath with her adulterer, and this gentile government is now a place for unclean vultures and demons with all the dead casualties. So don't unite with the world or the false church).}

B. 18:4-8— {Title: God Calls His People Out and Completely Judges the Harlot/Babylon. **4**-**"And I** (John) **heard another** (different) **voice** (unsure if God the Father, Son, or an angel) **from heaven, saying, 'Come out of her** (Harlot/Babylon) **my** (could be God's or possibly an angel like Michael, Israel's angelic prince, cf. **Dan. 10:21**) **people** (saved, probably mostly Jews), **that** (Gr:hina-purpose) **you be not partakers of her** (Harlot's/Babylon's) **sins, and that** (Gr:hina-purpose) **you receive not of her** (Harlot's/Babylon's) **plagues."** **5**-**"For her** (Harlot's/Babylon's) **sins have reached unto** (as far as) **heaven, and God has remembered** (Gr:mnemonic-exercise memory, recollect, [implies punish], rehearse, make mention, be mindful, remember; so God didn't forget, God has rehearsed or made mention to punish) **her** (Harlot's/Babylon's) **iniquities** (evil doings).**" 6**-**"Reward** (Recompense/requite) **her** (Harlot's/ Babylon's) **even as she** (Harlot) **rewarded you** (Israel and saved believers), **and double unto her** (Harlot) **double according to her** (Harlot's) **works: in the cup** (picture of judgment that must be drunk) **which she** (Harlot) **has filled** (poured out), **fill** (pour) **to her** (Harlot/Babylon) **double.'"** (A bad triple double, referencing double judgment 3 times. So, God's people are asked to doubly judge the Harlot/Babylon). **7**-**"How much she** (Harlot) **has glorified herself** (Harlot/Babylon), **and lived deliciously** (been luxurious), *so much torment and sorrow* (grief) *give her* (Harlot)*: for* (because) *she* (Harlot) *says in her* (Harlot's) *heart, 'I sit* (remain) *a queen, and am no widow, and shall see no sorrow.'" 8-"Therefore shall her* (Harlot's/Babylon's) *plagues come in 1 day, death, and mourning* (grief/sorrow)*, and famine; and she* (Harlot/ Babylon) *shall be burned* (down) *with fire: for* (because) *strong* (mighty/powerful/ valiant) *is the Lord* (Supreme authority) *God who judges her."* (The Harlot/Babylon).}

C. *18:9-10*— {Title: Earthly Kings Wail and Withdraw from Judged Harlot/Babylon. *9-"And the kings of the earth, who have committed fornication* (adultery/idolatry) *and lived deliciously* (luxuriously) *with her* (Harlot/Babylon) *shall bewail* (will wail aloud for) *her* (Harlot)*, and lament* (Gr:kopto-beat the breast in grief, lament, mourn, wail; worldly sorrow for their loss, not God's just anger) *for her* (Harlot/ Babylon)*, when they shall see* (behold) *the smoke of her* (Harlot's/ Babylon's) *burning,"* 10-"*Standing afar off* (was partying close with this Harlot, now standing back far away) *for the of fear of her* (Harlot's/Babylon's) *torment* (not fearing God or learning why just, but only fearing being a recipient of her torment)*, saying, 'Alas* (Woe)*, alas* (woe)*, that great city Babylon, that mighty* (Rome called Valentia by Romans, in Latin and in Greek both mean "*strong*") *city! For in 1 hour* (instant) *has your judgment come.'"*}

D. *18:11-20*— {Title: Wicked Merchants Wail, While Righteous Rejoice Over Babylon's Fall. *11-"And the merchants* (wholesalers) *of the earth* (again worldly) *shall weep* (wail aloud) *and mourn over her* (Harlot's/Babylon's)*; for* (because) *no man* (one) *buys their* (not just "*her*" [singular, the Harlot, City, or False Prophet], but plural, all those participating in "*her*" adulterous/idolatrous ways) *merchandise any more:" 12-"The merchandise* (cargo) *of gold, and sliver, and precious stones* (gems)*, and pearls* (Gr: margarites-pearl [because of the partying going on prior to destruction, thought you'd appreciate the drink word]. So 4 items of expensive jewelry, now 4 items of expensive clothing), *and fine linen, and purple* (expensive dyed garments)*, and silk, and scarlet* (crimson)*, and all thyine wood* (expensive fragrant wooden articles)*, and all manner vessels* (implements/equipment) *of ivory* (Gr:elephantinos-of ivory)*, and all manner vessels of most precious* (valuable wood)*, and of brass* (or copper)*, and iron, and marble,"* (6 expensive vessels to use or contain other things), *13-"And cinnamon, and odors* (incense)*, and ointments* (myrrh. 3 three expensive spices, oils or ointments)*, and frankincense, and wine, and oil (olive), and fine flour, and wheat (or corn), and beasts (domestic animals), and sheep, and horses, and chariots, and slaves (bodies), and souls of men (not eternal focus, but wailing over "Babylon's" evil selling of these things, trading in the very souls of men as they saw their soulful songs and cries. Rome commonly sold slaves). 14-"And the fruits that your soul lusted after are departed (gone) from you, and all things which were dainty (sumptuous) and goodly (radiant/bright/gorgeous) are departed from you, and you shall find them no more at all (Gr:ouketi ou me-now no more, then a double negative, emphatically no never; God's judgment of Babylon is sure and permanent). 15-"The merchants (wholesalers) of these things, which were made rich by her (Harlot/Babylon), shall stand afar off (2nd time stated, cf. 18:10; even world separates from the Harlot/ Babylon when she is receiving judgment) for the fear of her torment, weeping (wailing) and wailing," (Mourning/grieving), 16-"and saying, 'Alas (Woe), alas (woe), that great city (metaphorical Babylon or Daniel's revived 4th Beast and John's 7th King/Kingdom, Rome), that was clothed (arrayed) in fine linen, and purple (expensive), and scarlet (crimson), and decked in gold, and precious (costly) stones (gems), and pearls!'" (Wicked still amazed that someone/some place that looked that great on the outside is gone that quickly). 17-"For in 1 hour (instant) so great riches (wealth) is come (laid) to nought (waste/made desolate; repeats 18:2, 8 of her rapid fall again), and every ship-master (captain), and all the company (multitude/crowd, like travelers or slaves) in (or on the) ships, and sailors, and as many as trade by sea, stood afar off," (3rd time; repeating the distance from Babylon's judgment 18:10, 15), 18-"and cried when they (wicked partners) saw (beheld) the smoke of her (Babylon's) burning, saying, 'What city is ("city is" is supplied to make sure understand the focus, as seen by KJV italics) like unto this (the) great city!'" (This evil gentile symbolic city or empire, Babylon is called the "great city" 8 times in Revelation, 5 in chapter 18). 19-"And they (the wicked partners of Babylon's corruption) cast (threw) dust (or dirt) on their heads, and cried, weeping and wailing, saying, 'Alas (Woe), alas (woe), that great city (again the metaphorical Babylon or evil gentile government), wherein (in which) were made rich (wealthy) all that had ships in the sea by reason of her costliness (magnificence)! For (Because) in 1 hour (instant) is she made (laid) desolate (waste)." (Shows the response of the wicked to her surprising instantaneous and final judgment. Now he'll contrast with the righteous' response to God's patient justice). *20-"Rejoice* (Be in a good frame of mind; Present Passive Imperative, a continuous passive command) *over her* (Harlot/Babylon), *you* ("*you*" not in Greek, but supplied as personifying heaven by all its participants, so KJV supplies as seen by italics) *heaven* (so all in God's good place), *and you* (again supplied in KJV as are already in heaven too) *holy apostles* (NT spiritual leaders), *and prophets* (OT spiritual leaders); *for* (because) *God has avenged you* (plural; as all saints throughout the ages) *on* (or out of) *her* (judged by taking God's people out of metaphorical Babylon or the evil gentile governments that have oppressed all believers of all times, both Old and New Testament, especially the spiritual leaders).}

E. *18:21-24*— {Title: Violent Babylon, Violently Destroyed Never to Rise Again. *21-"And a mighty angel took* (lifted) *up a stone like a great milestone* (grinder), *and cast it into the sea, saying, 'Thus* (in this manner) *with violence shall that* (the) *great city Babylon be thrown down, and shall be found no more at all."* ("*Henceforth no never;*" emphatic double negative; certainty, no more evil world powers will ever be established). *22-"And the voice* (sound) *of harpers, and musicians, and of pipers* (flute players)*, and trumpeters, shall be heard no more at all* (after another "*no never*" or emphatic double negative) *in you* (singular, personal, as if speaking directly to Babylon/Rome in John's day, which was persecuting and killing all the Apostles, except John was now imprisoned); *and no craftsman* (artisan/builder), *of whatever craft* (art/occupation) *he be* ("*he be*" is supplied to make sure you understand it is talking about the different tradesmen), *shall be found any more* (after that "*no never*" or emphatic double negative again) *in you* (again very personal directly to evil government); *and the sound of a milestone* (grinder) *shall be heard no more at all* (again "*henceforth no never*" or an emphatic double negative; that dogmatically states that no more sounds of work or productivity will be heard ever again) *in you;"* (again very personal. So no musicians, no occupations, and no work will ever be found there again); *23-"And the light of a candle* (lamp) *shall shine* (lighten/be seen) *no more at all* (again "*no never*" or emphatic double negative) *in you* (again singular, personal); *and the voice* (sound) *of the bridegroom and of the bride shall be heard no more at all* (again an emphatic double negative; certainty; not only emphasizing no more great joy, intimacy and purpose of marriage of repopulating this city) *in you* (again, personal to this wicked worldwide gentile government city): *for* (because) *your merchants* (wholesalers) *were the great men* (lords) *of the earth* (worldly leaders); *for* (because; 2nd reason) *by your sorceries* (*Gr: pharmakeia-medication, magic, sorcery, witchcraft; where we get pharmacy*) *were all nations* (Gr:ethnos-races, gentiles, heathens) *deceived* (seduced/gone astray)." **24**-"*And in her* (leaves the personal you and reminds us that "*in her,*" the Harlot/ Babylon, the heart of the evil violent gentile world government/economy/ military) *was found the blood of prophets* (both OT, NT, and Tribulation believers that speak up in the truth), *and of saints* (all believers), *and of all that were slain* (butchered/slaughtered/ maimed) *upon the earth* (martyrs and persecuted/wounded by the worldly system; cf. **11:7**; **16:6**; **17:6**; **19:2**. Makes you long for God's just judgment on such evil of man's best attempts to rule his own wicked companions, but is corrupted to violently destroy the righteous and God's chosen nation and ultimate reign by His Son Jesus Christ, the righteous King of Kings and Lord of Lords).}

Application (Activity/Questions)

A. How do you see God's sovereign hand throughout the history of man's rule being a help for all to see whose way is best? {Yes, it's historically proven that man's absolute power corrupts absolutely, and leads to violent wars and judgment, while God's leads to peaceful praise and abundant eternal life with the only perfect benevolent ruler. Lots of historical examples, including the founding of America, Israel's becoming a nation and winning back Jerusalem...}

B. Why should we live separately from worldly people (**18:4**)? {So we don't receive any of her judgment or become like them; **2Co. 6:17**- "*come out from among them, and be ye separate, says the Lord...and I will receive you.*"}

C. What ways are you spending your life, free time, energy, thinking, concerns...that make you look like a citizen of Babylon and not a citizen of heaven? {Seeking money, fame or praise of man, comfort, my way, rejoicing more in economy that eternal...}

D. Do you love God more than you love the world or "*Babylon*" and what does that say about your inner allegiances and affections (cf. **James 4:4**)? {Yes, when I do separate, it shows by my heart and actions that I have chosen to love God enough to abandon anything or anyone that pulls me away from God.}

E. What desire, activity, time thief, or worldly thinking may God be calling you out of today? {Too much TV, not enough doing eternal things, too much working more money, security, or things...}

F. What will happen to a life lived for anything other than God? {Goes up in smoke or judgment in the end and loses joy and often even health now.}

Praise God; the Testimony of Jesus: His Wedding, 2nd Coming, and Wicked Defeated by the Word of the Lamb.

The Lamb's Heavenly Wedding and King Coming in Earthly Judgment {Jesus' Heavenly Wedding to the Church, His earthly 2nd Coming with the Church, and His judgment of the Wicked into Hell. Includes 4 Location, Role, and Action Tables for Christ, Church, and Israel in Relationship with His 1st and 2nd Comings and Rapture.}

Introduction

A. Who do you think would win in a fight, the Omnipotent Christ or all creation? {Not even a fight, Jesus would easily win; and we'll see today He does against all living wicked.}

B. What is the most exciting wedding you've ever been to, and why? {Mine, my beautiful wife, our promises to each other, the promise of a life together, and our intimacy to follow.}

C. What do you think is the most exciting testimony of Jesus? {His gospel and work in me, His Rapture of Church/me, His sanctification and glorification Christians/me, His promise of heaven with Him forever for all Christians and me.}

D. What religions or cults Do or Don't believe in Hell? {11 listed below from largest to smallest with approximate members, B=Billion, M=Million, K=Thousand; 6/11 "Don't" believe in Hell, and only 2/11 believe in Hell and that it is final and inescapable.}

1. **Christian/Christianity** (2.2B) {Do.}
2. **Muslim/Islamism** (1.6B) {Do.}
3. **Catholic/Catholicism** (1.2B) {Do, but believe 1 can escape after death from purgatory; some show as part of Christian.}
4. **Hindu/Hinduism** (1B) {Don't, believe in reincarnation.}
5. **Buddhist/Buddhism** (500M) {Do, but believe in only a temporary Hell (get reincarnated out of Hell).}
6. **Adventist/7th Day Adventist** (25M) {Don't, believe in annihilation, or soul sleep.}
7. **Mormon/Mormonism** (14.8M) {Do, but only believe in a temporary Hell.}
8. **Witness/Jehovah's Witnesses** (8.2M) {Don't, believe in soul cessation.}
9. **Unitarian/Unitarianism** (800K) {Don't, hold all go to heaven.}

10. **Wiccan/Witchcraft** (140K?) {Don't, believe in no punishment or reward.}
11. **Scientologist/Scientology** (25K) {Don't.}

<u>Scripture</u> (Observations/Interpretation/Commentary)
{17/21 verses begin with "*and*" showing continued action.}
A. _19:1-4_— {Title: Heavenly Praise of God's Truth and Justice on the Babylonian Harlot. **_1_-"And after these things** (the Fall of Babylon / the False Church and leader) **_I_** (John) **heard a great voice of much** (many) **people in heaven, saying, 'Alleluia** (*Gr:allelouia-Alleluia, Praise ye yah; from Hebrew-hallelu-yah*: Hallelujah, Praise Yah[wey]; only 4 times in Bible, all in **_Rev. 19_**, **_19:1, 3-4, 6_**; where we get the anonymous song, "*Hallelu, hallelu, hallelu, hallelujah! Praise ye the Lord! Praise ye the Lord, Hallelujah. Praise ye the Lord, Hallelujah. Praise ye the Lord, Hallelujah. Praise ye the Lord!*" We also get the famous "*Hallelujah Chorus,*" from Handel's Messiah, based on 3 Revelation verse phrases: "*Hallelujah! For the Lord God Omnipotent reigneth*" in **_19:6_**, "*The kingdoms of this world are become the kingdoms of our Lord, and of His Christ; and He shall reign for ever and ever*" in **_11:15_**, and "*King of Kings, and Lord of Lords*" in **_19:16_**); **salvation, and glory, and honor, and power, unto the Lord our God:'"** (4 great reasons to praise God): **_2_-"For** (why else praise God, because) **true** (truthful) **and righteous** (just) **are His judgments: for He** (God) **has judged the great whore** (Harlot)**, which** (who) **did corrupt the earth** (including its occupants) **with her fornication** (adultery/idolatry, again against God)**, and** (God) **has avenged the blood of His** (God's) **servants** (serving even unto blood and probably death, martyrs) **at** (out of) **her** (Harlot's) **hand." _3_-"And again** (2nd time) **they** (many heavenly people) **said, 'Alleluia.' And her** (Harlot's) **smoke rose up for ever and ever."** (A picture of eternal Hell coming in **_19:20_**). **_4_-"And the 24 elders** (all crowned and enthroned believers in white, cf. **_4:4_**) **and the 4 beasts** (living creatures; 6-winged, many eyed, angelic Seraphims) **fell down and worshiped God that sat** (present participle, "*sitting,*" showing continual rule) **on the throne, saying, 'Amen** (truly/let it be so)**; Alleluia** (Praise).'"}
B. _19:5-8_— {Title: Praise God for the Marriage of the Lamb and His Prepared Church. (Greek paragraph starts here, but some include verse 5 in prior paragraph). **_5_-"And a voice came out of the throne** (this voice commanding praise, seems a key believer as we're told is John's brother in Christ, cf. **_19:9-10_**), **saying, 'Praise our God, all you**

His (God's) *servants, and you that fear Him* (God), *both* (even) *small* (*Gr:micros-least, little, small*) *and great.'"* (*Gr:megas-big, great, strong*). **6**-*"And I* (John) *heard as it were the voice* (sound) *of a great multitude, and as* (just like) *the voice* (sound) *of many* (or great) *waters, and as* (just like) *the voice* (sound) *of mighty thunderings* (roarings), *saying, 'Alleluia* (Praise; because the true and right 1 reigns)! *For the Lord God Omnipotent* (praise as the 1 with all power can ensure justice) *reigns.'"* **7**-*"Let us* (Church age believers, cf. **19:14**) *be glad* (*Gr:chairo-be glad, joyful, rejoice*) *and rejoice* (*Gr:agalliao-be exceedingly glad, exceedingly joyful, greatly rejoice*; joy is building), *and give honor* (glory/praise-a reasonable response to such joy that God Who has all power reigns) *to Him* (Christ): *for the marriage* (wedding) *of the Lamb* (Jesus) *is* (has) *come, and His* (Christ's) *wife* (Church, was bride, now is wife) *has made herself ready."* **8**-*"And to her* (Church) *was granted* (given) *that* (*Gr:hina-purpose*) *she* (Church) *should be arrayed in fine linen, clean* (pure) *and white* (radiant/gorgeous): *for the fine linen is the righteousness of saints."* (Church, saved, dressed in white, without spot and blemish due to the righteousness given by Christ, cf. **Isa. 61:10**; **Eph. 5:26-27**. Obvious contrast of Christ's judgment on the filthy dressed in scarlet Harlot, due to the wicked works of the unsaved shedding blood/killing saints and even Jesus).}

C. **19:9-10**— {Title: The Testimony of Jesus is the Spirit of Prophecy; Blest if Invited to His Wedding (especially as Wife). **9**-*"And he* (a key believer, cf. **19:5, 10**) *says unto me* (John), *'Write, Blessed* (Happy) *are they which* (those who) *are called* (invited; Bible Study Fellowship (2018) notes say that the Bride=the entire Church and the Wedding Guests=individual believers) *unto the marriage supper of the Lamb* (Jesus)*.' and he* (key believer) *says unto me* (John), *'These are the true sayings* ("words;" *Gr: logos-word, reasoning, motive, doctrine*; Word used of Jesus by John in **John 1:1, 14**, and the very words of Jesus in the Parable of the Wedding Feast in **Mat. 22:1-14**) *of God.'"* **10**-*"And I* (John) *fell at his* (key believer's, probably with Christ's glory shining and reflected on his face) *feet to worship him* (key believer), *and he* (key believer) *says to me* (John), *'See you do it not* (Take heed not/never/forbear; don't do it)*: I am your fellow servant* (co-slave; servant with the same master)*, and of your brethren* (brothers, saved, maybe even Jewish, maybe even from the Tribulation Period) *that* (who) *have the testimony* (*Gr:marturia-testimony, witness, record, evidence given*) *of Jesus: worship God: for the testimony of Jesus is* *the spirit of prophecy."* (All Scriptural or other predictions point to Christ, *"who is our life,"* cf. **Col. 3:4** and our future. This is the answer and fulfillment of Jesus' High Priestly Prayer in **John 17** for the Church to be sanctified and glorified by the Word to be 1 with Christ, with the intimacy Jesus has with God, and receive eternal abundant joyful life as we believe in the testimony of Jesus. Our response can only be worship).}

D. **19:11-16**— {Title: The Eternal **King's 2ⁿᵈ Coming** with His Church in Judgment by His Word. **11-"And I saw heaven opened, and behold a white horse** (picture of a valiant just warrior)**; and He** (Jesus) **that** (Who) **sat** (present participle, *"was sitting"*) **upon him** (it, horse) **was called** (present passive participle, *"is being called,"*) **Faithful** (Trustworthy) **and True** (cf. **John 14:6**; Jesus always keeps His promises, His Character=Words=Deeds), **and in righteousness He** (Jesus) **does judge and make war." 12-"His eyes** (vision) **were as a flame** (flash) **of fire** (or lightening; cf. **1:14**; **2:18**; picture of consuming evil with a glance), **and on His** (Christ's) **head were** ("were" is supplied in KJV emphasizing He has always been crowned or authorized to rule and judge even when He hasn't judged and was merciful) **many crowns** (*Gr:diadema-royal crown, emphasizing His right to rule/judge*, not *Gr:stephanos-victory crown*); **and He** (Jesus) **had** (had and is having) **a name written** (Perfect Passive Participle-means completed action in the past with continuing results in the present, passive-not written by Him, but by God-the-Father), **that no man** (none/no one/nothing) **knew** (understood; Perfect Tense-in past and don't know today), **but He** (Jesus) **Himself."** (Only Jesus knows and understands the name that God has given Him). **13-"And He** (Jesus) **was clothed** (arrayed) **with a vesture** (garment/robe) **dipped** (stained) **in blood** (both clothed and dipped are Perfect Passive Participles-completed action with continuing results, demonstrating that Christ's past shed blood lasts forever and accomplished eternal results paying for all our sin and allowing us to be clothed in righteousness/white): **and His** (Jesus') **name** (authority/character) **is called** (Perfect Passive Indicative- *"has been and is being called,"* factually) **the Word of God."** (A name we can and do know, the final Revelation, *"the Word of His power"* [**Heb. 1:3**], by which He created the universe, the Word, and the embodiment of all the promises of God, Who is the Truth, and cannot lie—your sins have been and continue to be forgiven by the precious blood of Christ, God's Word has promised it, and God's Word, Jesus, has accomplished it. This is the *"testimony of Jesus"*). **14-"And** the armies which were ("which were" is supplied as implied to show saints on the move as Jesus moves; as **1Th. 4:17** promised us at the Church Rapture we would always "*be with the Lord*") **in heaven** (clearly the Church comes with Him at His 2nd Coming, possibly even angels) **followed** (union of true disciples) **Him** (Jesus) **upon white horses, clothed in fine linen, white and clean.**" (Pure; we never have to leave Jesus again; we go where He goes...). **15**-"**And out of His** (Jesus') **mouth goes** (proceeds) **a sharp** (swift) **sword** (Biblical metaphor for God's Word, cf. **Eph. 6:17**; **Heb. 4:12**; **2Th. 2:8**), **that** (*Gr:hina-purpose*) **with it** (sword of God's Word) **He** (Jesus) **should smite** (strike down) **the nations** (non-Jewish/ unsaved): **and He** (Jesus) **shall rule** (shepherd/feed, even the wicked during the Millennial Kingdom will have a benevolent and loving ruler whether they want Him or not) **them** (nations) **with a rod** (staff/ scepter) **of iron** (hard warring metal, symbolic of the revived Roman empire with the legs of iron and feet/toes of iron/clay that Jesus is conquering, cf. **Dan 2**): **and He** (Jesus) **treads** (or tramples) **the wine press** (a picture of divine judgment where wine represents the blood coming from evil people. Jesus 1st died for their sin in their place, but those rejecting His death and grace will justly die for themselves) **of the fierceness and wrath of Almighty** (Omnipotent/All Powerful; fully capable of crushing all) **God.**" **16**-"**And He** (Jesus) **has on His** (Jesus') **vesture** (robe) **and on His** (Jesus') **thigh** (place of strength) **a name written** (Perfect Passive Participle-"*having been written*" [by God] with continuing results today), **King of Kings, and Lord of Lords.**" (Greek is proper case, but the KJV shows in all capital letters, as Jesus is Sovereign ruler over all sovereigns and supreme master over all masters; a title that can only be applicable for God, found quoted exactly here in **19:16** and 1 other place in **1Ti. 6:15**; and once with the order reversed "*Lord of Lords, and King of Kings*" in **Rev. 17:14**. Interesting, Christ's 2nd Coming with the Church continues to emphasis Him as new Groom with His newlywed Bride, the Church, without switching back to Israel, which has been enduring, and is ready to be delivered from this terrible Tribulation Period of Seals, Trumpets, and Vial judgments. He chose not to emphasize the deliverance from this "*rod*" of testing-**Eze. 20:37**, that prepared the hearts of Israel, "*to look on Him Whom they pierced*"-**Joh. 19:37**, and repent, turn to Him, and say that they are with Him at His 2nd Coming, "*so all Israel shall be saved*"-**Rom. 11:26**. He could have punctuated the change of this country consciousness or national conscience from arrogant rejection crying "*crucify Him,*" thru guilt, repentance, and faith, where they will say *"crown Him"* or *"we're with Him"* as He delivers and saves all Israel from her enemies. However, instead of the lowly meek and mild baby not answering a word at His 1st Advent, here, He comes with the Church to save Israel on a white war horse with His eyes and sword blazing with the judging Word of God at His 2nd Advent).}

E. ***19:17-21***— {Title: Wicked War with Jesus so Fowls Fill with Flesh; Antichrist and False Prophet Thrown Alive into Hell. ***17***-"***And I*** (John) ***saw an angel standing in the sun*** (**Psa. 104:4**; **Heb. 1:7**): ***and he cried with a loud voice, saying to all the fowls*** (birds) ***that fly*** (flying) ***in the midst of heaven*** (sky), ***'Come and gather yourselves together unto the supper*** (feast) ***of the great God*** (cf. ***Eze. 39:17-23***, a prophecy of fowls feasting and how Israel and Gentile nations will understand more of God's plan. Fowls' feast is contrasted with Wedding feast that the wicked rejected Christ and his wonderful invitation; now they are dinner); ***18***-"***That*** (Gr:hina-purpose) ***you may eat the flesh of kings, and the flesh of captains*** (a commander of a thousand)***, and the flesh of mighty*** (valiant) ***men, and the flesh of horses, and*** (the flesh) ***of them that sit on them*** (horse riders)***, and the flesh of all men*** (men is supplied in KJV as the focus of God's judgment, although truly includes horses also)***, both free and bond*** (enslaved)***, both*** (Gr:kai-and, even, also, both) ***small*** (least) ***and great."*** (5 times he repeats *"the flesh of"* for effect of the things about to be eaten. The angel has already been told God's plan for the enemies of God's followers. Ever wonder how vultures know something is about to die before it does? -Here God's angel tells them). ***19***-"***And I*** (John) ***saw the Beast*** (1st Beast, the Antichrist, the evil world ruler), ***and the kings of the earth*** (the ones God already described as part of the final evil gentile world empire who give their power to the 1st Beast/Antichrist), ***and their armies*** (the wickedly controlled military)***, gathered together to make war against Him*** (Christ; this is the Battle of Armageddon, cf. ***16:12-16***) ***that sat on the horse*** (doesn't say the white 1 since all of us are on white horses also), ***and against His*** (Christ's) ***army."*** (Us, the Raptured Church, believers that have come from heaven with Him). ***20***-(he skips past any battle, because when Christ fights there isn't really a battle as it is over before it starts). "***And the Beast*** (1st, the Antichrist) ***was taken, and with him*** (Antichrist) ***the False Prophet*** (2nd Beast, the remaining leader of the False 1-World Church that was destroyed by the kings) ***that wrought*** (was doing) ***miracles*** (or signs) ***before him*** (Antichrist), ***with*** (by) ***which he*** (False Prophet) ***deceived*** (seduced) ***them*** (wicked/

unsaved) ***that had received the mark of the Beast*** (Antichrist's 666), ***and them that worshiped his*** (Antichrist's) ***image. These both*** (Antichrist and False Prophet) ***were cast*** (thrown) ***alive*** (clearly not soul sleep, nor soul cessation, but alive) ***into a lake of fire burning with brimstone."*** (A literal, burning, terrible Hell). ***21-"And the remnant*** (*Gr:loipoi-remaining ones, remnant, residue, rest*; of the wicked Antichrist's armies) ***were slain*** (killed) ***with the sword*** (again a metaphor of God's Word judging) ***of Him*** (Christ) ***that sat upon the horse*** (interesting he continues to repeat this phrase of "*Him sitting upon the horse,*" either an amazing horse or maybe so he doesn't have to spend lots of words trying to describe Christ's greatness), ***which sword*** ("*sword*" is KJV supplied as clearly implied and a direct contextual reference from ***1:16***; ***2:12, 16***; ***19:15, 21***) ***proceeds out of His*** (Christ's) ***mouth*** (metaphorical picture of the Living Word, Christ, and by His Words judging): ***and all the fowls*** (birds) ***were filled*** (gorged) ***with their*** (wicked unsaved armies fighting against Christ and Israel) ***flesh."***}

Application (Activity/Questions)

A. What you think is the climax: Christ's Wedding, Return, Defeating Wicked, or All; why? {All; as it is the testimony of Jesus, Who Jesus is, who He loves, when He returns, how He will give all justice, and that we are with Him for it all...}

B. What is your response to being invited to be married to Jesus (***19:9-10***)? {YES! Not feeling adequate, but worship based on the adequacy that Jesus gave and gives me; pure joy and excitement.}

C. How can we cultivate joy and engagement excitement with Christ before the wedding? {Praising Him, spending time with Him, praying, thinking, talking about, and looking forward to it...}

D. Why do wicked choose the white war horse, rather than the red peaceful lamb (***19:11-13***)? {They don't believe the testimony of Jesus—that He will Judge or Save, their most regrettable choice.}

E. Can God be good, loving, and yet create an eternal place of judgment called Hell for many? {Yes, the Bible says so. God is good and loves us and is not willing for any to go there (cf. ***2Pe. 3:9***). Jesus died in the place of all, so none would have to go there, people who blaspheme and reject God's gift/Jesus do go there.}

F. Will all evil ultimately fall, will God create a heavenly utopia for us? {Yes, yes, yea! **Wanted to provide some bonus application questions that also provide a good review. Might be good to do together with your class or in groups if teaching.}

G. Must any prophetic event proceed the Rapture? {No, the Rapture is Imminent, or could happen at any time or moment.}

H. At least how many prophesied judgments alone must proceed the 2nd Coming of Christ? {21; 7 Seals, 7 Trumpets, and 7 Vials.}

I. What are some differences between the Rapture and 2nd Coming? {The Rapture: Imminent, Christ returns in Air; For Church, Prior to Trib...; 2nd Coming: After many prophecies, Christ returns to earth, For Israel/With Church, After many Trib events.}

J. Which is most accurate for Christ's 1st Coming? {Have students circle correct answers; 1st column has all the correct answers.}

1	Christ comes as ____	Baby/Discipler	Bridegroom	Warrior
2	Church ___ by Christ	Started/Built	Retrieved	Brought
3	Israel _____ Christ	Rejects/Kills	Receives Anti-	Receives

K. Which is most accurate for Christ's Rapture? {Have students circle correct answers; 2nd column has all the correct answers.}

1	Christ comes as ____	Baby/Discipler	Bridegroom	Warrior
2	Church ___ by Christ	Started/Built	Retrieved	Brought
3	Israel _____ Christ	Rejects/Kills	Receives Anti-	Receives

L. Which is most accurate for Christ's 2nd Coming? {Have students circle correct answers; 3rd column has all the correct answers.}

1	Christ comes as ____	Baby/Discipler	Bridegroom	Warrior
2	Church ___ by Christ	Started/Built	Retrieved	Brought
3	Israel _____ Christ	Rejects/Kills	Receives Anti-	Receives

M. What is the main location for each in each Chapter (H=Heaven; E=Earth)? {Can have students circle correct answer; #1/2=H, E, E; #3/4=H, H, E; #5=E, E, E, and #6=H, H, H.}

#	Chapter	Christ	Church	Israel
1	*Rev. 1*	H or E	H or E	H or E
2	*Rev. 2-3*	H or E	H or E	H or E
3	*Rev. 4-5*	H or E	H or E	H or E
4	*Rev. 6-18*	H or E	H or E	H or E
5	*Rev. 19-20*	H or E	H or E	H or E
6	*Rev. 21-22*	H or E	H or E	H or E

The Millennial Kingdom with Christ, Without Satan and
The Great White Throne Judgment.

Satan Bound, Saints Rule with Christ, God Judges, Wicked in Hell.
{Includes Pre, A, and Post-Millennial Views and Proponents
of Christ's 2nd Coming, with Clarification of 1st and 2nd Death
and Resurrection Participants.}

Introduction

A. What do you think the Millennial Kingdom will be like when Jesus is ruling on earth? {As close to heaven on earth (even with sin and death) as possible...}

B. Did you know Covenant Theologians believe there isn't a Millennium Kingdom, or we are in it now? {They don't believe in a literal physical peaceful earthly rule by Christ but believe that He is spiritually over the Church today and that fulfills God's many specific Kingdom promises to the nation of Israel.}

C. Read only 9 non-Revelation Facts about the Millennial Kingdom; DOES GOD SAY THIS? AND DO WE SEE THIS TODAY?

1. ***Isa. 11:6-9***; ***65:25***—Predatory animals will get along and be peaceful vegans? {Yes; No.}
2. ***Isa. 11:8***—Nursing and young children will safely play on poisonous snake dens? {Yes; No.}
3. ***Isa. 65:18-19***—Israel's capitol (Jerusalem) will have joy and no more crying? {Yes; No.}
4. ***Isa. 2:2-4***—Nations will not learn war and come to Jerusalem to hear Christ's law? {Yes; No.}
5. ***Mic. 4:1-4***—Christ ruling the nations who forged their farming equipment from military equipment? {Yes; No.}
6. ***Zec. 8:3***—Christ will dwell in, and Jerusalem will be called Faithful/True? {Yes; No.}
7. ***Mat. 19:28***; ***Luk. 22:29-30***—Apostles on 12 thrones, judging 12 Tribes of Israel? {Yes; No.}
8. ***Zec. 14:16***—Nations going to Jerusalem to worship Christ, or will not get any rain? {Yes; No.}
9. ***Isa. 65:20***—People will live way past 70, well over 100 years? {Yes; like Methuselah; No.}

D. Why can't the Millennial Kingdom be happening now or never? {Verses above, 100's of specific promises to Israel, such as their regathering, peace, their *"promised land,"* Church hasn't been taken to heaven (at the Rapture), yet...}

Scripture (Observations/Interpretation/Commentary)
{13/15 verse begin with *"and,"* showing continued action.}

A. ___20:1-3___— {Title: Angel Seizes, Binds, Casts in Bottomless Pit, Locks Pit, and Seals Satan 1,000 Years, so He Can't Deceive Nations. ___1-___*"And I* (John) *saw an angel* (probably the angel of the bottomless pit, whose Hebrew name is Abaddon [means destroying angel], and Greek name is Apollyon [means destroyer], cf. ___9:11___ commentary) *come down* (descend) *from* (out of) *heaven, having the key of the bottomless pit* (*"the bottomless pit,"* 7 times in Bible, all in ___Rev., 9:1-2, 11___; ___11:7___; ___17:8___; ___20:1, 3___) *and a great chain* (fetter/bonds) *in his* (angel's) *hand."* ___2-___ *"And he* (angel with the key and chain) *laid hold* (seized/held fast) *on the dragon* (13 of 19 times in Bible are in ___Rev.___, most in ___Rev. 12___, picturing this 7-headed murderous deceiver of the world, Satan), *that old* (*Gr:archaios-original, primeval, old*; conjures memory of the Garden of Eden, the 1st temptation of man, cf. ___Gen. 3:1-6, 14-15___) *serpent, which* (who) *is the Devil* (*Gr: diabolos-Satan, false accuser, devil, slanderer*), *and Satan* (in case any doubt, it is Satan), *and bound him* (Satan) *1,000 years,"* (1st of 6 times in 6 verses, cf. ___20:2-7___, we are going to hear the time-frame that can't be seen in a vision, so this time-frame must be told directly and specifically. If God says a number once, it is true, if He repeats a number, it is important, if He repeats it twice it is very important, but when He tells us specifically 6 times in 6 verses when describing the Kingdom length, He is making sure we know that the Kingdom is how longs? That is right, 1,000 years. It is where we get the word Millennium, Latin:Mille-1,000, annus-year; Gr:chilioi-1000, etos-year, and that is why we call the Kingdom the Millennial Kingdom; where we get 3 main theological views of Christ's Return in relationship to the Millennium: 1) Pre-Millennial [Christ Returns prior to the Millennial Kingdom to rule during it, it literal interprets the future 1,000 years and many other Scriptures; most Baptists and Bible Churches]; 2) Amillennial [there is *"no"* Millennial or just a non-literal, symbolic of a long time, or spiritual kingdom now since Christ's resurrection where Christ is reigning over believers; most Catholics, Reformed, and Presbyterians], and 3) Post-Millennial [Christ returns at the end of the Millennium where the gospel gains momentum and Christ's reign in people's hearts is culminated by His return to reign eternally; fewer proponents since the World Wars didn't seem to reflect the world peace promised by God in His Kingdom; was held by some Reformed Churches, but most of them migrated to the Amillennial position after World War I and II]; ends verse with a "," as God's powerful angel is not done with Satan yet. See picture of the 3 main Millennial Views below.)

Figure 20 – 28.1 Main Millennial Views

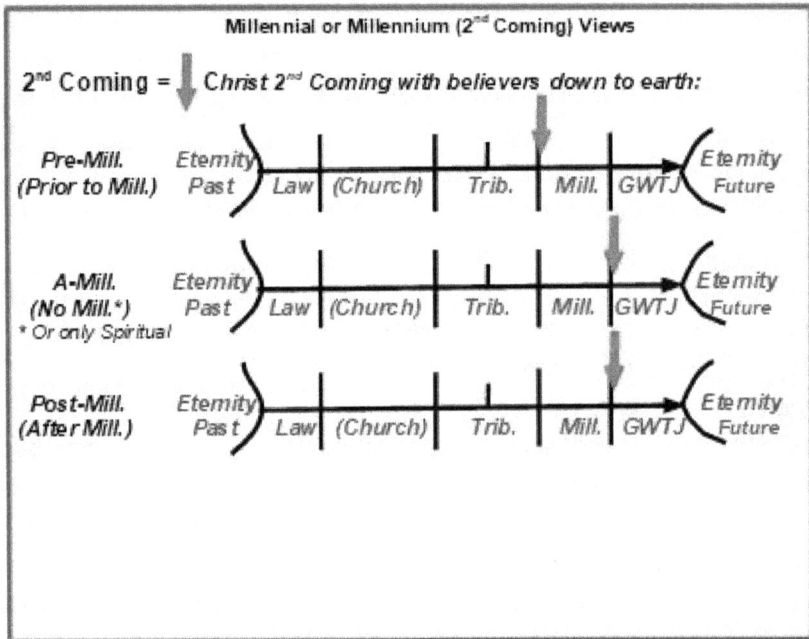

3-"**And cast** (threw) **him** (Satan) **into the bottomless pit, and shut him up** (closed him up in the pit, which does keep him quiet also as we'll see), **and set a seal** (stamp/signet attesting secure) **upon him** (Satan or possibly the lock on his chain or pit door), **that** (Gr:hina-purpose) **he** (Satan) **should deceive the nations** (wicked) **no more** (clearly shows Satan's involvement in deceiving the wicked now), **until the 1,000 years** (2nd time) **should be fulfilled** (completed/ expired/finished): **and after that** (1,000 years) **he** (Satan) **must be loosed** (released; from chains and the sealed pit) **a little season."** (Here Satan's being released timeframe is not specific, only a very short season or time).}

B. **20:4-6**— {Title: Believers Ruling with Christ 1,000 Years, While Wicked Await 2nd Death. **4-"And I** (John) **saw** (beheld) **thrones, and they** (saved) **sat upon them** (thrones), **and judgment** (legal decision) **was given to them** (Jesus, cf. **Mat. 25:31-46**; and saved church, cf.

178

5:10; *1Co. 6:2-3*; a little hint of 1 of our roles during the Millennium; and we'll see saved dead/martyred/resurrected and currently living Trib saints in verses to follow)*: and I saw the souls of them that were beheaded for the witness* (testimony) *of Jesus* (so, not the Church, but the other saved that had died)*, and for the Word of God* (not only God's Word, but another name for God's Son; both the name of Jesus and speaking the Word of God is offensive to a Satanically deceived world that doesn't want to hear the truth or about the Truth, which is the only Truth that has, will, and can eternally save)*, and which* (saved, who) *had not worshiped the Beast* (1st, Antichrist)*, neither* (nor) *his image, neither* (and not) *had received his* (Antichrist's) *mark upon their* (saved) *foreheads, or in* (or upon) *their* (saved) *hands; and they* (saved) *lived and reigned* (ruled) *with Christ a 1,000 years."* (3rd time; it is clear that the glorified married Church will always be with Christ and will rule as judges and priests...in the millennial Temple that Ezekiel describes in detail in *Eze. 40-48*; and here it tells of both Church and Israel, all saved of all times resurrected and ruling with Christ during this 1,000-year Millennial Kingdom). *5-"But the rest* (remaining) *of the dead* (unsaved wicked) *lived not* (didn't resurrect or live) *again until the 1,000 years* (4th time, Millennial Kingdom time-frame told; and here we are told the specific time-frame between the resurrection of the just and unjust) *were finished* (completed). *This is the first Resurrection."* ("*The 1st Resurrection*" only stated specifically twice in Scripture, *20:5-6*, is also referred to as "*the resurrection of the just,*" *Luke 14:14*; cf. *Acts 24:15*. it is timed with Christ's Comings, e.g. 1st, Rapture, and 2nd Coming; it is only for the saved, it includes all the saved, the 1st Resurrection has several phases, e.g. it includes the resurrection of Christ at His 1st Coming that made all others possible, it includes the resurrection of the Church at the Rapture, it includes all the remaining just, especially called out are God's martyrs, many from the Trib, at Christ's 2nd Coming. The 1st Resurrection is for all those that only die once and we all resurrect once, as Christ died in our place, and we resurrect 1st in the 1st Resurrection). *6-"Blessed* (happy/well off) *and holy* (*Gr:hagios-sacred, holy, saint*) *is he* (the one) *that has part of the 1st Resurrection* (only for saved)*: on such* (these; saved) *the 2nd Death* (Only for unsaved who die twice, once physically, and once spiritually, and as they rejected Christ's death for them, so they must spiritually die for them self) *has no power* (authority/strength), *but they* (saved) *shall be priests* (*1:6*; *5:10*; *1Pe. 2:9*; a hint of another 1 of our/Church's role with Christ and others during the Millennium) *of*

God and of Christ ("*anointed;*" Messiah and King), **and shall reign** (rule) **with Him** (Christ) **a 1,000 years."** (5th time, Millennial Kingdom timeframe is stated).}

C. 20:7-10— {Title: After 1,000 years, Satan is Released, Deceives Nations and God Destroys Nations and Casts Satan into Hell. **7**-"**And when the 1,000 years** (6th time God emphasizes the time-frame; He writes a lot of detail in the OT about the coming King and His peaceful Kingdom, but doesn't mention many specifics of it in **Revelation**, except re: the Churches inclusion, Satan's complete removal, and the specific time-frame, it is a Millennial Kingdom with the Church and without Satan, on earth) **are expired, Satan shall be loosed** (released) **out of prison** ("*guarding, prison;*" where he was chained in the locked and sealed bottomless pit)," **8**-"**And** (he, Satan) **shall go out to deceive** (his purpose; Satan is a deceiver, cf. **12:9**) **the nations** (heathen, non-Jewish), **which are in the 4 quarters** (corners) **of the earth, Gog and Magog** (Gog is found 11 times in Scripture, once in **1Ch. 5:4**, once here in **20:8**, and 9 times in **Eze. 38-39, 38:2-3, 14, 16, 18**; **39:1, 11**; Magog is found 5 times, **Gen. 10:2**; **1Ch. 1:5**; **Eze. 38:2**; **39:6**; **Rev. 20:8**; Gog is mentioned as an evil person or "*the chief prince of Meshech and Tubal,*" **Eze. 38:3**; **39:1, 11**; who leads a multitude against Israel/Christ and gets destroyed, and Magog is referred to as a person who settled in a place, "*the land of Magog,*" **Eze. 38:2**, where most believe Meshech and Tubal are in Turkey or part of the armies of the North or Russian providence; but clearly refer to the evil leader and followers of the wicked nations that come against Christ and Israel's peacefully ended Millennial Kingdom), **to gather** (assemble) **them** (nations) **together to battle** (Satan is a murderer, cf. **John 8:44**): **the number of whom** (wicked deceived nations) **is as the sand of the sea."** (Simile for huge number almost impossible to count, normally used to describe God's promised blessing of the nation of Israel, cf. **Gen. 22:17**; **32:12**; **Isa. 10:22**; **Jer. 33:22**; **Hos. 1:10**; **Rom. 9:27**; **Heb. 11:12**, but here describes Israel's enemies). **9**-"**And they** (deceived wicked leader and nations referred to collectively as Gog and Magog) **went up** (ascended; Jerusalem is up on a hill, and it is elevated in prominence as Christ's throne is there) **on the breadth** (width) **of the earth, and compassed** (encircled/ surrounded) **the camp** (encampment/battle array) **of the saints about, and the beloved** (Gr:agapao-loved; in a social or moral sense, because God chose it, cleansed it, and dwells in it, the same word John referred to himself when he said 5 times he was the disciple "*whom Jesus loved,*" **John**

13:23; *19:26*; *20:2*; *21:7, 20*, truly the same root as *Gr:agape-God's unconditional love, loved*) **city** (the saved Holy city and capital of Israel, Jerusalem, where Christ's Temple is, where we His priests are, which is contrasted with the evil gentile world destroyed government/city, Babylon)*: and fire came down* (descended) *from God* (clearly this is God's judgment protecting His people) *out of heaven, and devoured them* (ate them down; we would say "*ate them up*," but this is from God's perspective. Some associate this final battle with the battle of Armageddon in the plains of Megiddo, but *Eze. 39:11, 15* makes it clear that this is "*the valley of Hamongog*," where the final destruction of the Devil's deceived armies are defeated by Christ, the ruler over all; and we had just seen the final Battle of Armageddon in *Rev. 19:17-21*). *10*-"*And the Devil* (Satan) *that* (who) *deceived* (seduced) *them* (wicked people/nations. Deceiving Devil seduces Nations away from God/Christ to have them share in his fate) *was cast* (thrown) *into the lake of fire* (for judgment, pain, and purification; 4 times in Bible, all in *Rev. 19:20*; *20:10, 14-15*; and a 5th time in *21:8*, "*the lake that burns with fire*") *and brimstone* (this is Hell)*, where the Beast* (the Antichrist) *and the False Prophet are* (cf. *19:20*, both Beast/Antichrist and False Prophet have "*the*" preceding them as there have been many anti-Christs and false prophets, but these are "*the*" 2 specific ones during the Tribulation period)*, and shall be tormented* (again no soul sleep or just death and burial in the grave, but experiencing torment/pain) *day and night for ever and ever.*" (Hell is real, a place of conscious torment, and lasts forever—please don't go there. Trust in the testimony of Jesus: Christ died and was buried for your sin and was resurrected to prove He conquered sin and death for you. Believe on the Lord Jesus Christ and you will be saved, now and forever, cf. *Acts 16:31*).}

D. *20:11-15*— {Title: God Judges All Works at Great White Throne Casting Wicked into Hell. *11*-"*And I* (John) *saw* (beheld) *a Great White Throne* (an impressive literal place and picture of righteous judgment)*, and Him that* (Who) *sat* ("*sitting;*" a present participle) *on it* (more impressive than this great white throne is the great just God judging on it)*, from Whose* (God's) *face the earth and the heaven* (both singular, not all heavens, but the sky/atmosphere as God's throne is in heaven) *fled away* (vanished. What the wicked here wish they could do here)*; and there was found no place for them.*" (Heaven and earth; *2Pe. 3:10-13* reminds us, "*But the day of the Lord will come as a thief in the night; in the which the heavens shall pass away with a great* noise, and the elements shall melt with fervent heat, the earth also and the works that are therein shall be burned up. Seeing then that all these things shall be dissolved, what manner of persons ought ye to be in all holy conversation and godliness, Looking for and hasting unto the coming of the day of God, wherein the heavens being on fire shall be dissolved, and the elements shall melt with fervent heat? Nevertheless we, according to his promise, look for new heavens and a new earth, wherein dwells righteousness." Don't be too sad for the old heaven and earth as the next chapter describes the new heaven and earth as far better, eternal, and Jesus is there!). *12-"And I* (John) *saw* (beheld) *the dead* (saved and unsaved?-some think both, all, some think only unsaved as the saved already stood at the Judgment Seat of Christ, *2Co. 5:10*, as Christ received our judgment for all bad, and we received rewards for all good), *small and great stand before God* (the Father. He is starting to describe the 2nd Resurrection, that only includes the unsaved)*; and the Books were opened* (presumably those containing all works or actions)*: and another* (different) *Book was opened, which is the Book of Life* (cf. *Rev. 13:8*; *17:8* commentary, only saved are still written in Book of Life as unsaved were blotted out. Notice this is the 3rd pregnant pause in this verse with colon and semi-colons at this fearful judgment of the universe by God)*: and the dead* (unsaved) *were judged* (sentenced/condemned) *out of those things which were written* (Perfect passive participle-written about the dead in past with continuing results) *in the Books, according to their works."* (Works /Actions. Those which the unsaved pridefully depended upon to vindicate them in life are the very things demonstrating their sin's sentence is just in death; and even with God's terrible Tribulation plagues wicked men still did not repent, cf. *9:2* to receive the mercy and grace of God paying for all their wicked works by His Son Jesus Christ, cf. *John 3:16*; *Gal. 3:22*; *1Jo. 1:7*). *13-"And the sea* (both literal, a place of burial for many sailors...and figuratively like *17:15* says, the waters are *"peoples, and multitudes, and nations, and tongues"* on the earth. Both 1st and 2nd Resurrections are bodily resurrections for the earthly body to be reunited with the spirit into an immortal body) *gave up the dead* (unsaved) *which* (who) *were in it* (sea)*; and death* (an adjective used as a noun, literally or figuratively everyone who has died; where many have postulated a *"Death Angel"* that guards Hades so none can escape and now this *"Death"* delivers up his dead at this Great White Throne Judgment) *and Hell* (Gr:hades-place of departed souls, Hell, Hades; the place of torment for the unsaved/wicked until this 2nd Resurrection) ***delivered*** (gave) ***up the dead*** (unsaved) ***which*** (who) ***were in them*** (sea, death, Hades)***: and they*** (unsaved) ***were judged every man*** (one/person) ***according to their works.”*** (Actions/deeds. Again, repeating this is just like in **_20:12_**, not arbitrary, but judged based on their works, that they once depended upon for their own standard of right and wrong will be found lacking compared to God's holiness/perfect standard of Himself and His Son Jesus Christ). **_14_**-”***And death and Hades*** (there is no reason for, so neither will exist any longer, yea!!!) ***were cast*** (thrown) ***into the lake of fire.*** (Hell. A “.” for finality and thought-provoking pause, there is still time to accept Jesus as your Savior now before you die or He returns, please...). ***This is the 2nd Death.”*** (“*The 2nd Death*” is only for unsaved; found 4 times in Bible, **_2:11_**-where He promises the Church/believers won't die a 2nd time, **_20:6_**-where He says that all just/saved or those in 1st Resurrection won't die a 2nd time. Here in **_20:14_**-where He says this is the final death, and only for the wicked, and **_21:8_**-where He again describes all wicked/unbelievers /unsaved mankind, angels, death, and Hades will be thrown into Hell). **_15_**-”***And whosoever*** (frequent plea in John's Gospel/good news of the testimony of Jesus in **_3:16_**, where He begs all with “*whosoever believes in Him* [Jesus], *should not perish, but have everlasting life*”) ***was not*** (as they willed not to believe, they willfully rejected God's love) ***found in the Book of Life*** (all rejectors of Christ death in their place are blotted out from this Book that God had them written in) ***was cast into the lake of fire.”*** (Hell, where **_20:10_** tells us is torment forever and ever. Oh, that we would get John and God's heart, to beg many to miss that eternity and the forfeited blessings and rewards of Jesus' abundant life now. Most unsaved don't see the testimony of Jesus in us, so they reject Him, because of the life they believe He gives now. Oh, may the unsaved trust Jesus now and be saved. Oh, may we saved, live the joyful abundant life now that Jesus will ensure in heaven for all eternity).}

Figure 21 – 28.2 The Angel with the Key of the Bottomless Pit[34]

Application (Activity/Questions)

A. When/what is Jesus' <u>Rapture for the Church</u> before? {The 7-year Tribulation Period.}

B. When/what is Jesus' 2nd <u>Coming for Israel</u> before? {The Millennial Kingdom.}

C. During the Millennium, how can the earth have so many years of perfect peace when Satan is deceiving and murdering (**_20:1-7_**)? {Satan is locked up and unable to deceive and murder and Christ is physically ruling on earth.}

D. How many years will the saved rule and reign with Christ during the earthly Kingdom (**_20:4_**)? {1,000 years.}

E. Who is included in the 1st <u>Death</u> (Saved/Just, Unsaved/Unjust, or Both; cf. **_Heb. 9:27_**)? {Both.}

F. Who is included in the 1st <u>Resurrection</u> (Saved/Just or Unsaved/ Unjust)? {Saved/Just.}

G. Who is included in the 2nd <u>Resurrection</u> (Saved/Just or Unsaved/ Unjust)? {Unsaved/Unjust.}

H. Who is included in the 2nd <u>Death</u> (Saved/Just or Unsaved/ Unjust)? {Unsaved/Unjust.}

I. How scary is the <u>Great White Throne Judgment</u>? {For unsaved, it is the scariest place and event ever. For the saved, our fear will be replaced with total faith, though we will all wish we had played a bigger part in sharing the testimony of Jesus to the unsaved...}

New Heavens, New Earth, and New Heavenly City with God and
the Lamb's Glory, Light, and Life.

Heaven.
_{Describes Heaven with God and the Lamb's Glory, Light, and Life with
"streets of gold," "12 pearl" Gates, Glorious Music, "precious stone
walls" and Foundations Including "emerald."}_

Introduction
A. **_John 14:1-3_** tells us Jesus is preparing a heavenly place for us. What
do you think it will look, sound, feel, and smell like? {Wow, _"streets of
gold," "pearl"_ gates, precious gem walls, glorious music, light,
wondrous smells, perfect temperature, feel like home...}
B. Why is there less than 2 chapters in the Bible that describe Heaven
(cf. **_1Co. 2:9_**; **_Isa. 64:4_**)? {Nothing compares to heaven; some emerald
foundations, pearl gates, gold streets, Jesus...There are 716 times the
word _"heaven"_ or _"heavens"_ is in the Bible, though some of those refer
to the sky.}

Scripture (Observations/Interpretation/Commentary)
{22/27 verses begin with _"and"_ showing continued action; Could have as
many as 5 Groups; 1 team lead that you provide this commentary; have
group come up with and present Title and Commentary/Insights.}

A. **_21:1-4_**— {Title: God Destroys Death and Pain and Dwells with Us in
the New Heaven and Earth. **_1_**-"**_And I_** (John) **_saw_** (beheld) **_a new
heaven and new earth_** (new heaven and new earth, 4 times in Bible:
_21:1_; **_Isa. 65:17, 22_**-tell they are so good we won't ever think about
this old 1 and they will be eternal; **_2Pe. 3:13_** tells us this was promised,
and we look forward to them where righteousness dwells/remains)**_:
for the 1st heaven and the 1st earth were passed away_** (perished); **_and
there was no more sea._**" (Oceans. So, John begins with a thesis
statement of a new heaven and earth. 2 main views: 1) Literal new
heaven and earth-as it says, or 2) Symbolic, non-literal, a
"recapitulation," or summarizing of the Millennial Kingdom of **_Rev. 20_**-
since it has a Jewish sounding Jerusalem with 12 tribes inscribed, and
they think the new heaven is where the glorified Church rules and
resides during Israel's earthly reign with Christ. Due to view 2's
popularity, I provide 9 reasons I do not hold a symbolic/spiritual/non-

literal or recapitulation view. 1) In the Millennial Kingdom, people still die, cf. *Isa. 65:20*; *Rev. 20:8-9*, where *21:4* says they won't die in this Heavenly Jerusalem. 2) In the Millennial Kingdom, there will be an elaborate Temple, cf. *Eze. 40-48*, where *21:22* says there's no temple in the Heavenly Jerusalem. 3) *21:1, 4* says, "...*the 1ˢᵗ heaven and the 1ˢᵗ earth were passed away...the former things are passed away.*" 4) In *21:6*, Jesus says, "*It is done,*" seeming concluding the earthly timeline, which includes the earthly Millennial Kingdom, and then speaks in terms of heaven and the heavenly city. 5) A literal new heaven and new earth logically follows *Rev. 20*'s old earth passing away with fervent heat and the following judgment, as it says in *Rev. 20:11*, "*...the earth and the heaven fled away; and there was found no place for them.*" 6) A literal new heaven and new earth are consistent with the rest of Scripture, cf. *2Pe. 3:7, 10-13* says, "*But the heavens and the earth, which are now, by the same word are kept in store, reserved unto fire against the day of judgment...the which the heavens shall pass away with a great noise, and the elements shall melt with fervent heat, the earth also and the works that are therein shall be burned up. Seeing then that all these things shall be dissolved...the heavens being on fire shall be dissolved, and the elements shall melt with fervent heat? Nevertheless we, according to His promise, look for new heavens and a new earth, wherein dwells righteousness.*" *Heb. 11:10* says that Abraham did not look for another earthly city, "*For he looked for a city which hath foundations whose builder and maker is God.*" *Heb. 12:18, 22* says, "*For ye are not come unto the mount that might be touched...But ye are come unto mount Sion, and unto the city of the living God, the heavenly Jerusalem.*" *Heb. 13:14* says, "*For here have we no continuing city, but we seek one to come.*" *Gal.4:25-26*, refers to the earthly Jerusalem in bondage as the "*Jerusalem which is now*" and calls this free heavenly Jerusalem, the "*Jerusalem which is above...*" 7) All physical measurements, materials, and descriptions of the city's walls, foundations, gates, streets...are precise, normal, natural, and encouraging for us to know will be available for our future physically resurrected bodies. 8) All enemies are in Hell after the Millennial Kingdom, cf. *20:15*, so the heavenly Jerusalem gates can stay open, cf. *21:25* in safety without fear. 9) No one could get the blessing of reading and understanding, cf. *1:3* these last 2 chapters if everyone thinks the heavenly Jerusalem means something different to them than the literal description God wrote). *2-"And I John* ("*I John,*" only 3 times in Bible, all in *Rev.*, *1:9*; *21:2*; *22:8*; where John includes his name after talking in the 1st person to be personal, the 1st time when He saw and heard Jesus and mentions his brotherhood in tribulation, standing for God's Word, and the testimony of Jesus, the 2nd here when he sees the New Jerusalem, and the 3rd and final time where Jesus tells him He's coming quickly and he that guards these prophecies will be blessed) *saw (beheld) the holy city, new Jerusalem* ("*new Jerusalem,*" twice in Bible; *3:12*; *21:2*. In *3:12*, Jesus calls it "*the city of my God*"), *coming down* (descending; like a gift from the Father above) *from God* (the Father) *out of heaven, prepared as a bride* (a simile normally describing the Church, but here the new heavenly city named after Israel's capitol implicit of the intimacy and promise of both Israel and the Church believers) *adorned* (Gr:cosmeo-in proper order, decorate, adorn, garnish, trim; where we get the word cosmetics) *for her husband."* (Kind of double spousal imagery for Christ and the Church and God and Israel. So John continues with this sub-thesis that a new holy city is like a gift from God to believers). *3- "And I heard a great voice* (doesn't tell us whether this is God, Jesus, or a key angel or believer) *out of heaven saying, 'Behold, the tabernacle* (habitation) *of God is with men* (saved/righteous. God's house is with men)*, and He* (God-the-Father) *will dwell* (reside. God's presence is with men. Talk about elevating man's position, communion, protection...to actually live with God in His mansion. So God will dwell) *with them* (saved)*, and they* (saved) *shall be His* (God's) *people, and God Himself shall be with them* (saved. Repeats again that God Himself, not an angel, nor any substitute, but God will be with man)*, and be their* (believers') *God.'"* (The highlight of heaven is that God will be fully with us, praise Him, yea!). *4-"And God* (this is intimate, not an angel) *shall wipe away* (blot out; never blot out their name, but will) *all tears* (every single one, and didn't remove source of their pain, which God has already paid for and plans to always protect them from, as He has judged sin forever) *from their* (all saved) *eyes* (as we'll see with God's clear perspective for the 1st time); *and* (Gr:kai-and, even, also) *there shall be no more death* (as Christ crushes our enemies as God says in *1Co. 15:26*, "*the last enemy that will be destroyed is death*")*, neither* (not even) *sorrow* (grief)*, nor crying, neither* (not even) *shall there be any more pain* (God removes all causes of our pain and tears): *for the former* (prior) *things are* (have) *passed away."* (What a day...).}

B. 21:5-8— {Title: Ruling Jesus Began and Concludes Man's History— Saved Heirs with Christ, and Wicked Rejectors in Hell. *5-"And He that*

sat (was sitting/residing) **upon the throne** (Jesus, the rightful King, so this paragraph is red in a red letter edition Bible) **said, 'Behold, I** (Jesus) **make all things new.'** (All things—our home, our bodies, thinking, desires, our ability to love and be loved, worship, work, our fulfillment, communication, intimacy, laughter, music...) **and He** (Jesus) **said to me** (John), **'Write: for these words** (Revelation) **are true and faithful.'''** (Trustworthy/sure; just like Jesus). **6-''And He** (Jesus) **said unto me, 'It is done.** (Finished/ fulfilled/performed; Perfect-ongoing results from completed action in past, Indicative-Factual; like **John 19:30** also quoted Jesus on the cross of His suffering salvation work, "*It is finished.*" Sovereign God fulfilled and accomplished all His purposes in the details of time. At this line between time and eternity, He encouragingly reminds us) **I am Alpha** (1st letter in Greek Alphabet) **and the Omega** (Final/last letter in Greek Alphabet; He's the final letter and Word!), **the beginning** (commencement/chief) **and the end** (conclusion/goal). **I will give unto him that is athirst** (those thirsty) **of the fountain** (original spring/well) **of the water of life freely.''** (For nothing; at no cost to you, though it cost Him His life. Jesus has given true life and will satisfy all the need and longings of our soul. This beautiful picture of the Good Shepherd also being the living water that is the only one Who "*restores my soul,*" **7:16-17**; **Jer. 2:13**; **17:13**; **John 4:14**; **7:10-11, 37-39**; **Psa. 23:1-3**). **7-''He that** (who) **overcomes** (Gr:nikao-subdue, conquer, overcome, prevail, get the victory; used 10 times in Bible all by John; **1Jo. 5:4-5** says overcomers are "*born of God*" by "*faith,*" believing "*Jesus is the Son of God;*" in **Rev. 2:7, 11, 17, 26**; **3:5, 12, 21**; **21:7**, there are 18 promises, all by Jesus, for us to be given: 1) "*to eat of the Tree of Life,*" 2) "*will not be hurt by the 2nd death,*" 3) will be given "*to eat of the hidden manna,*" 4) "*a white stone,*" 5) with "*a new name,*" 6) "*power over the nations,*" 7) "*clothed in white raiment; and I will* 8) *not blot out his name out of the Book of Life, but I will* 9) *confess his name before My Father, and* 10) *before His angels,*" 11) "*will I make a pillar in the temple of my God, and* 12) *he shall go no more out: and* 13) *I will write upon him the name of my God, and* 14) *the name of the city of my God,*" 15-"*grant to sit with me in my throne,*" and 16) **shall inherit to all things; and** (17) **I will be his God, and** (18) **he shall be my son.''** (cf. **John 1:12**; which is probably the most awesome promise to be God's son, which entitles us to it all!). **8-''But** (contrasting the great news and blessings of the saved with the unsaved) **the fearful** (faithless), **and unbelieving** (faithless and unbelieving are 2 plural adjectives describing the type of disgusting wicked-unbelievers), **and the abominable** (disgusting/detestable/abhorrent; Perfect Participle-completed action with continued results. in their life they sinned and now the results continue since they refused to believe and accept the testimony of Jesus that would have saved and delivered them from all sin and its consequences), **and murderers** (intentional), **and whoremongers** (prostitutes), **and sorcerers** (drug pushers), **and idolaters** (false god worshipers), **and all liars** (deceivers; after 4 plural nouns of life takers, sex sellers, drug pushers, and god worshipers, he uses 2 more adjectives of "*all*" and "*liars*" or "*deceivers*" for each of these disgustingly deceived wicked, showing that sin deceives the sinner in all categories), **shall have their** (wicked/unsaved) **part** (allotment) **in the lake which burns** (burning; continuous) **with fire and brimstone** (eternal literal Hell)**: which is the 2nd Death.**" (Only for the wicked/unsaved, all 4 times in Bible found in **Rev. 2:11**; **20:6, 14**; **21:8**; even though horrible news for evil, some encouragement for good as the saved will be free from the actions and influence of the wicked. 2 verses say that the saved won't go to Hell and 2 say the wicked/unsaved will. All 4 of these verses in this paragraph are quotes from Jesus).}

C. **21:9-14**— {Title: Heavenly Jerusalem-God's Glory, High Walls, Guarded Gates, and Sure Foundations. **9**-"**And there came unto me** (John) **1 of the 7 angels which** (who) **had the 7 vials** (or bowls) **full of the 7 last** (final) **plagues, and talked with me** (John)**, saying, 'Come hither** (here; imperative/a command)**, I will show you the bride, the Lamb's** (Jesus') **wife.'**" (Clearly contrasted with the corrupting earthly city of Babylon like a harlot in **Rev. 14:8**; **16:19**; **17:5**; **18:2, 10, 21**; John sees the new holy Jerusalem in **21:2**, like or similar to a pure bride prepared for her Groom. Here the angel says that he will show John the bride, the Lamb's wife, and seems to focus on this new Heavenly city of Jerusalem, full of God's glory and all the unified individual Jewish and Church believers, a picture of the Church, still in white and still wearing her veil, just married to Christ, the Lamb, the 1 Who gave His life to purify and redeem us. Also metaphorically pictures her as the Ephesian [**2:14-22**] building, temple, holy habitation, or walled city of the Groom, the Lord). **10**-"**And he** (1 of 7 angel's) **carried me** (John) **away in the spirit** (probably John's spirit, not the Holy Spirit, another Charles Dickens type picture with the angel) **to a great and high** (lofty/esteemed) **mountain, and showed me that great city, the holy** (sacred) **Jerusalem, descending out of heaven from God,**" **11**-"**Having the glory of God: and her** (Jerusalem's) **light** (brilliancy) **was like unto** *a stone most precious* (costly stone/gem), *even like a jasper stone* (gem), *clear as crystal;"* (emphasizing God's glory is illuminating the entire heavenly city thru this crystal clear jasper like gem); *12-"And had* (having) *a wall great and high* (esteemed), *and had* (having) *12 gates, and at* (or upon) *the gates 12 angels, and names written* (inscribed) *thereon* (on the gates), *which are the 12 tribes of the children* (sons) *of Israel:"* *13-"On the east 3 gates; on the north 3 gates; on the south 3 gates; on the west 3 gates."* (Can enter or exit using any of 3 gates on any and every side). *14-"And the wall of the city* (holy heavenly Jerusalem) *had* (having) *12 foundations, and in them* (the foundations) *the names of the 12 Apostles* (cf. Mat. 10:2-4; Mar. 3:14-19; Luk. 6:13-16; 1-Simon-surnamed Peter, 2-Andrew-Peter's brother, 3-James-son of Zebedee-surnamed Boanerges/son of thunder, 4-John-son of Zebedee-surnamed Boanerges/son of thunder, 5-Philip, 6-Bartholomew, 7-Thomas-called Didymus, 8-Matthew-the publican, 9-James-son of Alphaeus, 10-Judas-the brother of James/Lebbaeus-surnamed Thaddaeus/ some say Jude, 11-Simon-the Canaanite also called Zelotes, and 12-Matthias-cf. Acts 1:26, since Judas Iscariot betrayed Jesus and committed suicide) *of the Lamb."* (Emphasizing both Jew (as most Apostles were Jewish) and Church (as were foundational Church leaders), and Jesus Christ is the Chief Cornerstone, cf. Eph. 2:20, and *"the Lamb"* emphasizes His perfect sacrificial saving work that unites us all in one happily ever after location together as the new bride and her handsome royal Groom have a secure protected palace and city).}

D. **21:15-21**— {Title: The New Holy Jerusalem, Walls, Foundations, and Gates. *15-"And he* (the angel) *that talked with me* (John) *had a golden reed* (like a yard stick) *to* (Gr:hina-purpose) *measure the city* (New Jerusalem), *and the gates thereof* (of it), *and the wall thereof* (of it)."* *16-"And the city* (New Jerusalem) *lies foursquare* (has 4 corners or square), *and the length is as large as the breadth* (width; true square, not rectangle): *and he* (angel) *measured the city* (New Jerusalem) *with the reed, 12,000 furlongs* (Gr:stadium, race course, race; 1 furlong=660 feet; 12,000 furlongs=7,920,000 feet, or 1,500 miles, or about half way across or 63.6% of the land area of America). *The length and the breadth* (width) *and the height of it are equal."* (Showing not only square, but also cube-shaped, although some postulate that could technically even be pyramid shaped, though would imply a non-stated ceiling). *17- "And he* (the angel) *measured the wall thereof* (of it, the city), *144 cubits* (Gr:pechus-the forearm, *cubit*, 1½ feet or 18 inches; 144 cubits=216 feet), ***according to the measure of a man, that is, of the angel."*** (In other words, the wall was 144 cubits that was about the length of a man's forearm, but actually the length of the angel's forearm). ___18___-***"And the building*** (structure) ***of the wall of it*** (city-New Jerusalem) ***was of jasper*** (opaque variety of chalcedony-multicolored with many unique patterns, bands, speckles; see ___4:3___ commentary describing 7 times found in Bible): ***and the city was pure*** (Gr:katharos-pure, clean, clear) ***gold, like unto*** (similar to) ***clear*** (pure/clean) ***glass."*** ___19___-***"And the foundations of the wall of the city*** (New Jerusalem) ***were garnished*** (decorated/ trimmed) ***with all manner of precious stones*** (gems). ***The 1st foundation, jasper; the 2nd, sapphire*** (9 times in Bible, ___Exo. 24:10___; ___28:18___; ___39:11___; ___Job 28:16___; ___Lam. 4:7___; ___Eze. 1:26___; ___10:1___; ___28:13___; and ___Rev. 21:19___; describing under God's feet, also the 2nd row and 2nd stone in the holy priestly breastplate of judgment, highly valued, highly polished, and around the glory and throne of God; a precious gemstone, normally blue, but can be yellow, purple, orange, and/or green; 9/10 on Moh's hardness scale); ***the 3rd, a chalcedony*** (only here in Scripture; a waxy luster, may be semitransparent or translucent, a wide range of colors, mostly white to gray, grayish-blue or a shade of brown ranging from pale to nearly black); ***the 4th, an emerald;"*** (found 5 times in Bible; here as the foundation of the wall; twice re: high priest's breastplate gemstone representing the 4th tribe, ___Exo. 28:18___; ___39:11___; once again of Satan's covering, ___Eze. 28:13___; and once of God, ___Rev. 4:3___; normally green, rare, expensive, and 7.5/10 on hardness scale). ___20___-***"The 5th, sardonyx*** (only here is Scripture, Gr:sard-reddish brown and Gr:onyx-claw, fingernail); ***the 6th, sardius*** (4 times in Bible; ___21:20___-the foundation of the wall; ___Exo. 28:17___ and ___39:10___-where it is the 1st gem in the 1st row of the priest's breastplate; and ___Eze. 28:13___-of Satan's precious covering in the Garden of Eden; maybe Ruby); ***the 7th, chrysolite*** (only here in Bible; Gr:chrusolithos-gold stone, yellow gem); ***the 8th, beryl*** (8 times in Bible; ___21:20___-8th wall foundation; ___Exo. 28:20___ and ___39:13___-4th row, 1st stone in priests breastplate; ___SoS. 5:14___-bride describing her beloved's hands; ___Eze. 1:16___ and ___10:9___-the color of the Cherubims wheels; ___28:13___-Satan's covering in the Garden; ___Dan. 10:6___-described an angels body like the beryl; usually green, also blue, rose, white, golden, opaque and transparent); ***the 9th, a topaz*** (5 times in Bible; ___21:20___-the foundation of the wall; ___Exo. 28:17___ and ___39:10___-4th row, 1st stone of priests' breastplate; ___Job 28:19___-good ones found in Ethiopia; ___Eze. 28:13___-Satan's covering in the Garden; pretty, 8/10 hardness, but not as valuable or rare); *the 10ᵗʰ, chrysoprasus* (only here in Bible; a greenish yellow gem, 7/10 hardness*); the 11ᵗʰ, jacinth* (twice in Bible; *9:17*-horse riders with breastplates of fire, jacinth, and brimstone; and *21:20*-New Jerusalem 11ᵗʰ wall foundation; *Gr:huakinthinos-hyacinthine, jacinthine, deep blue, jacinth-golden, red-brown, purple); the 12ᵗʰ, an amethyst."* (3 times in Bible; *21:20*-the wall foundation; and *Exo. 28:19* and *39:12*-the 3ʳᵈ row and 3ʳᵈ stone in the priest's breastplate). *21-"and the 12 gates were 12 pearls; each several* (and every) *gate was of 1 pearl* (the most expensive pearls ever seen, strong and beautiful; not to mention must have been enormous clams/oysters. *21:12* told us their gates have 12 angels and the 12 tribes of Israel engraved on them)*: and the street* (plat/open square) *of the city was pure gold, as it were* (like) *transparent glass."* (So, *20:15*-talks about the angel measuring: *20:16*-the overall city, *20:17-18*-the walls and their structure, *20:19-20*-the walls' 12 gem foundations, *20:21*-the 12 gates and streets of pure gold. Wow, I can't wait to live there).}

E. *21:22-27*— {Title: No Temple, Sun, Closing. nor Sin, but the Glory of God and the Lamb. *22-"And I* (John) *saw no temple therein* (in it; New Jerusalem)*: for the Lord God Almighty* (Omnipotent-the Father) *and the Lamb* (Jesus the Son, our sacrifice to be able to be with a perfect holy God in a perfect place) *are the temple of it."* (They are the object/place of worship. The temple was built with walls of separation from a holy God in holy heaven. Because of Jesus, there will be no temple, no temple walls, no walls of separation; we can truly live together with God). *23-"And the city* (New Jerusalem) *had no need* (requirement) *of the sun, neither of the moon* (we'll see as there is no more night or day only light from God/Jesus)*, to* (Gr:hina-purpose) *shine in it* (New Jerusalem): *for the glory of God did lighten* (illuminate/enlighten/ light; the Shekinah Glory or glory of God's presence; *James 1:17* says God is *"the Father of lights, with Whom there is no variableness, neither shadow of turning,"* since God is the Light source, there can't be a shadow or any lighting change when He turns. *Gen. 1:3, 14-19*-God created light, sun, moon, and stars. *Mat. 5:14*-God made us *"the light of the world"* through Christ) *it* (the heavenly city)*, and the Lamb* (Jesus is *"the light of the world," Joh. 8:12; 9:5) is the light* (illuminator/illumination) *thereof."* (Of it; the heavenly city). *24-"And the nations* (races, tribes, peoples; lots of diversity) *of them which are saved* (all in heaven will be saved, as *21:8* has already shown us the wicked are in Hell. But this emphasizes all the people in this heavenly city are good, but are good and there because Jesus saved them and gave them His righteousness) *shall walk in the light of it* (heavenly city; people will conduct themselves in the light of God and the Lamb's glory)*: and the kings of the earth do bring their glory and honor into it* (new heavenly city; emphasizes a royal procession of the glory of good leaders, from every nation and tribe walking in the light of Jesus, not in the deception of Satan and his evil rulers). *25-"And the gates of it* (new heavenly city Jerusalem) *shall not be shut at all* (no never) *by day: for* (because) *there shall be no night there."* (Heaven; complete safety and no need to fear or ever close the gates for no evil will ever come, will never come). *26-"And they* (heavenly citizens) *shall bring the glory and honor of the nations* (races, tribes) *into it."* (New heavenly city Jerusalem; similar to *21:24*, but here emphasizing the nations themselves will be honorable, like their leaders in *21:24*). *27-"And there shall in no wise* (no never) *enter into it* (the heavenly city) *anything* (or anyone) *that defiles* (Gr:koinoo-profane, common, defile, pollute, unclean*; something the Jews spent much of their time trying to keep themselves and those around them clean, undefiled and ready and able to worship), *neither whatsoever* (anything or anyone) *working* (doing/making) *abomination* (detestable/idolatry)*, or making a lie* (lying)*: but they which* (who) *are written* (perfect passive-written in the past by God with continuing results; *"have been and continue to be written"*) *in the Lamb's Book of Life."* (Only includes the eternally saved, those who trusted and received the Lamb and didn't reject His miraculous drawing and free gift of eternal life will all, ultimately enter the heavenly city. No one or nothing unclean, detestable, or even a lie will make it into heaven. Please trust in Jesus so you make sure you are in Jesus' Book, the Lamb's Book of Life, so you too can be forever in such an awesome perfect place with God's glory and good all around).}

Application (Activity/Questions)

A. Why should John write the Book of Revelation (*21:5*)? {Commanded by God and It has true/faithful Words.}

B. Why should we ask God to deepen our thirst for Jesus/the living water and be salt for unsaved? {So we can be eternally satisfied, and unsaved can be saved and not dry out and perish.}

C. What do you think makes the new heavens and new earth so special? {God with us; Jesus, no sin, death, pain, or sorrow; no divisions, gorgeous walls, gates, streets, mansions, glorified body...}

D. Why do you think God tells us so many specifics about the Heavenly city? {It's real, touchable, understandable, incredible by even things we do know, much less the things we'll learn and see...}

E. Why did the earthly temple have different courts, walls, restrictions, and the ark? {To restrict sinners [those farthest from God] with most sin from getting consumed by God's holiness.}

F. Why is there no need for a temple after all sinners/sin has been removed for eternity (*20:22*)? {Doesn't have to be separation from our holy God with those He has made completely holy.}

G. What gives you the most hope now from God providing this picture of heaven? {It's reality, the fact we can enjoy walking with God and Christ now; helps endure hardship now for unspeakable unheard wonders for all eternity. I can only imagine...}

Keep God's Word and Be Blessed, Jesus is Coming Quickly,
Please Come Lord Jesus.

The Final Chapter of the Bible—Come Quickly Lord Jesus.
{5 finales—The final: 1) Invitation, 2) Warning, 3) Promise, 4) Prayer, and
5) Provision. Includes the Crescendo of the Coming Christ, and also
Summarizes How Revelation Reveals Jesus Christ.}

Introduction
A. What is your guess of how long until Jesus comes? {<10 years.}
B. Is your greatest prayer/wish that Jesus come now? Why/Why not?
{Yes, though don't think about it as much as I should. We get to be
with God, love ones, incredible angelic creatures, we get to be in
heaven for ever with no sin, pain, sickness, or death...}

Scripture (Observations/Interpretation/Commentary)
{10/21 starts with _"and"_ showing continued actions, but interrupted
action, by an event that will soon interrupt all actions; the most
paragraphs of any chapter, 9, but only slightly more verses or words
than average; and 5 verses directly from Jesus.}

A. **22:1-5**— {Title: God, the Lamb, and Saved Reign in an Eternal
Paradise. (Truly this paragraph continues the heavenly description and
could have continued as part of **Rev. 21**. Remember, chapter and verse
numbers were added later for ease of reference and finding a passage,
though not inspired). **1**-"**And he** (1 of the 7 angels with 1 of 7 last
plagues who showed and measured the heavenly city, **21:9, 17**)
showed me a pure (clean/clear) **river of water of life** ("_water of life,_" 3
times in Bible, **21:6**; **22:1, 17**; never defined, Jesus says that the water
He will give will eternally quench thirst in **John 4:14**; this verse says it's
a river and the other 2 say the thirsty saved can take of it freely, and
similar to how earthly water is life giving or water of life), **clear as
crystal, proceeding** (coming forth) **out of the throne of God and of the
Lamb.**" **2**-"**In the middle of the street** (plait/open square/place) **of it**
(heavenly city), **and on either side** (both sides) **of the river, was there
the tree of life** ("_tree of life,_" 10 times in Bible, **Gen. 2:9**; **3:22, 24**-the
original tree for Adam and Eve, **Pro. 3:18**; **11:30**; **13:12**; **15:4**-a
metaphorical tree of life referring to the results of wisdom,
righteousness, fulfilled desires, and a wholesome tongue, and **2:7**;

22:2; *22:14*-this heavenly tree of life that Christians may eat and live forever)*, which bare 12 manner of* ("manner of" are supplied words by KJV, to indicate different types, not just 12 in number) *fruits, and yielded* (yielding) *her* (its) *fruit every month* (not just seasonal and not just 1 type of fruit, unsure if it has 1 type of fruit a month or 12 types to choose from all the time; "*tree*" is singular as in 1 tree, though many think singular as in a grove based on being on both sides of the river, but it could be 1 huge tree with branches and fruit on both sides of the river also)*: and the leaves of the tree* (of life) *were* (are) *for the healing* (Gr:therapeia-cure, healing; since no sickness in heaven, many say this is for initial health or continued strong health, not restoration from sickness) *of the nations."* (Races/peoples; cf. *21:24*-all saved; some believe the nations are outside the New Jerusalem in their own heavenly cities, others, including me, maintain we are all in complete unity in one heavenly celestial city). *3*-"*And there shall be no more curse* (a reminder of the completely removed curse from sin in the original terrestrial paradise, cf. *Gen. 3:14, 17*): *but* (or also; in contrast with sin's curse and rule is holy God-the-Father and Son's rule) *the throne of God and of the lamb* (Jesus) *shall be in it* (heaven); *and His* (God's/ Jesus') *servants shall* (do 3 things: serve/worship, see/gaze, and rule/reign; 1st) *serve* (worship) *Him:"* (God/Jesus; sadly now we want to serve Him, but slip up and fall down; in heaven, when we have a full understanding of what's best and most joyous we will chose to do that freely for Him in complete joy): *4*-"*And they* (God's servants and believers; 2nd) *shall see* (Gr:optanomai-gaze at with wide open eyes, at something remarkable; *Exo. 33:20*-where once no man can "*see My face: for there will no man see Me, and live.*" We will be amazed and never be able to take Him all in, so truly we will be continually, *Heb. 12:2*-"*looking unto Jesus,*" and *Eph. 1:18*-have "*the eyes of our understanding* [deep thoughts/ imaginations] *enlightened,*" as only looking at Jesus can do, and we will truly look and live; and by doing so, we will have our faces and perspectives changed forever reflecting His glory, as Moses was after only seeing the backside of God's glory, cf. *Exo. 33:18-23*; *34:29-35*. Jesus completely will fulfill His Beatitudinal promise that by faith we received a pure heart and "*will see God,*" cf. *Mat. 5:8*; *Heb. 10:22*; so truly *1Jo. 3:2*-"*we will be like Him; for we will see Him as He is,*" with holiness, truth, love, intimacy, unity...) *His* (God's/Jesus') *face* (appearance/person)*; and His* (God's) *name shall be in their* (normally doesn't refer to the saved in the third person, but does here to tie back to the 3 things God's filled and fulfilled, healthy and living, servant-leaders are preoccupied with: worshiping, gazing, and ruling; and reminding they are in God's house with God, with God's name, in their) *foreheads* (a sign of ownership; as the Father's name was in the 144,000 witnesses' foreheads in *14:1*). *5-* *"And there shall be no night* (cf. *21:25*) *there* (heaven)*; and they* (saved) *need no candle* (lamp/light)*, neither light of the sun; for the Lord* (emphasizing more reasons we serve Him, He is Lord) *God gives them* (saved now in Heaven) *light* (cf. *21:23*, shows both God's Glory and Lamb-Light)*: and they* (saved) *shall reign* (the freedom of Christ-looked-like servant-leadership is the highest rule/reign, and when you serve God, you truly reign the most, and the longest) *for ever and ever."* (Eternal rule with God).}

B. 22:6-7— {Title: Angel Affirms this Book; Jesus is Coming with Blessing to Keepers of Book. *6-"And he* (the angel) *said unto me* (John), *'These sayings* (Gr:logos-words, sayings, tidings) *are faithful and true* (truthful)*: and the Lord* (again God's sovereignty) *God of the holy prophets sent* (Gr:apostello-sent out, set apart, set at liberty, put in; a picture of the angel affirming the truth and faithfulness of the OT and NT through God's prophets and apostles. *Gr:apostolos-one that is sent*) *His* (God's) *angel to show unto His* (God's) *servants the things which must shortly* (in haste) *be done."* (All Scripture speaks of the testimony of Jesus and His soon coming and reigning forever). *7-*(Jesus says) *"'Behold, I come quickly* (Gr:tachu-shortly, without delay, soon, suddenly, quickly*; not necessarily now-as some atheists have suggested is a contradiction since Christ has not yet returned. But suddenly, where we get the doctrine of imminence, that Christ could come at any moment, there is nothing prophetically required to occur before His Rapture; 3 times in Bible, all in Revelation, *Rev. 3:11*; *22:7, 12*): *blessed* (happy/well off) *is He* (the one; Jesus speaking to each individual personally) *that keeps* (who is keeping/guarding/holding fast; an invocation to persevere in trusting servant-like obedience) *the sayings* (words) *of the prophecy of this Book.'"* (Keep/Guard the Word. Surely prophecy of the Book of Revelation and truly can be said of all Scripture).}

C. 22:8-11— {Title: Keepers of Book Worship God and Stay Just and Holy. (Scofield calls this *"The Last Message of the Bible."*[35] What message would you have given?-I think I would have talked about the importance of keeping God's Word and being ready for Jesus' coming). *8-"And I John saw* (person testimony and beholding) *these things, and heard* (hearing; both beholding and hearing are present participles)

them (showing that John is still seeing and hearing these visions, angels, heaven, and Jesus' prophetic and exciting Words), **and when I** (John) **had heard and seen, I fell down to worship before the feet of the angel, which showed** (showing) **me these things."** **9**-"Then (or and) **says he** (the angel) **unto me, 'See you do it not** (Take heed/ Discern clearly/Stop/Forbear): **for I am your fellow-servant** (co-slave; servant with the same master) **and of your brothers the prophets and of them which keep** (those keeping/guarding/holding fast) **the sayings** (words) **of this Book** (surely obeying Revelation and all Scripture to encompass John's Old and New Testament prophetic brothers): **worship God.'"** (Stop worshiping a fellow servant and keeper of God's Word and start worshiping God/Jesus; same message as angel in **19:10**. We may all need to hear this when we see some impressive men and angels in heaven. This incredible angel was reflecting God's glory and showing John some amazing places, people, and promises, but still not to be worshiped, only worship God). **10**-"**And he** (the angel) **says unto me** (John), **'Seal not** (Don't keep secret; write/ communicate) **the sayings** (words) **of the prophecy of this Book: for** (because) **the time** (occasion/set time) **is at hand.'"** (Near; a picture of the very words John is writing are about to come to pass. The angel told Daniel to "*Seal up*" and "*write them not*" in **Dan. 10:4**, there was still a long time to wait, but here the angel tells John to let people know these prophecies because the time is near; the angel continues). **11**-"**He** (The one) **that is unjust** (doing wrong), **let him be unjust** (wrong) **still: and he which** (the one who) **is filthy** (morally dirty), **let him be filthy** (morally dirty) **still** (progressively doing more evil, with less and less time left to change):**.and he that** (the one who) **is righteous** (innocent/just), **let him be righteous** (innocence/justice) **still: and he that** (the one who) **is holy, let him** (that one) **be holy still.'"** (Progressively doing greater good. You can see **22:11**'s emphasis on "*be*" filthy, righteous, or holy, not "*do*" [the focus of **22:14**] as this gets at their character and standing before God. This is a warning; evil and good stay that way, because **22:10** says that time has run out. Time=mercy, time will end, so all will stay in the state they have chosen. The unjust=unjust, just=just, holy=holy; time/mercy will suddenly end).}

D. 22:12-13— {Title: Jesus Comes Quickly with Believer's Reward. **12**-"**And behold, 'I** (Jesus) **come quickly** (soon; 2ⁿᵈ of 3 times quoted, 6 times total; a warning for unsaved and encouragement for saved); **and my** (Jesus') **reward is with Me** (Jesus), **to give every man** (one) *according as his work shall be.*" (Cf. **2Co. 5:10**, the Judgment Seat of Christ is not like the terrible Great White Throne Judgment for the unsaved in **20:11-15**, but is a reward ceremony for the saved, where bad deeds are burnt up in the fire like wood, hay, and stubble, and good works are rewarded eternally like when gold, silver, and precious stones pass through fire and are refined, cf. **1Co. 3:11-15**). **13**- (Jesus continues). "*I am Alpha and Omega* (4 times in Bible, all about and by Jesus, all in Revelation, **1:8, 11**; **21:6**; **22:13**, the 1st and last letters in the Greek alphabet, which is what the original Revelation manuscript was written in, Koine Greek, cf. similar OT verses: **Isa. 41:4**; **44:6**; **48:12**), *the beginning and the end, the 1st* (Gr:protos-foremost-in time, place, order, importance; He's before, best, chief, former, first) *and the last.*'" (Gr:eschatos-farthest, final, ends of, last, later end; it is impossible to be both former and later end, unless you're the eternal God/Jesus).}

E. 22:14-15— {Title: Blessed Obedient Live In Heaven and Evil Can't Come In. **14**-"*Blessed* (happy) *are they that do* (are doing; now the focus for the saved is to continue to "*do*," since they already are or "*be*" [cf. **22:11** focus] in Christ) *His* (Jesus') *commandments* (cf. **Joh. 14:15**; **Eph. 2:8-10**; **Tit. 1:16**; **3:3-8**; **1Pe. 2:7-8**; **1Jo. 3:5-10**, where these verses clearly do not teach a "*works*" salvation, as "*it is not of works*," "*it is a gift*," a person is saved "*by grace*," "*through faith*," will evidence their eternal life by obedience to their Lord, Who saved them. Everyone in love is happy and Jesus says you will obey His commandments, if you love Him, cf. **John 14:15**), *that* (Gr:hina-purpose) *they may have the right* (privilege/authority. God has given the right/authority to claim His promise of eternal life by Jesus' obedience unto death by faith, which Scripture also shows that our faith is demonstrated by a believer's works or obedience, cf. **John 14:12**; **James 2:18**) *to the tree of life* (once banned or prohibited by an angel from this tree. cf. **Gen. 3:22-24** through disobedience, but now promised access when we overcome sin by our faith), *and may enter in through the gates into the city* (Heaven, where pearly gate angels now welcome believers now perfectly doing His commandments and serving Him forever). **15**-"*For* (or But) *without* (outside; not in heaven, told elsewhere is in Hell, cf. **21:8**; **Mat. 8:12**) *are dogs* (Gr:kuon-dog; a dog, often shown in Scripture as an unclean ravenous pack animal, not the domesticated pet you think of today; but as those that need to be separated from clean or holy. **Isa. 56:9-11**-describes dogs as those that "*devour*," "*beasts*," "*ignorant*," mute, "*sleeping, lying down*," "*loving* to slumber," "greedy," "can never have enough," "cannot understand," "look to their own way;" cf. **_Pro. 26:11_**. In **_2Pe. 2:22_**-"*returns to his vomit,*" and a pig washed "*to her wallowing in the mire,*" showing it is part of their nature to be gross, filthy, and unclean. **_Mat. 7:6_** shows dogs as unholy. **_Php. 3:2_** says "*beware of dogs*" and lumps them in with the pack of "*evil workers,*" and numerous verses describe them eating and licking unclean things like dead bodies, blood, sores, e.g. **_1Ki. 21:24_**; **_22:38_**; **_Luk.16:21_**)**, and sorcerers, and whore-mongers** (fornicators/prostitutes)**, and murderers, and idolaters, and whosoever loves** (loving) **and makes** (making/doing) **a lie."** (So after encouraging the faithful with life and great fellowship, those practicing and loving evil will not enter into heaven; which **_22:11_** called unsaved, "*unjust*" and "*filthy*").}

F. 22:16-17— {Five Finales in the Bible—The Final Invitation, Warning, Promise, Prayer, and Provision. 1st - The Invitation. Title: Jesus' Great Testimony and Heavenly Invitation, Come. **16**-"**_I Jesus_** ("*I Jesus,*" only found once in Bible where His name is found more than a thousand times, no one else can say, emphatic, personal, but Jesus Himself) **have sent my angel** (as an aside, all saved have been given guardian angels and not sure if Jesus is referring to a personal angel given Him, or the fact that He owns and created them all, or just one that He specifically sent on this personal errand) **to testify unto you** (plural; all saved) **these things** (prophecies, the Book of **_Revelation_**) **in the churches. I am** ("*I am,*" here Jesus uses a title for God in **_Exo. 3:14_**, already claimed by Jesus in **_John 8:58_**) **the Root and the Offspring** (*Gr:genos-kin, born, offspring, stock;* although a different word, *Gr:sperma-"seed"* in **_Gal. 3:16_** says that this "*seed*" was singular or "*one*" seed, "*which is Christ*") **of David** (**_2Sa. 7:12-16_**-a reminder of the coming King fulfilling the Davidic Covenant; **_Jer. 23:5_**; **_33:15_**-In OT Jesus is called the "*Righteous Branch*" of David's family tree coming, in the NT called "*the Root of David*" preceding David in the family tree-**_Rev. 5:5_**, and here in **_22:16_**-"*the Root and the Offspring of David,*" emphasizing "*the Root*" or His Deity/pre-existence before David and His humanity/royal lineage later as "*the offspring of David*")**, and the bright** (radiant) **and morning star.'"** ("*Morning star,*" twice in Bible, **_2:28_**-promising Christians Jesus Himself and here in **_22:16_**-saying this inspired Message is from Jesus, the morning star, which is the brightest as can be seen even with the sun shining. Jesus, Who gives the brightest light and synthesizing sustenance to all family trees and is the radiant dawn/beginning of all eternity). **_17_**-"**And the Spirit** (Holy

Spirit through the Scripture, in our hearts, and our intercessory prayers, "*which cannot be uttered,*" cf. **Rom. 8:26**) *and the bride* (Church and even Heaven) *say, 'Come'* (Gr: *erchomai-come, accompany, come enter*; Present Imperative-a Command to do now, don't wait, don't linger, come, accompany Me into Heaven). *And let him that hears* (the one hearing) *say, 'Come'* (All of us should invite all to come to such a glorious heavenly place). *And let him* (the one) *that* (who) *is athirst* (thirsty), *'Come.'* *And whosoever will* (the one choosing/wishing /desiring/intending), *let him take* (receive; the Imperative Mood-a command) *the water of life* (here Jesus gives the eternal water of life quenching to the very depths of your soul) *freely."* (Salvation, heaven is a "*free gift,*" cf. **Rom. 3:24**; **5:15-18**. Take it, please Come into heaven with me...The angel testifies of Jesus that Jesus sent to you for you to Come; the Spirit calls you to Come; the Church invites you to Come, Heaven beckons you to Come; anyone who hears says, Come; if you are thirsty, Come; anyone who wishes to come take of the eternal water of life, Come; and Come quickly, without delay, while there is still time; this is the final Biblical invitation; you never know which invitation will be your very last).}

G. **22:18-19**— {2^nd – The Warning; Title: John Affirms this Book; God Severely Punishes Changing this Book. **18**-"*For I* (John) *testify* (Gr: *summartureo-testify jointly, corroborate by concurrent evidence*) *unto every man* (one) *that hears* (hearing; can be by various senses, not just the ears) *the Words of the prophecy of this Book* (clearly **Revelation**, and surely the entire Bible as this is the final Book), *If any man* (one) *shall add unto these things, God shall add unto him the plagues that are written in this Book:"* (**Revelation** and surely all Scripture as in **Deu. 4:2**): **19**-"*And if any man* (one) *shall take away* (remove) *from the Words of the Book of this prophecy, God will take away* (remove) *his part out of the Book of Life* ("*the Book of Life,*" **3:5**; **20:15**-unsaved get their name blotted out of), *and out of the holy city* (removed from Heaven), *and from the things which are written* (perfect passive participle-have been written in the past, with the result that Scripture stays written [as it was in the past] today) *in this Book."* (You don't want to lose all the great promises to believers. God is very serious where God's Word promises plagues if you add to Scripture, and loss of heaven and all His Word's promised blessings, if you take away from it. Hear it and believe it, never change it).}

H. **22:20**— {Title: Jesus Is Coming Quickly, Come Lord Jesus. (3rd and 4th - The Final Promise and Prayer). **20**-"*He which* (The One Who) *testifies* (is testifying) ***these things says*** (you would think this is John, but this is testimony from Jesus, about testimony of Jesus), **'Surely** (Truly/Yes), **I** (Jesus) ***come quickly'*** (Soon/suddenly. What a promise; the 3rd time Jesus says He comes quickly in this chapter-**22:7, 12, 20**, and 3 times prior-**2:5, 16**; **3:11**). **'Amen** (Surely/Truly. Now John's response). ***Even so*** (Yes; same word as Jesus' Surely/ Truly/Yes)**, Come, Lord Jesus.'"** (What a prayer. Are you ready, is that your desire, is He your desire? Is He your Lord? He is, even if you don't know Him yet. Is He your Savior? He died for you and calls you to accept Him as such. Please make Him so now...).}

I. **22:21**— {Title: Jesus' Grace Be With You, Amen! (5th - The Final Provision, God's grace). **21**-"***The grace*** (Jesus giving us something we do not deserve, a gift) ***of our Lord*** (Master, the One we should obey. If Jesus isn't your complete Lord, you won't receive all the grace He is trying to give you) ***Jesus*** (Savior) ***Christ*** (Messiah, anointed One) ***be with you all*** (proves John is a southerner :)). ***Amen.***" (Surely/Truly/Let it be so!).}

Application (Activity/Questions)

A. If you don't long for Jesus' Coming, what does that say about you? {Unsaved, immature Christian, in sin, or maybe haven't heard or understood...}

B. What does it mean to keep the words of this prophecy (**1:3**; **22:7, 14**)? {Guard, obey, know and understand, listen to, tell...}

C. What aspects of the curse are you most excited that in heaven will be no more (**22:3, 15**)? {No: sweaty work, thorns, thistles, pain, weight gain, sin, sickness, guilt, depravity, deception, disease, night or darkness, defense mechanisms, negativity, cursing, depression, bad memories, evil or evil doers, punishment...}

D. How does God showing you about the future encourage you to live better now? {Builds trust; encouraging to know; shows God has a plan; makes me want to use time wisely...}

E. What is the most important, sincere invitation, and command of Jesus' Words, His angel, His Church, His hearers, and those thirsting (**22:16-17**)? {Come! Come to Jesus. Come into Heaven. Come now. **Acts 16:31**-"*Believe on the Lord Jesus Christ and you shall be saved.*" Play (https://www.youtube.com/watch?v=PANivelKVX0 on laptop or phone...best with projector-3:49) video song of one of my favorite songs, "*Come to Jesus.*"[36]}

F. Why has Jesus sent so many to tell about the future? {To warn and encourage and maybe change the eternal destiny of many. The testimony of Jesus is that He is coming soon. Are you ready? What is your testimony? What is your testimony of Jesus?}

G. Who is Jesus revealed as in the Book of Revelation? {The entire Bible has what is called the Scarlet Thread running through it, where OT and NT prophecies tell us of Jesus Christ, His shed blood, resurrection, redemption, and eternal plan. The OT primarily prophesies about His 1st Coming as baby to die for our sin. The NT reveals Christ fulfilling these 1st Coming events and prophesies of His 2nd Coming in justice with a powerful earthly and eternal reign. Revelation has one of the thickest and most complete scarlet threads of any book, even including John's other Book, the Gospel of John. Jesus is revealed in Revelation:

Rev. 1—Jesus Christ, the Resurrected (was dead, but now living), glorified Lord (Almighty, the prince of the kings of the earth), eternal (alpha and omega, beginning and ending, 1st and the last, alive forevermore, was, is, and is to come), the faithful witness (reveals Himself and His prophetic plan), Judge (Who sees all, has a strong bright face, mighty voice, judges with a 2-edged Sword; has the keys of Hell and death), Who loves and is Savior (washed those receiving Him from their sins by His own blood), is coming soon, and sends His message to the Churches.

Rev. 2-3—The Eternal One (1st and last, the beginning, was dead and is alive) in the middle of the Churches holding them in His strong right hand and warns the church to stay in His Truth (by sharp 2-edged Sword coming from His mouth), and promises Churches heaven and rewards (heavenly food, crowns, a new name, stone, rule over the nations, white raiment, a heavenly city, sit on thrones...), Confesses believer's names before God and angels, the Morning Star, Has the only key to the Davidic/Millennial Kingdom, Faithful and true, Standing ready to let anyone who comes to Him into heaven to dine with Him, sits on His throne, Jesus Christ is coming very soon.

Rev. 4-5—The only holy one, Worthy to Judge others (or open the 7-year Tribulation Seals, Trumpets, and Vial Judgments), the Lamb (or only perfect sacrifice without sin Who could and did die for man's sin or unholiness), Who redeems (buys back from sin and its consequence of physical and spiritual blindness and death) believers by His blood (Jesus' death and burial), Lion (from Israel's tribe of Judah-as prophesied) and descendant of David (as prophesied from royal lineage), prevailed over sin and death (resurrected as He is the resurrection and the life), so is worshiped by all saved creatures in heaven and worthy to receive power, riches, wisdom, strength, honor, glory, and blessing...

Rev. 6-19—Lamb (the only sacrifice for all who will believe), also pictured as born of a woman, a man child (showing His humanity) ascending back to heaven (prior to ruling on earth) and sitting on the throne (ruling), being praised and thanked (for His saving, His feeding, His living waters, His wiping away all tears), sealing His witnesses, believers, and the nation of Israel (protecting believers during judgment that He took in their place), opening God's Book calling forth 7-years of the worse Seal, Trumpet, and Vial judgments in human history on wicked (unrepentant unbelievers, still rejecting Jesus' salvation) providing His promised justice, but Jesus sends an angel with *"the everlasting gospel"* (God loves you, took on flesh to die for your sins so you would not have to, Jesus Christ was buried, and rose again from the dead proving He is righteous and has power to resurrect you, if you will only receive Him by grace through faith to be eternally saved and be able to have a truth filled, purposeful abundant life living the way God desires you to be—the happiest, the most blessed, now and forever); so naturally angels, other heavenly creatures, and all in heaven repeated sing *"the song of the Lamb"* about how great and marvelous are His works and how just and true are His ways, and call Jesus *"Lord God Almighty;"* and Jesus Christ (even during the Trib) is called *"King of Kings and Lord or Lords,"* though the wicked on earth continue to reject Him.

Rev. 19—He is the Rider on the White Horse (not on a baby donkey like His 1st Coming, but in battle at His 2nd Coming) for *"in righteousness He does judge and make war,"* He has a name written that none knows, but He is *"Faithful and True,"* His clothes were dipped in blood (reminding us this Judge died and tried to take the death coming even to His rejectors), His name is called *"the Word of God,"* He smites and rules the nations by the truth, He has a name written on His outfit King of Kings, and Lord of Lords. There is singing and rejoicing in heaven for Jesus, saying, *"Alleluia; Salvation, and glory, and honor, and power to the Lord our God: For true and righteous are His judgments...Alleluia, for the Lord God omnipotent reigneth. Let us be glad and rejoice, and give honor to Him."* This all happens while Jesus' intimacy with the Church is described changing Him from finance to husband, where Jesus's High Priestly Prayer of John 17 is answered of the perfect unity of believers with God through Jesus Christ our Savior.

Rev. 20—Jesus is described as the Millennial, Earthly, or Kingdom King ruling, reigning, and judging the earth with Israel and the Church. He is also pictured sitting on God's right hand at the Great White Throne Judgment where all are resurrected, and all wicked men, creatures, and even death are cast into an eternal Hell fire, based on their sin and personal rejection of Jesus Christ.

Rev. 21-22—Reveals Jesus as creator (of a new heavens and earth), He is still and will always be Faithful and True, He is the Alpha and Omega, the beginning and the end, the 1st and the last, says He is a descendant of King David (showing His humanity and prophesied right to rule Israel), He gives believers living water, which comes directly from Him and His throne, He gives an inheritance to believers, He again is described as Husband (due to such intimacy and unity with believers), He is described as the Lamb (perfect holy sacrifice), He is our spiritual Temple (though no need for a physical temple in heaven as we have perfect unity with God through Jesus, and no unforgiven sin separating us from holy God), He is described as the Light of heaven (no sun or moon is needed and there is no night because He is so bright), says we get to see Him face-to-face, He is *"the Bright and Morning Star,"* it describes the Lord Jesus Christ's grace (undeserved giving, especially giving eternal life), and says in the final chapter that Jesus Christ comes quickly.

H. Who is Jesus Christ to you? Are you ready for His soon Coming? {All the above; my Savior, Lord, Healer, Life, Truth, God; Yes...}

v. End Notes

[1] Wikipedia. "Apocalypse (Dürer)." Wikipedia, Wikimedia Foundation, 20 May 2019, Web. en.wikipedia.org/wiki/Apocalypse_(Dürer). 26 June 2019. Public Domain, originally cited from www.britishmuseum.org, a woodcutting by Albrecht Durer, 31 December 1497.

[2] Schaff, Philip, **History of the Christian Church**. Vol. II, Anti-Nicene Christianity, AD. 100-825, 8th edition, revised and enlarged (New York, New York: Charles Scribner's Sons, 1901), 670.

[3] Wikipedia. "Apocalypse (Dürer)." Ibid.

[4] fxswan Last. "*Revelation Chapter 5/Lion/Judah/Root of David/Angels/Seals.*" *YouTube*. lamb2lionfilmation, 29 May 2009. Web. 20 March 2019.

[5] Copp, Dennis. "*The Revelation of Jesus Christ: Chapter Five.*" *Youtube*. YouTube, 18 December 2009. Web. 20 March 2019.

[6] ILoveJesus-Jazmin. "*The Revelation of Jesus Christ: Chapter 5.*" *YouTube*. YouTube, 29 October 2016. Web. 20 March 2019.

[7] Wikipedia. "Apocalypse (Dürer)." Ibid.

[8] *Wikipedia. "Apocalypse (Dürer)." Ibid.*

[9] *Wikipedia. "Apocalypse (Dürer)." Ibid.*

[10] *Wikipedia. "Apocalypse (Dürer)." Ibid.*

[11] Lewis, C.S. **THE SCREWTAPE LETTERS: LETTERS FROM A SENIOR TO A JUNIOR DEVIL** (Oxford, United Kingdom: Samizdat University Press, 1941), 1.

[12] Wikipedia. "Apocalypse (Dürer)." Ibid.

[13] Cheng, David. "*Scorpion Envenomation.*" *Medscape*. Medscape, 09 November 2018. Web. 30 April 2019.

¹⁴ Wikipedia. *"Apocalypse (Dürer)." Ibid.*

¹⁵ Dadax. *"Current World Population."* Worldometers. Worldometers, 30 April 2019. Web. 30 April 2019.

¹⁶ Dadax. *"Countries in the World by Population (2019)."* Worldometers. Worldometers, 30 April 2019. Web. 30 April 2019.

¹⁷ Pew Research Center. *"The Global Religious Landscape: Muslims."* Pew Research Center. Pew Research Center, 18 December 2012. Web. 30 April 2019.

¹⁸ Dadax. *"Top 20 Largest Countries by Population (2019)."* Worldometers. Worldometers, 30 April 2019. Web. 30 April 2019.

¹⁹ Wikipedia. *"Apocalypse (Dürer)." Ibid.*

²⁰ Wikipedia. *"Apocalypse (Dürer)." Ibid.*

²¹ Wikipedia. "*Woman of the Apocalypse*." Wikipedia. Wikipedia Foundation. 27 April 2019. Web. 01 May 2019.

²² Wikipedia. *"Apocalypse (Dürer)." Ibid.*

²³ Scofield, C.I., **The New Scofield Reference Bible** (New York, NY: Oxford University Press, Inc., 1967), 1364-1365.

²⁴ Smith, Uriah, **The United States in the Light of Prophecy**, 4ᵗʰ edition (Battle Creek, Michigan: Seventh-day Adventist Publishing Association, 1884), 224.

²⁵ Wikipedia. *"Apocalypse (Dürer)." Ibid.*

²⁶ Peterson, Andrew. *"Is He Worthy?"* YouTube. YouTube, 15 March 2018. Web. 01 May 2019.

[27] Adams, John. *"A Dissertation on the Canon and Feudal Law"* Teaching American History. Teaching American History, 1765, Web. 05 May 2019.

[28] Newell, William R. **Revelation: Chapter-by-Chapter** (Grand Rapids, MI: Kregel Publications, 1994), 377-379 (was also detailed in his The Revelation, on p. 271).

[29] Scofield, C.I., **The New Scofield Reference Bible** (New York, NY: Oxford University Press, Inc., 1967), 1364, 1369.

[30] Aldrich, Roy. L, *"Facts and Theories of Prophecy,"* Unpublished Doctor's Dissertation, Dallas Theological Seminary, Dallas, TX, 1942, 120-21.

[31] MacArthur, John, **The MacArthur Study Bible** (Nashville, TN: Word Publishing, 1997), 2016.

[32] Pentecost, J. Dwight (1964) **Things to Come**. Grand Rapids, MI: Zondervan Publishing House, 323-25.

[33] *Wikipedia. "Apocalypse (Dürer)." Ibid.*

[34] *Wikipedia. "Apocalypse (Dürer)." Ibid.*

[35] Scofield, C.I., **The New Scofield Reference Bible** (New York, NY: Oxford University Press, Inc., 1967), 1376.

[36] kelsey06712. *"Come to Jesus – Chris Rice (Lyrics)."* YouTube. YouTube, 16 October 2008. Web. 06 May 2019.

vi. Bibliography (with notes)

Adams, John (1765) *"A Dissertation on the Canon and Feudal Law,"* Teaching American History. Teaching American History, 1765, Web. 05 May 2019. Great treatise dealing with why church and state should be separate to ensure liberty.

Aldrich, Roy. L (1942) *"Facts and Theories of Prophecy,"* Unpublished Doctor's Dissertation, Dallas Theological Seminary, Dallas, TX, (198 pages). Good title covering key prophetic questions.

Beale, G. K. (2013) **NIGTC: The New International Greek Testament Commentary, The Book of Revelation**. Grand Rapids, Michigan: Wm. B. Eerdmans Publishing Co. A massive and scholarly Revelation commentary (over 1,300 pages) from an Amillennial perspective maintaining some future events are actually in the OT.

Beale, G. K. and David H. Campbell (2015) **NIGTC: The New International Greek Testament Commentary, Revelation: A Shorter Commentary**. Grand Rapids, Michigan: Wm. B. Eerdmans Publishing Co. Beale condenses his prior exhaustive work on Revelation and adds more reflections to help the reader apply, Amillennial (still over 500 pages).

Caird, George B. (1984) **A Commentary of the Revelation of St. John Divine**, 2nd Edition, London, England: A & C Black. A provocative interpretation of Revelation (318 pages).

Cheng, David (2018) *"Scorpion Envenomation."* *Medscape.* Medscape, 09 November 2018. Web. 30 April 2019. Interesting medical information regarding scorpions.

Copp, Dennis (2009) *"The Revelation of Jesus Christ: Chapter Five."* *YouTube.* YouTube, 18 December 2009. Web. 20 March 2019. Good narrated free video with images of Revelation 5.

Dadax (2019) *"Current World Population."* Worldometers. Worldometers, 30 April 2019. Web. 30 April 2019. Good site for world statistics, especially population related.

Ibid. *"Current World Population."* Good site for world statistics, especially population related.

Ibid. *"Top 20 Largest Countries by Population (2019)."* Good site for world statistics, especially population related.

Darby, John (1862) **John Darby's Synopsis of the Bible**. Public Domain; free download from eSword. Written from a Dispensational perspective.

Exell, Joseph S. (2008) **The Preachers Complete Homiletical Commentary**, 38 volumes. Bellingham, WA: Logos Research Systems. 1st written in 1892 by a preacher for preachers with commentary illustrations, including Revelation.

Exell, Joseph S. and Spence-Johnes, H. D. M. (1897) **The Pulpit Commentary**. Public Domain. One of the largest and best-selling homiletical commentaries written by over 100 authors over 30 years, provides at least 3 treatments of every verse, designed for conservative preachers and teachers.

Fee, Gordon D. (2010) **Revelation: A New Covenant Commentary (NCCS)**. Eugene, OR: Cascade Books. Stimulating on Revelation, over 300 pages, from a Covenant or Amillennial perspective.

fxswan Last (2009) *"Revelation Chapter 5/Lion/Judah/Root of David/Angels/Seals."* YouTube. lamb2lionfilmation, 29 May 2009. Web. 20 March 2019. Good narrated free video with images of Revelation 5.

Guzik, David (2014) **David Guzik's Enduring Word Commentary**. Free download from eSword; also on blueletterbible.com. A great concise practical verse-by-verse commentary by a pastor and professor from Pre-Millennial perspective, includes Revelation.

Hamilton, James M. (2012) **Revelation: The Spirit Speaks to the Churches**. Wheaton, IL: Crossway. A helpful exposition of Revelation from a Pre-Millennial perspective with 37 sermons and their homiletical idea.

Henry, Matthew (1714) **Matthew Henry's Commentary on the Whole Bible**. Free download from eSword. Important 6-volume devotional commentary with eloquence and practical application, including Revelation, frequently elaborates on his view, but doesn't include views of others.

Henry, Matthew (1714) **Matthew Henry's Concise Commentary**. Free download from eSword. Important concise devotional commentary with eloquence, practical applications, and outlines, including Revelation, frequently elaborates on his view, but doesn't include views of others.

ILoveJesus- Jazmin (2019) "*The Revelation of Jesus Christ: Chapter 5.*" *YouTube*. YouTube, 29 October 2016. Web. 20 March 2019. Good narrated free video with images of Revelation 5.

Jeremiah, David (2014) **Agents of the Apocalypse: A Riveting Look at the Key Players of the End Times**. Carol Stream, IL: Tyndale House Publishers, Inc. Does a good job of the key players of Revelation along with fictionalized dramatizations consistent with these Biblical figures that helps bring the Book together.

Jeremiah, David (2018) **Escape the Coming Night: A message of Hope in Time of Crisis**. Nashville, TN: W. Publishing. A best seller providing Revelation urgency in 20 chapters of dramatizations to have hope midst today's chaos and the terrible judgments of Revelation. Not a commentary.

Jeremiah, David (2016) **When Christ Appears: An Inspirational Experience Through Revelation**. Nashville, TN: Worthy Publishers. 60 chapters, 196 pages, including his study Bible notes, and ways to apply the Book of Revelation.

Johnson, Dennis E. (2001) **Triumph of the Lamb: A Commentary of Revelation**. Phillipsburg, New Jersey: P & R Publishing. Written for Presbyterians and a Reformed publisher showing an Amillennial theological interpretation, but clearly written explanation of Revelation for busy pastors.

Kelsey06712 (2008) *"Come to Jesus – Chris Rice (Lyrics)."* YouTube. YouTube, 16 October 2008. Web. 06 May 2019. Awesome worship video song compelling unsaved and saved to come to Jesus.

Ladd, George E. (2018) **A Commentary of the Revelation of John**. Grand Rapids, Michigan: Wm. B. Eerdmans Publishing Co. A literal verse-by-verse interpretation of Revelation from a Pre-Millennial perspective.

Lewis, C.S. (1941) **THE SCREWTAPE LETTERS: LETTERS FROM A SENIOR TO A JUNIOR DEVIL**. Oxford, United Kingdom: Samizdat University Press. Includes a letter where "Wormwood" is considered a demon, not a meteor.

MacArthur, John (1997) **The MacArthur Study Bible**. Nashville, TN: Word Publishing. NKJV is one of the most accurate translations of Scripture and John MacArthur's study notes are excellent on all Scripture and Revelation.

Meyer, F. B. (1914) **Through the Bible Day by Day**. Public Domain. He comments and outlines Revelation with review questions and applications.

Mounce, Robert H. (1997) **NICNT: The New International Commentary on the New Testament, The Book of Revelation** (Revised). Grand Rapids, Michigan: Wm. B. Eerdmans Publishing Co. A critical scholarly commentary and interpretation of Revelation, in 475 pages, lots of references, Pre-Millennial perspective.

Newell, William R. (1994) **Revelation: Chapter-by-Chapter**. Grand Rapids, MI: Kregel Publications. An excellent, Scriptural summation from a Pre-Millennial perspective, referencing many great Christians, and thoroughly explaining how the Church is the not in the Tribulation.

Osborne, Grant R. (2002) **Revelation (Baker Exegetical Commentary on the New Testament: BECNT)**. Grand Rapids, Michigan: Baker Academic. A clear exposition of Revelation from a Pre-Millennial perspective intended for a broad evangelical audience, over 800 pages.

Pew Research Center (2012) *"The Global Religious Landscape: Muslims."* Pew Research Center. Pew Research Center, 18 December 2012. Web. 30 April 2019. Great non-profit site for religious statistics.

Pentecost, J. Dwight (1964) **Things to Come**. Grand Rapids, MI: Zondervan Publishing House (633 pages). One of the most comprehensive and scholarly Biblical works on prophecy in existence, providing many views and Scriptures.

Peterson, Andrew (2018) *"Is He Worthy?" YouTube*. YouTube, 15 March 2018. Web. 01 May 2019. Great free worship song and video that goes perfect with Revelation 5 or any chapter.

Schaff, Philip (1901) **History of the Christian Church,** Vol. II, Anti-Nicene Christianity, AD. 100-825, 8th edition, revised and enlarged. New York, New York: Charles Scribner's Sons. Scholarly history of the Christian Church, helpful on 7 Asian church background and figures.

Scofield, C.I. (1967) **The New Scofield Reference Bible**. New York, NY: Oxford University Press, Inc. Great reference notes for the KJV Bible, including cross-references, abbreviated concordance, chapter titles, and concise commentary.

Smith, Uriah (1884) **The United States in the Light of Prophecy**, 4th edition. Battle Creek, Michigan: Seventh-day Adventist Publishing Association. Represents the 7th-Day Adventist prophetic perspective.

Thomas, Robert L. (2016) **Revelation Exegetical Commentary**, 2 volumes. Chicago, Illinois: Moody Publishers. A thorough Revelation commentary from a literal dispensational Pre-Millennial perspective.

Unknown (1896) **<u>Expositor's Bible Commentary</u>**. Free download from eSword; Public Domain. Written by 29 scholars from interdenominational Protestant perspective focusing on the essentials of the Christian faith.

Wesley, John (1766) **<u>John Wesley's Notes on the Bible</u>**. Public Domain. As the founder of the Methodist movement, he writes in simple, plain, and practical language.

Wikipedia (2019) "*Woman of the Apocalypse.*" Wikipedia. Wikipedia. 27 April 2019. Web. 01 May 2019. A descent free encyclopedia on the Internet, but sometimes inaccurate.

Ibid. "Apocalypse (Dürer)." Wikipedia, Wikimedia Foundation, 20 May 2019, Web. en.wikipedia.org/wiki/Apocalypse_(Dürer). 26 June 2019. Public Domain, originally cited from www.britishmuseum.org. The Apocalypse, properly Apocalypse with Pictures (Latin: Apocalypsis cum Figuris) is a famous series of 15 woodcuts by Albrecht Dürer of scenes from the Book of Revelation, published simultaneously in Latin and German at Nuremberg in 1498, now public domain. I chose to exclude the 1st woodcut in this series of 15, as it was the Martyrdom of St. John, which did not occur until after the Book of Revelation had been completed.

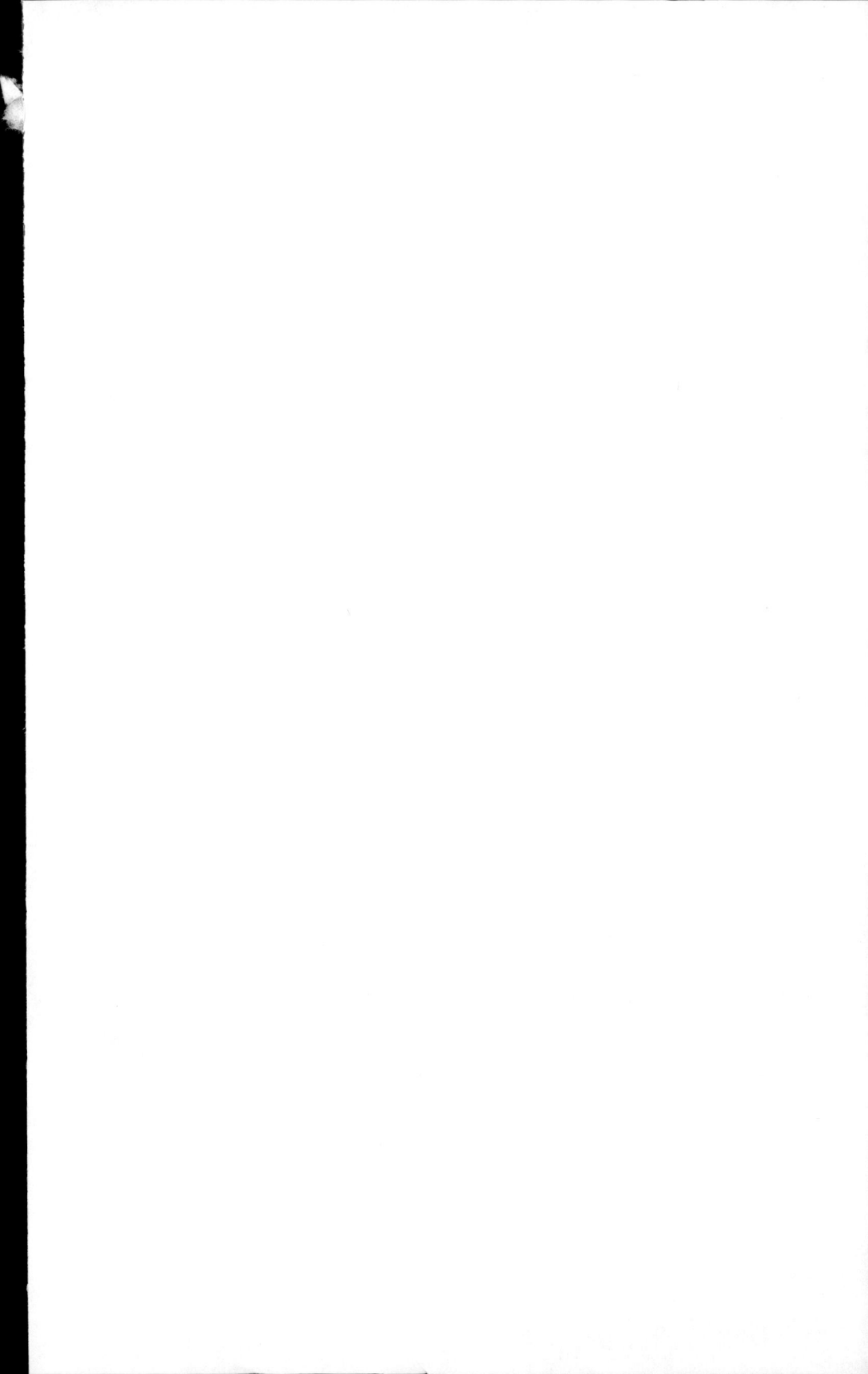

www.ingramcontent.com/pod-product-compliance
Lightning Source LLC
Chambersburg PA
CBHW060317050426
42449CB00011B/2516